The Young Artist as Scientist

The Young Artist as Scientist

What Can Leonardo Teach Us?

Mary Jo Pollman

Foreword by Judy Harris Helm

TEACHERS COLLEGE PRESS

TEACHERS COLLEGE | COLUMBIA UNIVERSITY
NEW YORK AND LONDON

Published by Teachers College Press, 1234 Amsterdam Avenue, New York, NY 10027

Copyright © 2017 by Teachers College, Columbia University

Original cover design by Jennifer Pollman. Cover child's drawing by Helen Field, iStock by Getty Images; Leonardo Da Vinci helicopter courtesy of Wikimedia Commons.

Library of Congress Cataloging-in-Publication Data is available at loc.gov

ISBN 978-0-8077-5795-6 (paper)
ISBN 978-0-8077-7650-6 (ebook)

Printed on acid-free paper
Manufactured in the United States of America

24   23   22   21   20   19   18   17   8   7   6   5   4   3   2   1

In memory of the late Dr. Marjorie Milan, who was a colleague, collaborator, inspiring educator, and true advocate for the creative arts. Many of her ideas live on in this book.

CONTENTS

FOREWORD

We think we know, as early childhood professionals, what we should espouse and what we should think. We believe that all children are curious and creative. All children can invent, think in very complex ways, and solve problems. We believe that arts are important, and yes, we are learning that we need to also provide science, technology, engineering, and math experiences. However, is our practice congruent with our beliefs? Do we recognize that a magnifying glass, a few rocks, and a plant do not constitute science teaching or that paint on an easel and markers at a table do not constitute teaching the arts? One might wonder why we would give creative children directions, models, and even precut parts to make egg carton caterpillars in the spring and paper plate spiders in the fall? When we find parents impressed by showy craft ideas found on Pinterest or when an administrator purchases another canned "prescribed curriculum" for us to follow, do we step up and say that these may damage children's dispositions to be creative and solve problems? Many educators are at a loss for words.

The book you are about to read, *The Young Artist as Scientist: What Can Leonardo Teach Us?*, will help you think through these dilemmas by documenting "why" we should do what we say we believe and alternative ways of thinking about "how." Mary Jo Pollman presents a coherent, well-researched argument for replacing meaningless activities with engaging creative art and STEM experiences, which have the potential to become cohesive, integrated adventures in learning. Summarizing everything from 21st century skill development to the push for developmentally appropriate practice to technology to multiple intelligences, she builds a case for the importance of creative arts and STEM experiences not just for individual student achievement but also for the betterment of community and societies. The concise summaries of research help the reader understand important educational initiatives and how, in some cases, these have led to a compartmentalization of teaching in the early years. By carefully reviewing these separate isolated conclusions, we can see how they each connect and build on one another.

I urge you not to skip through Part I but to think about the work that others have done to lead us to where we are. You will want to store away some of the nuggets of wisdom, such as why coloring books are not a good idea, so you can draw upon them when you need them. You will want to especially pay attention to the discussion of the creative ecosystem of the classroom and how the powerful forces of climate, space, and time affect life in the early childhood classroom.

The vignettes that tell of Leonardo DaVinci's development are enlightening and informative. Pause, as you read, and consider how this young boy came to be an intensely creative artist/scientist who gave so much to the world. You will be reminded that teaching is about individual children—one by one—and supporting their development into functioning adults. We go astray when we plan if we focus on teaching "reading standards" or "21st century skills" and act like we are accomplishing great things when we have everyone do the same thing at the same time. Our job is to be there, as the adults were for little Leonardo, to facilitate individual growth and provide an opportunity for each child to reach his or her potential. Each individual in the classroom is on a trajectory of growth and development. That trajectory begins to take shape in the early years, and the success of this endeavor depends on the child being awakened to his or her potential as a powerful learner. To do this we need to introduce children to the arts, science, technology, engineering, and math by providing instruction and opportunities to experience and learn about them. As they become engaged in topics they find interesting, children develop the motivation to learn—to apply and to use their skills through integrated investigations such as deep project work. Part I provides wonderful guidance on exactly how this might be done. There are rich descriptions of learning experiences and projects, including the bridge project, that show what happens when there is an attempt to integrate the arts and STEM into classroom life.

The life story of Leonardo DaVinci provides an inspiring description of what a person can become when immersed in a community that values art and scientific learning. This book can also be an inspiration to do things in a better way. We do not know how many children in our classrooms today have the potential to become a Leonardo DaVinci or a Steve Jobs. I am pretty sure, however, that egg carton caterpillars and paper plate spiders are not what they need now.

—Judy Harris Helm, EdD

PREFACE

In this book I demonstrate how the arts—creative movement, drama, visual arts, and music—are connected to and support the STEM fields—science, technology, engineering, and math—particularly in early childhood, The book is based on the ideas that all children are creative beings, that both the arts and sciences require creativity, and that it is incumbent upon teachers to recognize the connection to STEM as children engage in artistic endeavors. Further, I show teachers and administrators how to create a spectrum of tools for thinking about the creative process and the connections between art and science. I seek to enable educators to become instigators in expanding the opportunities for creative thinking in the arts and sciences.

As a visitor to the preschools in Reggio Emilia, Italy, in 1996, I saw children's participation in the arts develop into in-depth, project-based study of topics with profound extensions into science and math. This experience, along with my exposure to the insightful project approach of Helm and Katz (2016) and Helm (2015), have since been emphasized in my teaching.

While in Italy, I also saw paintings and drawings of inventions of Leonardo da Vinci (1452–1519) and became profoundly interested in his life. This fascination led me to research his work and spend hours in exhibits dedicated to him in the United States. Leonardo da Vinci, one of the greatest artists of the Renaissance era, was also an accomplished scientist and inventor.

As I progressed in my understanding of the arts–science connection, I also became a student of the work of Friedrich Froebel, a German architect, mathematician, and mineralogist whose theory of unity permeated the kindergarten movement in Europe and America in the 1800s. Through my study of his theory of unity in nature, design (art), and knowledge (math and science), I came to fully appreciate the concept that everything in nature has design (art), as well as math and science in it. The design, math, and science just need to be discovered. These strong interconnections became a part of my teaching, my professional workshops, and my writing (see Pollman, 2010).

My interest in Leonardo da Vinci's designs and Froebel's philosophy helped me realize that becoming a scientist starts with the keen observation and study of nature. Just as a lobster or insect uses its antennae to explore, feel, and discover its surroundings, so too does an artist-scientist like Leonardo use his creative thinking and art media to understand the world. His work exemplifies how the artist-scientist's mind expands through exploration. In this book, I draw on

Leonardo's imaginative work to show why the arts constitute a powerful and efficient method for communicating interests, feelings, and ideas to others, as well as for developing a strong base in early childhood for creative thinking in the STEM fields.

Every chapter in this book begins with a vignette from Leonardo da Vinci's life and work, which I created based on adult and children's books by R. Edwards (2005), Gelb (1998), Osborne and Boyce (2009), Phillips (2008), Shlain (2014), Strom (2008), and White (2000). In the chapters I relate Leonardo's experiences and insights to the development of children's ideas in the arts and STEM fields. I then present background research and material that are traditionally taught in the expressive arts and creativity courses in early childhood education programs and emphasize how they can be expanded to teach concepts needed in STEM, similar to how Leonardo developed his artistic and scientific skills.

The book is organized into two main parts, followed by a conclusion. The three chapters in Part I present the concepts fundamental to understanding the Arts–STEM connection. In Chapter 1 I explain the different terms that are used by others for the Arts–STEM connection, and why I use Arts–STEM to refer to integrating the arts in STEM activities. I also examine the creative arts and link them to the STEM movement, 21st century skills, developmentally appropriate practice, and the Next Generation Science Standards. Chapter 2 describes the issues related to creativity and the forces influencing creative expression. It provides examples of how teachers can expand the possibilities of creative thinking in young children for the arts and sciences. Chapter 3 focuses on conditions surrounding the creative environment in the classroom. I explain each condition with examples from the life of Leonardo da Vinci, a creative early childhood classroom, and a Reggio Emilia preschool classroom. The chapter also discusses forces at work in the classroom environment that promote creativity.

Each of the chapters in Part II takes up one of the arts in depth and provides guidance for linking it to STEM. Chapter 4 shows how the elements of creative movement are used in both movement and science and how creative drama in early childhood promotes STEM activities. Chapter 5 explains how teachers can examine art media and how they can use the media as a STEM lesson. Two- and three-dimensional forms of artistic expression are expanded into STEM activities. Chapter 6 builds on the design ideas of Leonardo and the theory of unity of Froebel to define the elements of art and the principles of design. Teachers are guided in using them in the arts and STEM. Chapter 7 provides background for promoting the connection between music and STEM. It discusses the elements of music and expands on experiences in music that should be made available to young children, with examples of the integration of math and science.

The Conclusion begins with a vignette of an afterschool primary program, *Thinking and Inventing Like Leonardo da Vinci*. This chapter gives specific tips on starting an Arts–STEM program in a preschool or primary program and how Arts–STEM can be enhanced in teacher education. It also gives innovative suggestions for the promotion of Arts–STEM in schools and the community through advocacy.

Throughout the book, discussions in the text are brought to life with vignettes of children and teachers (all names are pseudonyms) in early childhood classrooms and illustrative material. At the end of each chapter are exercises to enable readers to review and reflect on the content just presented.

This book can be used by colleges and universities that are developing STEM and/or STEAM concentrations in elementary and early childhood undergraduate and graduate programs, as well as in courses designed to promote a deeper, more interdisciplinary approach to learning through adoption of an expressive arts text with strong connections to STEM. The book can be used for book studies in child-care centers and preschools that are moving into STEAM programs and in kindergarten and primary programs that seek to promote a deeper understanding of how the arts support the implementation of the Common Core State Standards in Math (National Governors Association Center for Best Practices [NGA] and Council of Chief State School Officers [CCSSO], 2010) as well as the Next Generation Science Standards (NGSS Lead States [NGSS], 2013). With this book, home-schooling parents will be able to extend their understanding of the importance of the arts in connection with STEM. Children's museums, art museums, and science museums, which are developing Arts–STEM components in response to many grant requirements, can use this book with museum employees as well as teachers and parents to promote Arts–STEM. My message is that a strong connection between the arts and STEM makes both more effective and complete.

ACKNOWLEDGMENTS

First and foremost, I would like to acknowledge Dr. Marge Milan, who died in 2007, but who was a contributor to Chapters 2 and 7. Her understanding of the expressive arts has been an inspiration to me and to my college students who participated in field experiences in her classroom. She understood and provided the conditions for creativity that are expressed in this book in her preschool class before the Arts–STEM movement came into existence.

I am indebted to Dr. Esther Rodriquez, who asked me to join her team at Metropolitan State University of Denver's 21st Century College Readiness Center, a partnership between MSU Denver and Denver Public Schools. As a result of the partnership grant, I was able to implement many of the ideas in this book in afterschool programming in primary education for two low-performing schools. I am very grateful for Carla Mirabelli, who was always very supportive of Art–STEM programming and who continues the work of Esther Rodriquez, as well as Rachel Brazell for her time and creative efforts on behalf of children. Additionally, I would also like to thank the undergraduate collaborative team that worked with me at Cheltenham and Fairview elementary schools in Denver, Colorado, implementing programs with Arts–STEM: head tutors Rebeca Murray and Kimberly Aranda and Inez Garcia, Destinee Hughes, Arianne Ortiz-Lopez, Abelard Palmer, Guadalupe Torres, Adam Viglione, Sarai Williams, Dejchia Yang, and Kazong Yang. Additional gratitude goes to Brandon Mason and Lorraine Ortiz-Lopez, teachers in Denver Public Schools, who allowed the Arts–STEM Projects and Leonardo da Vinci inventions into their classrooms.

As my ideas grew for the connections in Art–STEM, I wanted to express these ideas, and the following special people contributed their expertise and time in various ways: Jessica Boyles, Jaclyn Knapp, John Knapp, Judy Knapp, Jan Pollman, Jillian Rhodes, and Michel Vallee. A special recognition goes to Jennifer Pollman, who helped with pictures and illustrations.

My appreciation goes to the members of the Teachers College Press team who worked collaboratively to produce this manuscript. I want to express my special gratitude to Sarah Biondello, who first demonstrated an interest in the manuscript at an NAEYC Conference and helped to support it throughout the publishing process. Susan Liddicoat, John Bylander, Kathy Caveney, and Karl Nyberg have also been helpful in an exceptional way with the editing and the bibliographic process.

Part I

FOUNDATIONS OF THE ARTS–STEM CONNECTION

CHAPTER 1

A MODEL FOR APPLICATION OF ARTS–STEM IN EARLY CHILDHOOD EDUCATION

Man is unique because he does science, and he is unique not because he does art, but because science and art equally are expressions of his marvelous plasticity of the mind.

—Jacob Bronowski

LEONARDO DA VINCI:
THE ARTIST WHO BECAME A SCIENTIST

Once upon a time there was a little boy who was separated from his parents. Undoubtedly, he was very sad and unhappy, but he did go to live with his grandparents and later with his uncle. His uncle loved nature and helped the little boy observe the birds carefully and notice how their wings worked. The young boy recorded the flight of birds, the plants he saw, the insects and their parts, the water and how it flowed. He drew pictures of all that interested him, and he tried to figure out how everything worked. A very curious learner, he was known to be a harp player and dancer, too. This boy later became an artist, scientist, and engineer. His approach toward science was based on his detailed observations and a point of view with roots in the artistic rather than the experimental realm. His name was Leonardo da Vinci (1452–1519).

The arts were a catalyst for Leonardo da Vinci to pursue his understanding of engineering and the sciences such as aeronautics, botany, and anatomy. They helped him develop an insatiable curiosity for how things worked. The arts, in the early childhood field—including creative movement, drama, visual art, and music—are often put into action through play and are used to express creativity. The use of creative arts is a way for children to communicate their imaginative thinking to others. Through the magic of play, children can become anyone and go anywhere in any time frame; they do this through role-playing and improvisations. They learn to see things from another point of view, and their knowledge is dramatically increased when they interact with others. Children generally express themselves spontaneously in the arts by using their imagination and creativity. Encouraging such creative expression in our schools will open endless realms of new knowledge and exploration for children of all ages. However, when this type of open-ended exploration begins in the earliest grades, with the youngest students, it can truly become second nature and continue through the rest of their lives.

Advocacy for the arts is especially critical today because many school systems are cutting arts programs to provide "more time" for teaching basic literacy. According to Ken Robinson (2009), an internationally recognized leader in creativity, elevating certain subjects (such as literacy) over other subjects and requiring a precise amount of time for specific subjects each day can prevent children from receiving the diversity of experiences that they need for developing their creativity.

THE ARTS: A CATALYST FOR 21ST CENTURY SKILLS, STEM, AND DEVELOPMENTALLY APPROPRIATE PRACTICE

The arts are an effective way to communicate interests, feelings, and ideas to others, and they lay the foundations for creative thinking in math and science. Mathematics and science can be enhanced and expanded as children express their imaginative thinking. As children focus on their own interests, they often become intensely motivated to express themselves spontaneously through play by utilizing creative movement, drama, visual arts, and music.

The arts are connected to 21st century skills; to science, technology, engineering, and math (STEM); and to developmentally appropriate practice in unique ways that promote a synergetic effect for curriculum development in inclusive settings, as illustrated in Figure 1.1 and discussed below.

What Are 21st Century Skills?

Creativity is needed more than ever in our schools. Major reports on the skills that are needed for the future have been spurred by the Partnership for 21st Century Skills (2008, 2009), which is composed of large corporations, national professional organizations, and state offices of education. These organizations have expressed concern because they foresee a need that goes beyond what is presently emphasized in our schools. The reports emphasize the importance of creativity, critical thinking, and problem solving, as well as communication and collaboration, as skills needed for the 21st century. These skills are already nurtured in tolerant, inclusive, and pluralistic societies (Chua, 2007; Florida, 2007, 2012; Zhao, 2009) and are further discussed in Chapter 2. These skills are utilized in the arts as well as in the sciences, yet few sources have linked 21st century skills, the arts, and the sciences together. An examination of developmentally appropriate practice principles of child development and learning (Copple & Bredekamp, 2009)

Figure 1.1. A Model for Early Childhood Arts–STEM and Its Components Utilizing Developmentally Appropriate Practice

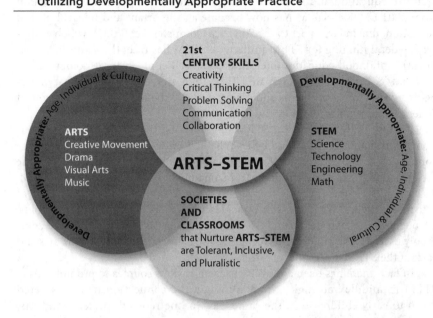

gives credence to a model that promotes an integrated approach based on cultural understanding. In this book my intention is to help the reader discover the Arts–STEM connection with 21st century skills and developmentally appropriate practice in an in-depth way so that the Arts–STEM movement can be practiced in early childhood at a more robust level.

Arts–STEM History and Emphasis

Innovation is the buzzword of the future because the world is moving into a creative conceptual age. According to Daniel Pink (2006), a conceptual age demands creativity, critical thinking, problem solving, collaboration, and communication with people of diverse backgrounds and thinking. The Arts–STEM connection has opened doors for artists and scientists to work together to produce innovative ideas and inventions for a global economy with diverse needs. This intersection has been called by various names, such as STEAM, STEM–Arts, ArtsSTEM, and TEAMS. It means an exchange between the arts (creative movement, drama, visual arts, and music) and STEM (science, technology, engineering, and math). These programs are scattered throughout the states. None are national programs, and very little has been done to promote them at the early childhood level in schools. However, it is in early childhood that interest in the STEAM fields starts to emerge, and the arts can be a catalyst for creativity in the fields of science, technology, engineering, and math. The arts are foundational to helping children express STEM concepts and dispositions (Piro, 2010; Sharapan, 2012).

The acronym STEM was first introduced by Judith Ramaley, assistant director of education and human resources at the National Science Foundation from 2001 to 2004. STEM has now become an important and integral part of education, due in large part to the America Competes Act (2007), which authorized federal funding for STEM initiatives. STEM has recently begun to appear in early childhood education literature (Counsell et al., 2016; Moomaw, 2013; Moomaw & Davis, 2010; Sharapan, 2012). The vision of STEM was that of recognizing real-world problems and giving students the tools to become the next generation of problem-solvers and innovators.

Because of the support for STEM in grants and the importance of innovation for our national economy, I believe that it is critical that an interdisciplinary connection to the arts be developed. This book is based on the thesis that the arts, particularly in early childhood, are an adjunct to and supporter of STEM. As such, it is incumbent upon teachers to recognize the connection to STEM as artistic endeavors take place. This book describes how such recognition unfolds. Throughout the text, the term Arts–STEM has been used rather than the commonly used STEAM in order to recognize the connections between the arts and each of the STEM disciplines.

In fact, there has been a movement from various sources to promote Arts–STEM in middle and high school, although the connection has not filtered down to early childhood in the same way. In one research project, students, ages 9 to 10, were trained to carefully observe pictures and reason about pictures in a museum setting. They were later asked to transfer to a similar task of looking at and reasoning about an image from the biological sciences. Their ability to complete the task presented clear evidence of the transfer of observational skills from art to science (Tishman, MacGillivray, & Palmer, 2002). The National Science Foundation is now funding science and art projects, such as the Learning Worlds Project (www.learningworldsinstitute.org), which emphasizes sciences and arts working together to promote scientific breakthroughs.

The STEM initiative is morphing into STEAM, according to Eger (2011). This idea was first expressed by Frans Johansson (2004) in the book *The Medici Effect*, and refers to the creativity enabled by the Medici family of Italy during the Renaissance. This was the time when Leonardo da Vinci grew up, and he would have been exposed to the arts and their importance in STEM. Johansson reports that during the Renaissance there was an intersection of different fields, cultures, and, ultimately, an explosion of new discoveries. These ideas have been reinforced by Weiner (2016). Many people think that the arts and sciences are mutually exclusive because the sciences are about knowledge and objectivity while the arts are about self-expression and nonobjectivity. In reality, there are many similarities between the two disciplines that draw on the creative processes. Collaboration of the arts and STEM in early childhood education may be the dawning of a new renaissance that provides a breakthrough of ideas, concepts, and cultures.

How Is Developmental Appropriateness Related to Arts–STEM and 21st Century Skills?

The National Association for the Education of Young Children (NAEYC) provides guidance on what constitutes research-based curriculum in several of its position statements, particularly on developmentally appropriate practice (DAP). It is important for directors, teachers, and principals to refer to DAP when choosing a curriculum. In thinking about the Arts–STEM approach, one should look at each of the DAP principles and contemplate how an Arts–STEM connection meets those principles. Especially noteworthy are the principles encompassing the following actions (Copple & Bredekamp, 2009):

- Exposing children to a wide range of teaching strategies and interactions in supporting all kinds of learning (Number 9, p. 14)
- Using play for developing self-regulation as well as promoting language, cognition, and social competence (Number 10, p. 14)
- Challenging children to achieve at a level just beyond their current mastery (Number 11, p. 15)
- Having children's experiences shape their motivation and approaches to learning such as the development of persistence, initiative, and flexibility—dispositions and behaviors that affect children's learning and development (Number 12, p. 15)

These principles along with the core decisions of age appropriateness, individual child appropriateness, and cultural relevance (Copple and Bredekamp, 2009) make an Arts–STEM connection important in helping create a developmentally appropriate curriculum that is intentional.

HOW ARE THE CREATIVE ARTS CONNECTED TO STEM?

There are many ways in which the creative arts can connect with STEM. This section focuses on the following specific areas of integration between arts and STEM: creative problem-solving commonalities; the similar personal characteristics of artists and scientists; similar philosophical approaches to arts and STEM; mutual pursuit of interests in artistic media, design, and nature; interdisciplinary concepts that enhance the Arts–STEM relationship; and cultural connections.

Creative Problem-Solving Commonalities in Arts–STEM

Inquiry. When art techniques are used with or encouraged in young children, they will help them develop curiosity, which is a skill needed to excel in STEM areas. A child who asks, "What if I mix these two colors together?" is actually producing art, but this curiosity is leading to a major component of the sciences: cause and effect. In other words, when "what if" questions are asked while children are doing art, this stimulates their ideas in STEM courses and vice versa. Inquiry is an essential part of all educational endeavors, including the arts and STEM. (See Chapter 2 for a detailed discussion of curiosity and how it is important in scientific investigation.)

Problem Solving. Questions and problems, which are part of the artistic process, are also part of the acquisition of new ways of designing in the science and engineering fields. Artists ask: How can I use shapes to make this plane beautiful? Scientists ask: Why does this paper airplane go faster than the other? The scientist uses rigorous methods to discover and verify the answers within the scientific method. An engineer asks: How can I make this paper airplane go farther and safer? Engineers use a slightly different method to design, build, and test solutions. The arts, science, and engineering have propelled people to solve puzzling problems, develop useful inventions, and introduce innovation. (See Chapter 2 for a discussion of the stages of creative problem solving.)

Imagination. The arts with young children stimulate imagination, which is also necessary in STEM-based projects. *Imagination* is the ability to see things other than the way they are. It is the ability to visualize the future and foresee what might happen, plan to anticipate it, and represent it in some form. Artists and scientists perceive what is but imagine what could be. They use their awareness, knowledge, and technical skill to develop what could be. Michelangelo "saw" David in the stone before he carved it. Ben Franklin saw electricity in lightning, and he proved it was there by using a key. (See Chapter 2 for a further discussion of imagination.)

Learning from Mistakes. The arts in young children help with a positive approach to failure and a willingness to change. With art that young children make, it is generally easy to change, cover up, or redo. A mistake can usually be fixed, but most of all, an artist or a scientist must take advantage of the mistake and realize there are lessons to be learned—this is also referred to as "trial and error." Children show persistence in their creative arts, and this quality is needed in STEM. The arts and STEM require that one continually assess, recognize challenges in a process, and identify what further needs to be done. A mistake is not the beginning of learning; it is the continuation of learning and the impetus to learn something new. (See Chapter 3 to further understand the importance of allowing a child to make mistakes.)

Discovery. The environment of the creative arts is one of discovery, just as the laboratory of science is one of discovery. Children should have an environment where discovery can take place in the arts and sciences. The environmental conditions that promote creativity and discovery are discussed in Chapter 3. Children discover the science of sound by using string, wind, and percussion instruments in Chapter 7.

Process Skills. The process skills aid in helping children with the methods of learning both art and science. These process skills include, but are not limited to, observation, comparison, classification, measuring, communicating, inferring, predicting, and hypothesizing. The arts help the child develop the detailed observation skills that are needed in STEM courses. Children *observe* using their senses to gather information in both art and science. Children *compare* similarities and differences in both art and STEM. Psychologist Reuven Feuerstein and his colleagues (2006) say that making comparisons helps the child focus on detail, develop a schemata, and draw conclusions. Children *classify* in creative arts and in STEM fields by color, shape, size, and so on, and notice the intricate details of two- and three-dimensional figures. Children *measure* in creative arts as well as STEM projects with a measuring tool, either standard or nonstandard, and see how the measurements fit the project. Children *communicate* and share their ideas on paper with pictures, graphs, and journals in the arts and sciences. When children *infer* in art and science, they recognize patterns and note when they reoccur or deviate. Children *predict* in both art and science by making reasonable guesses. They even *hypothesize* by making, "if, then" statements or "if I do this, that will happen." (For further discussion of process skills, see Chapters 2, 3, and 5.)

Similar Personal Characteristics of Artists and Scientists

Intuition. Both the arts and sciences draw on the knowledge, passions, and intuition of the artists and scientists. It is a myth that scientists only think logically. They use intuition gaps to make great inventions. (See Chapter 2 for an in-depth discussion of intuitive gaps and insights.)

Aptitude and Passion. The excitement of an artist completing a work of art and a scientist making a discovery is driven by commitment, and both engage the knowledge, feelings, and intuitive powers of the person. The creative moment in the arts and sciences occurs when an artist or scientist is working in his or her element (Robinson, 2011). This element according to Robinson (2009) has two main features, and there are two conditions for being in it. The features are aptitude and passion, and the conditions are attitude and opportunity. Aptitude and passion for creativity can be developed in children in an environment that provides conditions for creativity to exist, as described in Chapter 3.

Intrinsic Motivation. The arts teach that intrinsic motivation is important and that immersion in the act of creating is essential. This quality is also essential in the scientist who needs to continue to learn in order to inquire. The cultivation of conditions that promote intrinsic satisfaction is a way to increase the probability that such motivation will be developed in STEM. In a school system where students are only extrinsically motivated by grades, this quality of intrinsic value will not be seen. Creative ideas, according to Eisner (2002), whether they are qualitative as in the arts or abstract as in mathematics, should be experienced as beautiful with an attentive and constructive mind.

Need for Expression. Artists and scientists distinguish themselves by a strong need to express themselves; the artist expresses emotion, beauty, and intuition, whereas the scientist expresses scientific knowledge. The scientist can also see beauty in the organic life and the organization of the universe. According to Bronowski (1973), who traced significant scientific and artistic inventions since the beginning of recorded history, the most powerful drive in the ascent of humans is pleasure in their own skill. Both artists and scientists love what they do and strive to do it better. Throughout this book are vignettes of children expressing themselves in the arts and sciences. The need for self-expression is particularly strong in young children, and it should be encouraged.

Similar Philosophical Approaches to the Arts and STEM

Desire to Discover Beauty and Organization in the World. The arts and STEM are driven by what drove earlier artists, scientists, and innovators such as Leonardo da Vinci and Albert Einstein—the desire to discover beauty, organization, and meaning in the world. Bronowski (1973) says that Leonardo took an artist's vision into science; that is, he gave science the detail of nature. Leonardo emphasized that the ability of the artist is predicated on the scientific study of the form. This book will demonstrate how Leonardo expressed his desire to know the organization of the world through his intense study of form, which led to his detailed art and inventions.

Unity of Nature, Design, and Knowledge. The arts and STEM fields are driven by the philosophical belief of Friedrich Froebel (1887/2001), the father of kindergarten, that there is a unity of nature, design, and knowledge. This belief helps one see that the organization of the universe can be understood through art, science, and math instead of through isolated subjects. A discussion of Froebel's theory of unity can be found in Chapter 6.

Connections Throughout History. The arts and STEM have produced and can produce some of the greatest inventions, and this same inventive behavior is necessary for innovation in the future. Leonardo is the consummate example of the connection between arts and sciences. While his primary profession was that of artist, at the same time he possessed intense observation skills and love of learning that helped him employ the skills of the scientist in his inventions. These connections are particularly relevant now in light of advancing technology. Steve Jobs, the late inventor of the Apple computer, employed art and design together with technology in his work. The arts and STEM both look closely at the unsolved problems of the world and work to solve them. Creativity is about making connections, and these connections take place in the arts and sciences.

Beauty and Its Relationship to Science. Many scientists who marveled at art in nature began in-depth studies of certain species. Haeckel, a German artist and scientist, drew hundreds of radiolarians, a type of sea organism. He realized that beauty was important to study in natural science. According to Rothenberg (2011), "the beautiful is the root of science and the goal of art, the highest possibility that humanity can ever hope to see" (p. 285). To Leonardo da Vinci, the pursuit of beauty and the pursuit of truth are not incompatible. He had vision, logic, imagination, and an unrelenting desire to know truth and beauty (Gelb, 1998). Beauty and its relationship to science is discussed in Chapter 6.

Mutual Pursuit of Interest in Artistic Media, Design, and Nature

Design. The elements of art (line, color, shape, texture, light) and the principles of design (emphasis, balance, pattern, scale, emphasis, unity) are used in the STEM fields. The arts are a way of communicating the STEM fields. Chapter 6 provides detail on the elements of art and the principles of design and how they are useful in the arts as well as in the sciences. The elements of movement (space, shape, time, flow, force) are found in Chapter 4, which shows how these elements can be useful in artistic movement and transferred to the sciences.

Topics of Interest: Nature. Artists and scientists can be interested in the same elements of nature, for instance, seascapes, landscapes, or flowers. However, artists and scientists may be interested for different and varied reasons. The artist could be interested to understand the detail and beauty of the form of nature, whereas the scientist may want to understand the function and why the particular element exists. Chapter 6 provides connections between the way artists and scientists think about a topic of interest such as nature.

Use of Media and Technology. Many different media are used in the arts, and many different media are used in STEM fields. The tools used in the early childhood arts (crayons, pencils, scissors, chalk, blocks, computers, iPads, and so on) were invented by people from the STEM fields in collaboration with artists or designers. Technology does not consist only of advanced forms of machines such as computers and iPads; it is any of the tools that have been invented to help people do their work, including the tools available in the arts. In Chapter 5 the media connection to the arts and sciences is discussed. The media of technology in the visual arts promotes interest in STEM. Computer programs and apps are forms of technology that exist in media for young children in the visual arts as well as in STEM projects. Just as photography evolved as an art form, yet artists continue to draw and paint, other technology will evolve as art forms, and artists will continue to enhance programs and applications by incorporating the old forms along with the new. Children will be able to participate in these developments, and as they mature, many will become creative artists and scientists. Art, architecture, communication, and design operate together with technology to involve and produce interdisciplinary projects of interactive design. New areas of technology require an interdisciplinary approach, opening up new creative digital designs.

Interdisciplinary Concepts That Enhance Arts–STEM Relationships

Classroom Standards. Students synthesize and relate personal experiences to make art (National Coalition for Core Arts Standards [NCCAS], 2014). The *Next Generation Science Standards* (NGSS, 2013) state that structure (form) and function are complementary properties in the crosscutting concept of structure and function and that students should observe the natural world and designed objects and note how the form is related to its function. These standards are basic to the understanding of the Arts–STEM connection and are discussed throughout this book.

It should also be noted that the Next Generation Science Standards have transdisciplinary crosscutting concepts, which are explained later in this chapter and illustrated with the Bridge Project, which includes the arts (visual arts, movement, music), math, engineering, and physics.

Spatial Development and Its Importance in Arts–STEM. Spatial thinking is a skill that is needed in the arts and lays the foundation for STEM (National Research Council [NRC], 2006; Pollman, 2010). Spatial thinking is essential to understanding locations, maps, distances, directions, shapes, and patterns. Good spatial development has been found to be a very high predictor of people who pursue STEM fields as well as the visual arts. People, nature, and human-made objects and structures exist in space, and shapes and patterns play a significant role in both art and STEM. Studies have shown that students who score high on spatial skills are attracted to software engineering, airplane design, architecture, mechanical engineering, industrial design, surgery, advanced math, physics, biology, astronomy, and chemistry (Xie & Shauman, 2003). Students in the visual arts also use a certain kind of spatial thinking, and the preschools of Reggio Emilia, Italy, have designed a program in which multiple experiences of the arts as extensions of thinking and spatial understandings take place. Furthermore, reports in mathematics from the National Research Council (2009) and the National Mathematics Advisory Panel of the U.S. Department of Education (2008) point out that attention to spatial development is necessary and children require formal instruction. Spatial development is discussed in Chapter 4 via examples in body and spatial awareness and in Chapter 6 via the Design–STEM connection and Froebel's curriculum.

Cultural Connections

Art helps individuals appreciate and develop empathy for the different cultural aspects of a society. There is some evidence that diversity helps create more ideas and that creative cultures promote an inclusive environment for ideas (Weiner, 2016). This diversity in turn promotes ideas for inventions in STEM. The arts are a way of communicating though artistic design. By understanding cultural needs and expressions in the classroom and the general culture, inventors in STEM can better meet the needs of various cultures and express the desires of those cultures. In an early childhood classroom, more learning can take place when there is more variation in culture and therefore more diversity of thought. These cultural aspects are emphasized throughout this book.

HOW ARE THE NEXT GENERATION SCIENCE STANDARDS CONNECTED TO THE ARTS?

The Next Generation Science Standards (NGSS, 2013) are national standards that have been adopted across all STEM areas and grade levels. The NGSS *crosscutting concepts* represent the kind of support for learning that results in deep, interdisciplinary learning of science and can be connected to the arts. Although the crosscutting concepts are not shown in the model in Figure 1.1, it is important to see how they promote an interdisciplinary approach. The crosscutting concepts include: (1) patterns; (2) cause and effect; (3) scale, proportion, and quantity; (4) systems and system models; (5) energy and matter; (6) structure and function; and (7) stability and change. These concepts will be explored below with applications to practice taken from the Bridge Project, a 3rd-grade project described in the next section. Also provided are references to chapters later in the book where there is more detailed discussion of these crosscutting concepts.

Patterns

According to the Next Generation Science Standards (NGSS, 2013), patterns guide organization and further classification in the sciences. The understanding of patterns is a necessary step in the artistic process as well as in the scientific method. A good example of this is understanding the patterns in leaves, whether they are alternate (leaves arranged in an alternate fashion along a stem); opposite (leaves arranged on a stem directly across from one another); or whorled (three or more leaves attached at a node along a stem).

An example of the alternating pattern from the Bridge Project can be seen in the design of triangles on a truss bridge, which are essential to the bridge structure. Patterns are further studied in Chapter 6 by looking at the principles of design seen in nature.

Cause and Effect

Although cause and effect is a major activity in the sciences and engineering, the arts can contribute to an understanding of cause and effect by their visual representation of the topic. An example of cause and effect would be the construction of ramps of various heights and a determination of the various outcomes of a ball that is rolled down each ramp (further questioning would determine why different outcomes occurred). Using a visual representation of the ball and its relation to the various ramp sizes would be helpful for facilitating learning.

Cause and effect can be seen in the study of bridges by the testing of weights on the various bridges in the Bridge Project. Cause and effect is studied in the discussion of art media exploration in Chapter 5.

Scale, Proportion, and Quantity

Scale, proportion, and quantity are important in both art and science. Size is critical in understanding a change in scale, proportion, or quantity. Although very young children do not completely understand scale and proportion, they can learn these concepts at a basic level with block playing, particularly with unit blocks. They begin with the basic unit block and discover that two basic unit blocks fit into the double unit block. Then they see that four basic unit blocks fit into the quadruple unit block and two double unit blocks fit into the quadruple unit block.

Block play is a tool for learning that supports children's understanding of geometry and spatial development, as discussed further in Chapter 5. Children in the Bridge Project are able to support their understanding of proportion by utilizing unit blocks and discussing the basic blocks and how they relate to one another. Beginning perspective and vanishing point can be taught to primary-age children by helping them notice that things that are farther away are smaller.

Systems and System Models

A system comprises multiple views, such as planning what is required, analysis of it, and the design and implementation. A system model describes and represents a system.

The building of bridges requires a system model that includes site considerations, people and environmental issues, structural issues, material availability, and economic issues. This system model is used in the Bridge Project and can be used in engineering and architecture in the block play area. (See also Chapter 5.)

Energy and Matter

Energy is a force, such as heat, that can cause a physical change. Matter is anything that takes up space and has mass, such as a solid, liquid, or gas. Children can see the effects of melting ice (solid) turning to water (liquid) in the classroom. In a video they can see the effects of ice turning to water in the mountain streams because of the sunlight. As young children see how water flows downhill from the mountaintop, they can understand that water flows downward and could possibly be a danger if too much of it flows in a steep mountain stream, due to the melting snow on the mountain peak. Energy or force is given off by the sun as well as the slope of the hills or mountains.

The building of a bridge in the Bridge Project might include energy and force issues such as what happens if a certain amount of weight is placed on the bridge, a large wind comes in contact with the bridge, or a huge amount of water comes under it. This understanding of energy and matter is promoted through the study of shapes and lines in the Earth sciences, as discussed further in Chapter 6.

Structure and Function

The structure, or shape, of an object will help a child see its function. For example, the shape of a bird's beak will help one see that the function of the beak is to assist the bird in getting food. Further and deeper observation of the bird will show the function of the bird's beak in more precise ways. For instance, the spear-shaped beaks of the kingfisher and heron help them spear fish. The short, thick, conical shape of the sparrow's and cardinal's beaks are for cracking seeds. The hooked beaks of the hawk and owl are useful for catching and tearing prey. The long and tubular beak or probe of the hummingbird is useful for sucking nectar from the flowers. The chisel-shaped, flat, and pointed beak of the woodpecker is necessary for drilling into wood to find insects.

The structure of a bridge is somewhat determined by its function. A lift bridge may have one side that moves up vertically, allowing ships to pass. A pontoon bridge floats so it can be moved from one part of the river to another. The swing bridge, on the other hand, has a steel cantilever that pivots on a support to move it when ships pass by. Structure (form) and function are further explored in Chapter 6.

Stability and Change

It is important for children to study how the natural world changes. They can record the changes they observe in specific areas of sciences. In biology, for example, children can do this with the life cycle of plants by recording what transpires when a seed is planted.

In the Bridge Project the children could see what happens to an iron bridge, or to a bicycle, when snow or water with salt come into contact with parts of the bridge or bicycle. Salt and water cause rust, and teachers can orchestrate a discussion of how too much salt used on the highways in the winter to prevent sliding can also cause rusting to bridges. Natural-world changes are studied in Chapters 5 and 6.

THE PROJECT APPROACH: TEACHING STRATEGY FOR ARTS–STEM CONNECTIONS

Although there are many types of integrated curriculum, such as units, thematic teaching, and learning centers, the project approach affords additional opportunities for growth of knowledge, skills, and dispositions. Because children ask their own questions, conduct their own investigations, and make their own decisions, the project approach provides a more viable opportunity to naturally practice Arts–STEM connections along with 21st century skills. These connections are illustrated in the following description of the development of the Bridge Project.

Ms. Sterling's 3rd-grade students expressed an interest in learning more about bridges after she read them the traditional story, The Three Billy Goats Gruff. She used three versions of the story and pointed out the designs of three different bridges in the illustrations. The children seemed interested in bridges and talked about a bridge they had walked over. Two days later, Ms. Sterling took them on a field trip to see two bridges not far from the school. One bridge was an iron truss bridge that was rusting due to exposure to water and possibly some salt. The children wondered why this would happen. To illustrate, the teacher talked about what would happen if a bicycle was left outside. They visited another bridge, an arch bridge made of stone, over a stream. The children immediately noticed that it looked like the bridge in the story book, and that the stone was very heavy and curved like the arch blocks they played with in the unit block center. They also discovered it had a ramp, like the unit block ramps. She taught them the word "deck" (where you walk or drive). They learned the words "support" and "span." They learned that all supports rest on a foundation, and they paid attention to the approaches leading up to the bridge. They then discussed what the differences were in the designs of the two bridges they had seen.

Back in class, Ms. Sterling encouraged the children to choose any bridge and represent it exactly as they remembered seeing it. They had free choice of various media such as tempera paint, crayons, chalk, blocks, clay, and pastels. The children were amazed at the many different interpretations of bridges that were drawn or built. The bridges had different shapes and lines, and the children soon realized that there is not one way of representing a given object, but many different approaches. Each child's individual bridge was unique and valued, and provided stimulation for a more in-depth and long-term study of bridges and for learning science and engineering concepts such as balance, gravity, and opposite and equal forces, as well as types of bridges such as beam, arch, suspension, pontoon, covered, draw, and swing.

Children used active movement with a rope to show how a suspension bridge cable works with two children on one side and two children on the other side. They imitated being a stone in an arch bridge. To do this, four children lined up facing each other. The middle two children placed their hands on each other's hands. The outside players put their hands on the waist of the child in front of them. They began pushing and feeling the compression force.

So that they could learn about bridges that collapse, the teacher taught them the nursery rhyme London Bridge, which describes a very old bridge that fell down. Through this exercise, the students became convinced of the importance of safety as well as testing bridges for safety. Later, in small groups, the children built bridges of different materials (blocks, popsicle sticks, cardboard) and examined the type of bridge that was the easiest to make and the type of bridge that was the sturdiest by using the engineering design system of defining the problem, developing possible solutions, and comparing solutions, as recommended by the Next Generation Science Standards (NGSS, 2013, p. 22).

As time went on, they did tests on triangles and squares to see which was stronger so they could build a better trestle bridge. This was demonstrated by using three straws to make a triangle. The children laced a string through each end of the three straws and tied the ends together tightly to form a triangle. They then went on to use four straws to make a square by lacing the four sides together. They found that the triangle was the sturdiest. The triangle was not as flexible as the square. They then were shown pictures of a roof beam and a building crane. They noticed that these structures used triangles. When asked why, the children were able to explain that triangles are stiff shapes, and they don't change when a force is applied. The children understood this concept because they had previously studied it and they observed the rigid shape of the triangle in their experiment.

One group of children designed and built trestle bridges with popsicle sticks. A second group drew and assembled a drawbridge after seeing one in a book about medieval castles. A third group sketched and erected a swing bridge similar to the one Leonardo da Vinci had designed. The children were so excited about their bridges that they invited their families to come see a presentation of their designs. They shared their work and reported on their investigations and research from books such as *Bridges! Amazing Structures to Design, Build, and Test* (Johmann & Rieth, 1999). (See Figure 1.2.)

The Bridge Project that developed after children observed the bridges in their community is an example of how the arts can be integrated into the study of literacy, math, and science (engineering and physics) using investigative work in a 3rd-grade classroom. The project approach is particularly important because it encourages children to be curious, a trait that is important in both the arts and sciences. A project approach begins from the interest of the children and lasts only as long as the children continue to show an interest in the project. The Bridge Project motivated the children to integrate drama, art, movement, and music into their next project, the scientific study of ants. The project approach is not a unit of study previously planned for the children by the teacher. Helm and Katz (2016) have explained the *project approach* as a teaching strategy in which one or more children can apply the arts and other subject matter to a topic worth studying. Katz (2007, 2010) and Helm and Katz (2016) have written how the project approach has complemented the skills of the 21st century. They indicate that the intellectual

**Figure 1.2. Girls Sharing Their Knowledge of Bridge Building
    at Parent Night**

skills that are important for developing the mind to its fullest include reasoning, hypothesizing, predicting, and the quest for understanding and conjecturing, as well as the development and analysis of ideas, all of which can be accomplished through the project approach. They believe the early childhood curriculum should support the innate curiosity of children and provide a wide range of contexts in which children can use their curiosity. As teachers help children meet the content standards in preschool, teachers can ensure that children get the experiences that help enrich them in the skills of the 21st century.

The arts in the project approach can also be very valuable for second language learners since the arts can be a good way to convey feelings to others. Expressing themselves through the arts gives second language learners an outlet, especially when they are not adept at expressing themselves verbally in English. Through drama, second language learners are able to tell their personal stories to others by acting them out. The arts are a way to convey ideas across cultures because children can communicate both verbally and nonverbally and the scientific and artistic processes are also used.

One way to foster intellectual development through the expressive arts in the project approach is to be responsive to children's interests in science and math.

Children, from a very young age, are naturally interested in the way things work and in trial-and-error attempts. Children were particularly interested in bridge design, which later led into safe bridge design in the Bridge Project described above. The arts can be a methodology for studying the STEM courses. For instance, "representation (drawing, writing, building, constructing) challenges children to integrate concepts" (Helm & Katz, 2016, p. 4), and representation is useful in engineering and the sciences. The responsive teacher provides materials, space, and time for children to explore and discover things in their environment and ask questions. This gives children opportunities to construct their own knowledge, and they are then able to express their personal understandings and imaginations more effectively. The versatility of the expressive arts offers *all* children a way to express themselves, not just those who are proficient in the English language. All children with special needs, including gifted and talented, developmentally delayed, and second-language learners, can learn to express themselves competently in a child-centered expressive arts environment that promotes skills in math and science. The separation of the expressive arts from the sciences does not take place in the project approach, which provides an exemplar for developmentally appropriate practice.

SUMMARY

Early childhood teachers need an understanding of 21st century skills of creativity, critical thinking, problem solving, communication, and collaboration in inclusive settings in order to motivate their students in the arts and STEM. The arts include, but are not limited to, creative movement, drama, visual arts, and music; they are a way to communicate to others and are more connected to an understanding of the sciences than previously thought. This chapter examined how the arts can be a catalyst for the STEM subjects (science, technology, engineering, and math) and how the project approach is a curriculum that exemplifies the Arts–STEM connection. This approach is a developmentally appropriate, researched-based curriculum in line with the crosscutting concepts of the Next Generation Science Standards (NGSS, 2013). The principles of developmentally appropriate, research-based practice are at work in the model presented in Figure 1.1 and should provide a robust schema for thinking about curriculum for young children. Throughout this book, robust content across an integrated curriculum is enhanced with a strong arts–science base, not only for the content base but also for the dispositions and interdisciplinary connections that are both challenging and achievable for children and for future innovators in Arts–STEM. Meaningful connections are made that integrate children's learning within and across the domains (physical, social, emotional, cognitive) and the disciplines of the arts (creative movement, drama, visual arts, and music) and STEM (science, technology, engineering, and math).

REVIEW AND REFLECT

1. How are the creative arts related to the STEM courses? Why should the early childhood teacher use 21st century skills to improve teaching?
2. Why is the project approach an exemplar of Arts–STEM?
3. Read a biography of a creative person, such as Thomas Edison, Alexander Graham Bell, Frank Lloyd Wright, Brunelleschi, Galileo, Albert Einstein, or Leonardo da Vinci, and determine what early influences help develop the characteristics important for creativity. How were the arts and sciences instrumental in their creativity? Find out what they were punished for in school, if possible. For instance, both Einstein and Edison were punished for asking questions in school. Yet the parents of both Einstein and Edison knew that their children had a gift for penetrating deep into the body of human knowledge; their teachers were not aware of this gift. In the case of Einstein, his parents sent him to a new school where he could pursue his thoughts. In the case of Edison, his parents allowed him to drop out of school and pursue his dedication to scientific experimentation.

CHAPTER 2

CREATIVITY
The Propeller for Arts–STEM

What you can do, or dream you can, begin it; Boldness has genius, power, and magic in it.

—Goethe

THE DEVELOPMENT OF CREATIVITY IN LEONARDO DA VINCI

Leonardo da Vinci often wondered about the things that were around him. He was very inquisitive. He drew and designed, but never published, many innovations based on what he saw. The parachute, the helicopter, the bicycle, the life preserver, many types of water craft, the robot, and even solar panels were thought of and even drawn by Leonardo in his journals. He used his inquiring mind to imagine what could be. He might have studied dandelions to understand how the seed head opens like a parachute and then the breeze takes the seeds away. He might have seen how the sycamore and maple trees have seeds inside winged cases that look like helicopter blades. He wrote down his ideas and predictions and often experimented to see what would happen. He practiced flying his machines on the hills of Florence, Italy.

Creativity involves the ability of children to use their imagination to develop new and original ideas. All children are creative by nature. Like Leonardo da Vinci, children get their ideas from their imagination, and they often choose to display their imagination creatively through the expressive arts, science, and engineering inventions. Parnes (1967) compared imagination to a kaleidoscope where knowledge is in bits and pieces, and imagination is what enables children to turn the drum and create new patterns. More recently *creativity* has been identified as a combination of abilities, skills, motivations, and attitudes (Honig, 2006). Although creativity is often associated with the arts, artists are not the only ones who are creative. A scientist must be creative to make a new discovery. A computer programmer must be creative to make new programs. An engineer must be creative to make a new and innovative car. A mathematician must be creative to come up with new ideas for solving a problem. To encapsulate, *creativity* is a combination of abilities, skills, motivations, and attitudes used in the arts and STEM. It requires critical thinking, problem solving, communication, and collaboration. This chapter focuses on issues related to creativity and their impact on the arts and sciences, the cultural emphasis on creativity, and foundational concepts of creativity to help teachers understand the creative process and its connections to art and science.

ISSUES RELATED TO CREATIVITY

In the 1970s Ellis Paul Torrance developed the Torrance Tests of Creative Thinking. These tests are highly reliable and respected, as well as widely used. Kyung Hee Kim (2011) analyzed almost 300,000 Torrance scores and reported a serious concern: Creativity scores had been rising until 1990 but have consistently inched down since then. According to Kim, the decrease is significant, and of particular note, the decline is most serious in scores of children from kindergarten through 6th grade. A point that many researchers agree upon is that creativity has suffered a decline during the childhood years. Meador (1992) presents evidence that creativity declines in kindergarten, even though this may seem like a natural time to be creative. This apparent decline in creativity poses the question as to why this occurs.

Most kindergarten teachers today believe they do not have time to explore the creative arts because their curriculum is prescribed. Teachers more often than not focus predominantly on formal literacy and mathematics instruction in order to have their students meet the Common Core State Standards (NGA & CCSSO, 2010). Furthermore, this focus on academic skills in early childhood classrooms provides a major obstacle to the inclusion of classroom learning experiences designed to promote children's use of creative thinking skills (Copple & Bredekamp, 2009).

Despite the trend, there is an alternative to formal and prescribed kindergarten curriculum. Teachers can focus on teaching more informally using the creative arts in a transdisciplinary way to develop 21st century skills (creativity, critical thinking, problem solving, communication, and collaboration) and still meet the standards. The formal focus, frequently found in schools, may be a function of many school districts not requiring prior training in the expressive arts as a specialized field of early childhood education certification. Many states do not require certification in early childhood education for kindergarten teachers (National Association of Early Childhood Teacher Educators [NAECTE], 2008). Young children do not learn effectively or efficiently by sitting and listening to teachers during formal instruction; they learn by becoming actively involved in their own learning that is based on a foundation of direct experience. Yet in many kindergarten classrooms, there is little, if any, scheduled time for children to freely explore their environment through play. Creativity is an important tool for individuals and society, as it has lifelong cognitive and affective effects that promote innovation in a culture.

Until recently there has been no widespread agreement about applying the results of extensive brain research to education. However, in 2004 the International Mind, Brain, and Education Society was formed to integrate the diverse disciplines that investigate human learning and development—to bring together education, biology, and cognitive science to form the new field of mind, brain, and education (Tokuhama-Espinosa, 2011). This shared academic discipline includes psychologists, neuroscientists, and former teachers. Their work has shown that in any given creative task, individuals use both hemispheres of the brain (Aghababyan, Grigoryan, Stepanyan, Arutyunyan, & Stepanyan, 2007; Chavez-Eakle, 2007) and not just one side of the brain, the right hemisphere, as was once thought. This neural interconnectiveness has been verified as essential to creativity (Tokuhama-Espinsoa, 2011). Any creative task must tap into the knowledge that is known so that the unknown can be explored. Gruber and Bodeker (2005) have speculated that the brain's ability to learn is based, at least in part, on its ability to be creative. According to Tokuhama-Espinosa (2011), being creative could be more natural to humans than not.

Pink (2006) has said that we are moving into the Conceptual Age whereby creators and empathizers will be important. The wealth of the nations will depend on having designers who are creating innovative solutions, jobs, and enhancing life. In his book he explains how we have moved from the 18th-century Agricultural Age, where most jobs were in farming, to the 19th-century Industrial Age, where most jobs were in the factories, to the 20th-century Information Age, where most jobs were knowledge centered, and finally to the 21st-century Conceptual Age, where most jobs require creativity and empathic behavior. For this reason, creativity and the arts should lead the way for innovation in such areas as science and math.

Creativity is essential in the evolution of the individual and society (Eckhoff & Urbach, 2008; Lindqvist, 2003). Research by Eckhoff (2011) found that although preservice teachers viewed creativity as linked to multiple domains such as the arts, science, and math, as well as other fields, further research is needed on how to train teachers to actually implement science and math experiences that foster children's creative thinking. Additionally, the research showed that schools limit opportunities for young children to exhibit their creativity in the early grades.

CULTURAL IMPORTANCE OF CREATVITY

Howard Gardner (1993, 1999, 2006, 2008) defined *creativity* as the ability to solve problems or make original things that are of value to a culture. Those cultures that place a value on certain skills usually provide the motivation for children to learn to perform those skills. For example, in countries such as China, detail in art is rewarded and valued by the culture, probably because children must learn to write the intricate symbols of their alphabet. Very young Chinese children are taught specific brush techniques, and it is their high-quality artistic products, containing intricate and skillfully made symbols, that are regarded as creative by their culture.

Singapore's educational leaders have placed a high value on the development of creativity in their schools primarily because their economic survival depends on the intellectual and imaginative thinking abilities of their citizens. Singapore has few industries; since the technological revolution has increased competition among countries in our global society, creative ideas are essential for the economic survival of Singapore. This country has embraced the full inquiry method. It empowers students to use their knowledge in inventive ways. Very young children in Singapore are encouraged to express their creativity in schools using the expressive arts. The development of creativity in all areas of the curriculum is now a national priority (Sharp & Le Métais, 2000). Other countries such as South Korea and Japan have also embraced creativity as part of their national plans (Zhao, 2009). Finland, a high scorer on the PISA International tests, has also used creativity and encouraged risk taking, creativity, and innovation. If *creativity* is defined as coming up with original ideas that have value, then creativity can be treated as the same status as literacy. The Finnish system has tried to define a successful school as one in which both students and teachers further their development and go further than they could have gone by themselves (Sahlberg, 2011).

In Western cultures where individualistic thought is valued, creativity is often thought of as an individual problem-solving process (Lubart, 1990). Other cultures reward collectivism; that is, group creativity is more valued than an individual's creativity. In Japanese culture, ideas come about because of group thought in "quality circles." These groups promote fluency of ideas and flexibility in thinking. The groups also spend time incubating an idea before a decision is made. Torrance (1995) suggests that the Japanese have developed a national climate for creativity with their emphasis on creativity in preschool education and the development of the expressive arts.

Although the United States has embraced creativity as an important skill of the 21st century (Partnership for 21st Century Skills, 2008, 2009), Robinson and Aronica (2015) describe how changing metaphors are needed to promote creativity in our schools. Schools in the United States were developed and are still structured for industrial societies. Industrial societies demand compliance and certain requirements, and the academic curriculum pays little attention to an individual child's aptitudes, interests, and dispositions. Nonetheless, there are some schools in the United States and elsewhere in the world that encourage children's inner world of creativity and at the same time succeed in promoting overall achievement (Robinson & Aronica, 2015).

FOUNDATIONAL CONCEPTS ABOUT
CREATIVITY IN YOUNG CHILDREN

Teachers and schools trying to balance children's creativity and academic achievement may turn to not only Gardner's definition of creativity, cited earlier, but his broader theory of multiple intelligences. Gardner (1993, 1999, 2006, 2008) contends that people do not possess a general intelligence as reflected in one IQ score, but that each individual possesses various degrees of many different intelligences. What he is saying is that intelligence is not a single concept but a pluralistic one. He theorized that creativity could occur within and among eight or more different intelligences: linguistic, logical, kinesthetic, visual, musical, interpersonal, intrapersonal, and environmental–naturalistic. The implications of this view of multiple intelligences for teaching and learning will be discussed further in the pertinent chapters of Part II.

Additional concepts about creativity are reviewed in this section to enable teachers to become more skillful provocateurs for expanding the possibilities of creative thinking of children. Children are naturally creative, and learning is a creative act that needs to be understood and enhanced in the context of the arts and sciences.

Characteristics of Personal Creativity

Creativity can be viewed as societal (cultural) or personal creativity according to Gowan, Khatena, and Torrance (1981). Societal (cultural) creativity is creativity that is valued by a society and recognized by it; examples would be inventions such as the light bulb by Edison or the iPad by Apple and its founder, Steve Jobs. Personal creativity is expressed by children every day. It refers to producing something new or novel, extending an idea they have, refining an idea, or finding new ways of expressing an idea (Isbell & Raines, 2013). Early childhood teachers should see personal creativity as part of a developmental process that depends on age and opportunities for developmentally appropriate artistic and scientific expressions. Young children spontaneously express themselves without giving much thought to a final product they produce. The product is relatively unimportant to them. However, as they grow and develop, children often become interested in learning techniques for improving their finished personal products.

Characteristics of personal creativity include sensitivity, curiosity, flexibility, originality, and intuition (adapted from Guilford, 1984; Isenberg & Jalongo, 2014; Jackson & Messick, 1965). The following vignettes illustrate characteristics of personal creativity in highly creative children in early childhood and how they can be used by teachers to understand or promote an understanding of art, math, and science.

Sensitivity can be observed in children like Imelda who are aware or cognizant of the feelings of others and their own feelings and express them in their art.

Imelda, a preschooler, seldom visited the art area in early childhood. However, one day she became very focused on a painting she was creating. "Quick, Ms. Alfredo. See what I made." It was paper covered with blue paint. Ms. Alfredo couldn't see what Imelda was trying to create, but she knew she would discourage Imelda if she asked her what she had painted. So Ms. Alfredo said, "Yes, Imelda, I see. Can you tell me about it?" Imelda said, "I made a crayon picture of me jumping on my mother's bed. See, here I am high in the air and these lines show how many times I jumped. Since I knew my mother might not like me jumping on her bed, I covered the crayon picture with this beautiful blue paint. That's my mom's favorite color."

Imelda, a child who did not frequent the creative arts area, demonstrated that she could be brilliantly creative when so inclined. Her sensitivity to the problems she might face if her mother saw her "jumping on the bed" led her to cover that part of the picture with a color her mother loved. Imelda's behavior showed characteristics of a sensitive, creative child and an understanding of the concept of number and one-to-one matching by her indication of how many times she had jumped. Her teacher was perceptive enough to encourage her to talk about the picture and her experiences to help her deal with her conscience and see that she was using her math skills.

Curiosity, a skill needed in art, science, and math, can be observed in children like Monic who are always asking questions and are eager to know about many things.

Monic, a 1st-grade student from India, continuously asked his teacher questions such as, "Why did the magnet pick up metal?" "Why did the leaves turn different colors?" "Why did some glass not make things bigger like the magnifying glass?" He was interested in, among other things, magnets, trees, glass, animals, plants, leaves, shells, pumpkins, nests, gourds, pinecones, and tree bark. Examining things carefully delighted Monic, as he touched and felt the objects and used descriptive vocabulary to identify them.

All these experiences contributed to his understandings and knowledge of the new world around him, and helped him to develop an enduring curiosity for nature and science. He soon improved his usage of the English language as he explored and questioned things in his environment.

Flexibility can be observed in children such as Alexis who have the ability to change or be influenced by others.

Alexis, a preschooler, was flexible in her thinking and actions, and she would be the dog, the princess, or the firefighter in a play, depending on the suggestions of the other children. Being able to think flexibly helped Alexis become more prepared for school experiences that involve changes. An example in science would be a cooking experience in which the ingredients go through chemical changes in the process of baking a cake. Other examples are in mathematics, as numbers change through addition and subtraction, and in spelling, as words change with the addition of suffixes and prefixes.

Flexible thinking is basic to many of children's subsequent learning experiences in math or science. According to Piaget (1952), children gradually come to understand how things change as they explore different materials in various situations in their environment.

Originality can be observed in children like Alfonso who have one-of-a-kind ideas.

Alfonso, a 1st-grader whose family had emigrated from Mexico, had the ability to depart from his traditional ideas and come up with an action he had not done before. Alfonso regularly said, "I got an idea" and then proceeded to try out his idea. For example, one day when drawing a picture of himself, he drew the skeleton inside the body. He also discovered a clever block-building solution by putting a flashlight in the blockhouse for electricity. In the fall, when describing a round yellow leaf with brown spots, he said it looked just like a tortilla. He proceeded to find more "tortillas." He also spent a great deal of time examining the ladybugs in the grass and their dots.

Alfonso's original ideas in art and science reflected his awareness and exploration of his new environment.

Intuition or insight can be observed in children who have the ability to interpret things in a situation to try to understand or solve problems.

Harry, a preschooler, tried to explain things using his insight. When he cut his finger, he said, "Look, I'm leaking." When he found out how old his teacher was, he exclaimed, "Man! That's a lot of numbers!" Harry's mother told his teacher that Harry explained that the cat was falling apart when he discovered his cat giving birth to kittens. After that he told the class that his mother cat had "faucets."

Harry looked for reasons for happenings by using his insightful intuition. His perceptions, though not always scientifically accurate, reflected his age-appropriate ability to look for intuitive reasons for what was happening in his environment based on what he was learning.

Sensitivity, curiosity, flexibility, originality, and intuition/insight into problems are characteristics of young children from various cultures and are ways of expressing personal creativity. These characteristics provide a foundation for creative behaviors in children and later for creativity in the Arts–STEM fields. A teacher needs to be perceptive enough to encourage children to express their thoughts and to see value in them.

Creative Thinking and Problem Solving

Guilford (1950) conceptualized creativity in terms of the child's ability to imagine, and he identified a divergent thinking category of the mental abilities involved in developing the imagination. His well-known model is called the Structure of Intellect. For Guilford, creativity evolved in divergent thinking, the process of generating many different ideas about a topic that leads to novel and creative solutions. It is "thinking outside the box." Convergent thinking, on the other hand, is the process of looking for the best single idea or answer to a problem. Guilford observed that scientists prefer convergent thinking, whereas artists use divergent thinking. However, divergent thinking is also needed in science and math. Divergent thinking, also called creative thinking, displays fluency, flexibility, originality, and elaboration. *Fluency* refers to producing many ideas, *flexibility* refers to producing ideas of various types, *originality* refers to producing clever and original ideas, and *elaboration* refers to embellishing existing ideas. Note that there is some overlap between Guilford's list and the characteristics of personal creativity discussed above. However, Guilford took the discusssion of creativity to another level by focusing on children's collaboration in group situations to promote creativity.

Fluency may be explored by gathering many related ideas through brainstorming or web making. Young children can participate in oral brainstorming or create a web and categorize ideas to discuss or visualize a theme or project. Webs are a way to help children extend their association, since after their thoughts are put on paper, patterns and associations can be seen more easily. Webbing also appears to minimize linear thinking. Teachers who are sensitive to webbing can stimulate fluency by asking what they could make with a paper cup that could be useful in their bedroom, in school, in a hiding place, in a car, in a bicycle, or at the park.

Flexibility may be explored by examining children's responses to the question, "What can you make with this paper cup?" This could demonstrate their flexibility to adapt an idea or change it. If they say, "make a drum," "cut out a door," "make a house," "make a bird feeder," or "make a cup necklace for snacks at the movies," the children show that they have changed thought processes and adapted the specialized object, a cup for drinking, to serve a different purpose. Teachers could also stimulate children's thought even more by asking what would happen if they wore a cup, carried it upside down, floated it in the air or on water, rolled it, or connected it to something else.

Originality may be explored when asking children, "What can you make with this paper cup?" Children who come up with unusual ideas such as putting the cup on a stick to find out which way the wind blows or attaching it to a string to make a toy for their siblings are showing originality. As long as no one else in the group has previously come up with the same idea, such responses can be considered "original." To further promote originality, children can be encouraged to use a paper cup with other items such as a paper plate and straws. One of the 2nd-graders made a hat from a paper plate with cups on the top to collect rain, and then she made a hole in the cups and placed straws in them. She could actually drink water from the cups on her head (see Figure 2.1). One made a flying saucer with two plates and cups. One made them into earmuffs with soft material inside. Another child attached two cups with a string in between. On the string was a straw that moved along the string from one cup to another cup as a means of transportation.

Elaboration or expanding on an idea may be explored by asking for specific uses for an item. Ask a child who responds that the cup could be a house: "Who will live in the house?" or "To whom does this house belong?" This child should be encouraged to elaborate on this original idea, which imagined a real use for the repurposed object: the paper cup for drinking becomes a house with a door for a mouse that wishes to have a portable home. The girl who made a hat

Figure 2.1. Rainwater Drinking Machine. It Really Works!

for drinking water created a water-saving device that allows the owner to drink water from the sky and not get wet. The creator of the flying saucer imagined it as the first flying saucer to go to Mars. The child who attached two cups with a string described the invention as the "steep riding line swing" for people to use going up a hill or down a hill.

Children who amaze their teachers with unusual responses to questions, such as a house for a mouse, a water-saving hat, earmuffs, and a "steep riding line swing" have a keen sense of humor and may be thinking divergently. People use divergent thinking when they see things in original and imaginative ways, and convergent thinking when they select the most useful and appropriate ideas and solutions that were generated during the divergent thinking process. Divergent and convergent thinking are both necessary for the output of creative expressions in STEM. For example, children may use divergent thinking to imagine many ways to draw a house, but choosing the way they will finally draw the house requires convergent thinking.

Katz, Chard, and Kogan (2014) refer to both divergent and convergent thinking when webbing. Exhibiting divergent thinking, children can write down ideas about a project they are studying on sticky notes. The notes are then moved around so that similar ideas are grouped together. Katz suggests that slips of paper of a different color be used as headings or cluster-group headings. Later these ideas are recorded on a more permanent sheet. Once they have compiled cluster-group headings, the children are no longer the creators, but become the critics. As critics, they can often see better ways of grouping and organizing, and use convergent thinking to make their final decisions. Thus these two forms of thinking are interconnected in the creative expression process.

Stages of Creative Process

Many years ago, Graham Wallas (1926) theorized that creativity was developmental, that is, it progressed through stages. According to Wallas, there are four classic stages of the creative process: preparation, incubation, illumination, and verification. These stages in young children will be illustrated by vignettes from Ms. Meyer's kindergarten.

Preparation. The first step in the creative process, preparation is the process of research and brainstorming prior to the creative expressions. Wallas hypothesized that before people can have creative ideas "dawn on them," they must become prepared by gaining more knowledge in their field. He suggested that people explore creative ideas mainly in their own fields, for example, artists focus on art and scientists focus on science. The preparation process for children involves gaining knowledge of the world by actively exploring using their five senses. The children in Ms. Meyer's kindergarten were curious about dandelions.

Ms. Meyer watched the excitement and interest of the children in the dandelions changing from yellow to fluffy white, and the seeds flying away. As she observed the children, she became more sensitive as to how they were preparing themselves for ideas that may later be creatively expressed in aeronautics. Ms. Meyer and the children saw how the wind provides lift and thrust for the dandelion seeds to fly and how the fluffy ball is similar to a parachute. Ms. Meyer brought a small parachute to school to show the children how it works with wind, similar to how the dandelion seeds were lifted up and blown in the direction of the wind. The children later made parachutes out of string and paper plates and flew them. They could see how they flew just like the dandelion seeds.

Later, the children flew kites. Ms. Meyer asked the children how the wind made the kites fly. They said the wind came up behind the kites and under the kites. If the wind stopped, the kite fell down. They learned about lift, gravity (weight), thrust, and drag. As they were flying the kites, a helicopter came along, and Ms. Meyer asked them how the dandelion seeds, parachutes, and kites are similar to the helicopter. The children answered that they all fly. The teacher then asked how, and they replied that the wind made them fly. They then remembered to say the wind went under them, lifted them up, and thrust them forward. She asked them what pulled them down to Earth when the wind stopped. One boy said gravity (weight).

During this week of preparation, Ms. Meyer made available books about helicopters, airplanes, and rockets. The children became very interested in flight and began to design airplanes, helicopters, and rockets on drawing paper. Later they tried to make them at the block-playing center.

Incubation. The second stage in the creative process, incubation involves allowing ideas to develop without acting upon them. It is a temporary pause to allow subliminal processes such as daydreaming, relaxation, or time away from a situation to operate. During this stage of the creative process, a child's indecision and daydreaming can be a sign of creative thinking. Many young children have pretend playmates whom they talk to as they are developing creative ideas. When young children are daydreaming, many ideas go through their minds. Young children spend time daydreaming and imagining things before they clarify an unusual idea, such as a cat hammock out of a paper plate and rope or a bed-making machine out of pulleys and rope.

The children in Ms. Meyer's kindergarten started the process of incubation by using their bodies to play airplanes and helicopters outside. They pretended they were going places, and the planes were landing on the runway while the helicopter landed on the circular landing pad. They used scarves and other play materials to demonstrate the wind beneath the planes' wings. One day they asked the teacher if they could make some flying machines that would fly. One child, Jordan, told his teacher he dreamed about an airplane he was making.

Illumination. The stage of illumination refers to the hatching or the "aha" experience. This is the time imaginative ideas come forth. According to Wallas (1926), there appears to be a strong need in creative people to continuously improve upon or modify their work. In the illumination stage, people often refine their work and come up with more practical or novel ideas. For young children, after an idea comes forth, they often persist in expressing this idea repeatedly. For example, after discovering that they have the power to change colors, children may spend an excessive amount of time mixing various colors together. Teachers should allow children to continue to explore changing colors as long as their interest lasts, and in addition show them how to explore their power to change other things such as oranges to orange juice, or apples to applesauce. As explained earlier, the idea of change is an important thing for a child to know in art and science and is a concept that develops slowly. Children learn how things can change as they experience different materials in various situations; they learn that clay can change from soft to hard or plaster can change from liquid to solid. These changes continue when they see how iron can be broken down in the oxidation process and turned into rust if iron is left outside with water for a number of days.

Children in Ms. Meyer's class began to refine their aeronautics vocabulary in the block center. They thought about how the air goes under the wing. They used the word lift to talk about how planes are lifted up by the wind. They talked about how planes are thrust forward. They talked about how gravity brings them down to Earth. They were learning about the principles of flight: lift, gravity (weight), thrust, and drag. After Mrs. Meyer placed books on airplanes and helicopters in the block-playing area, she drew a plane runway and helicopter landing pad. Mrs. Meyer decided to have the children further refine their ideas by folding construction paper into helicopters and airplanes. She had labels for the airplanes that included propeller, cockpit, engine, wing, aileron, tail, and rudder; as well as labels for the helicopters that included cockpit, engine, large rotor blades, tail, small rotor blade, and skids. Children used the labels to identify the parts of the aircraft in the block-playing area. They flew their planes and helicopters and experienced many changes in their designs and then found an "aha" moment as they completed their designs. One boy designed his plane to be both a helicopter and airplane. This was his "aha" moment.

Verification. The fourth stage, verification, is when something is complete, and all parts seem to fall into place. Usually there is satisfaction with the final product. This stage is vital to any successful project. In early childhood, however, the process of verification is relatively unimportant to a young child when compared to the overall creative process. Children often do not value their ideas or *products* but rather just enjoy the *process* of creative expression. Early emphasis on producing a product may discourage the creative efforts of a young child, and producing a product should originate from the individual child and not be imposed by the teacher. However, group collaboration can enhance this work and make it easier to produce a product. Teachers should not show children how to draw or fold unless they need some help. They should provide the materials and the inspiration for them to make their designs. Teachers often verify the importance of children's ideas by displaying artwork or inventive creations on bulletin boards.

Later, the children in Ms. Meyer's class verified their work by having an "air show." The different designs of folded airplanes were tested to see which one flew the fastest and which one flew the longest distance. The helicopter was tested to see if it could land in the center of the landing pad. Children recorded what they observed. Children also described their aeronautical designs using the aeronautical words they had learned. Invitations were sent to the parents so that the children could share their creations.

Verification can take place as part of the scientific method whereby conclusions are made based on hypotheses that are tested, observed, recorded, and verified. These elements of the formal scientific method are seen in a very uncomplicated way in the stages of the creative process in the example above and the observation of what type of aircraft flew the quickest and the longest distance.

Wallas (1926) provided the framework for understanding how creativity develops in stages. However, it takes special kinds of thinking, both divergent and convergent, for a child to be able to come up with innovative ideas.

SUMMARY

This chapter began with the development of creativity of Leonardo da Vinci and the Arts–STEM connection. It emphasized that all children are creative and that learning is a creative act. Next, creativity issues and cultural influences were examined. Finally, foundational concepts about the characteristics of personal creativity, creative thinking and problem solving, and stages of the creative process were reviewed to help teachers think about the possibilities of creative thinking in young children who are naturally creative beings in the arts and sciences.

REVIEW AND REFLECT

1. Many characters in books and movies have been stuck in what is learned behavior rather that what is unique to their own self-expression. In many of the fairy tales, someone is in prison and tries to get out. Powerful figures such as the Queen of Hearts and the Red Queen try to stop Alice in Wonderland. In the end she says, "You are a pack of cards." She used her ingenuity and initiative, which is necessary for creativity. Go back through the vignette examples in this chapter and rewrite them with the main character a teacher or parent who does *not* value creativity. Then note which of the following barriers to creativity took place because of this adult's resistance to valuing creativity:

   - Not understanding the culture of the child
   - Comparing work to a model
   - Not allowing children to ask questions
   - Not giving children enough imagining time
   - Not giving children enough time to complete projects
   - Not making a variety of materials available
   - Not allowing play or exploration

2. This group activity is designed to help adults or primary-grade children improve their divergent thinking skills of fluency, flexibility, originality, and elaboration. Give the adults or children a straw. Then organize the adults' class or the children's class into small groups, and assign each group the following tasks:

   - Come up with as many creative ideas as you can for using the straw. Who came up with the most ideas? Adults or children who come up with many ideas have developed fluency.
   - Use the straw with something else in the room to develop more ideas. Adults or children who are able to come up with other ideas have developed flexibility.
   - Think about who came up with the most unique idea or ideas. Adults or children who come up with the most innovative idea have developed originality.
   - Think of a special title for one of their creations. Adults or children who come up with a special title have developed elaboration.

The above activity, which emphasizes the processes of fluency, flexibility, originality, and elaboration, can be introduced with a can, box, pencil, and other items instead of a straw. Research whether the adult class or primary class is able to produce more ideas each time. Does practice help with divergent thinking? Record the results and share them. How could the teacher enhance creativity? What questions or what webbing techniques could be used?

3. After reading the biography *Steve Jobs* by Walter Issacson (2011), make a web of some of the early experiences of Jobs, founder of Apple and inventor or contributor to the invention and revolutionizing of personal computers, animated movies, music, phones, tablet computing, and digital publishing. Then analyze what would have happened if one area of influence on his development had not taken place. Discuss the implications for schools in your district. Share with an administrator, and determine how some of these influences can begin in early childhood.

4. Invite a group of creative people from different domains to class, and ask them what made them creative. What characteristics discussed in this chapter did they have? Reflect on what they might have been like as children.

CHAPTER 3

Building a Creative Ecosystem in the Classroom

Children learn what they live.

—Dorothy Law Nolte

Invest in a creative ecosystem.

—Memphis Manifesto

A CREATIVE ECOSYSTEM:
FLORENCE DURING THE TIME OF LEONARDO DA VINCI

During the 1400s, Florence, Italy, was a flourishing city-state with its own government. It was ruled by the Medici, a powerful family, and it attracted some of the best thinkers, architects, and artists. This period is known as the Renaissance, with advances in art, literature, and science. Florence was a city full of ideas. Because Leonardo da Vinci lived in Florence during this time, this bursting forth of ideas would have been part of his life. He would have been able to share his own new ideas in an environment that promoted invention. The creative ecosystem that existed in Florence during the Renaissance is equaled in only a few other cities in the world.

An *ecosystem* is the interactions of a community of organisms with their environment. The interactions in a creative ecosystem—whether a city or a classroom—can help shape development of creative ideas. Creative cities, according to Florida (2007, 2012), are places that are diverse, tolerant, open to new ideas, and conducive to human interaction. This was true of Florence, and also Milan, when Leonardo da Vinci lived there. These characteristics have a synergetic effect on creativity in cities as well as in classrooms. Cities that promote creativity have "third spaces" where people neither work nor live but meet to discuss ideas. Such spaces can be cafés, bookstores, museums, music venues, and so forth. Leonardo da Vinci was able to discuss his ideas in the art studios and in the cafés of Florence and Milan. He associated with Michelangelo, Raphael, and possibly Amerigo Vespucci. Classrooms of today can be developed as a microcosm of the creativity found in the broader environment. A creative ecosystem in the classroom promotes interactions with other children and the environment.

The *ateliers* (studios) of the preschools in Reggio Emilia, Italy, have become known as places where children can explore with various tools, techniques, and materials, connecting art, architecture, and design. Vecchi (2010) describes the *atelier* of Reggio as a space but also a way of thinking that breaks down the closed-off disciplines and brings in connections across transdisciplinary subjects. This can be true in any classroom if teachers are attuned to the arts, and there are connections to other subjects, particularly the STEM courses that are being emphasized today.

The sensitivity of the teacher to nuances of the interactions in the classroom environment that shape creativity is important. This chapter will explore a theoretical model of conditions that promote creativity in the environment and three forces at work in the environment: climate, space, and time.

CONDITIONS OF A CREATIVE ECOSYSTEM IN THE CLASSROOM

Brian Cambourne (1988), a theorist trained in art education, conceptualized the conditions necessary for children to learn a complex series of literacy skills. These same conditions of learning can be used to explain how creativity develops in a classroom in the arts and sciences. Cambourne postulates eight interconnected conditions that generally support both children and their teacher in the pursuit of creativity. The conditions are immersion, demonstration, engagement, expectation, responsibility, use, approximation, and response. These conditions are discussed in this section as they were evidenced in Leonardo's time, in creative early childhood classrooms of today that nurture the young artist as scientist, and in the preschools of Reggio Emilia.

Immersion

Leonardo da Vinci was immersed in the arts and sciences in his environment in Florence. He was encountering the latest advances in the arts as well as science, technology, engineering, and mathematics. The journals he kept were filled with many detailed examples and demonstrations of the intersections of the arts and inventions in various fields.

When children and teachers are completely immersed in creative expressions in creative classrooms of today, all their time, energy, and concentration are devoted to that activity. Children in creative classrooms are immersed in the visual arts, music, play, drama, and movement, as well as in math and scientific inventions and discoveries in a stimulating environment. The process skills of observation, comparison, classification, measuring, communication, inferring, predicting, and hypothesizing are also emphasized. To promote immersion the classroom teacher provides many different art media, blocks, simple machines, live plants and animals, as well as many types of musical activities such as listening, singing, playing, moving, and creating. The elements of the arts such as line, color, and shape in the art area are explored as well as the elements of music and movement. The synergetic effect of the exploration of these elements takes over. There is an immersion of all the senses in science areas. There are pleasant aromas, sounds, colors, textures, and lights to stimulate children to become involved aesthetically.

The condition of immersion can further be seen in the atelier experience of the Reggio preschools, where children's immersion in the research of a project on a topic of interest promotes a transdisciplinary approach to learning and the development of in-depth understandings (Vecchi, 2010). Through the process of project documentation, as demonstrated in the Reggio preschools, families are also immersed in the creative processes that are appropriate for the child's world in the arts and sciences.

Demonstration

When Leonardo da Vinci was about 12 or 13 years old, he became an apprentice in the studio of Andrea del Verrocchio, a well-known Florentine artist. Verrochio provided formal demonstrations in art techniques for Leonardo, and he rose from apprentice to journeyman, to assistant, and later to master. Verrochio recognized the talent of Leonardo and encouraged him in his work. He would have been exposed to other artists who were also extremely talented and who contributed to the field.

Children in creative early childhood classes learn from many informal and formal demonstrations of the creative arts and sciences in their environments. They can watch the teacher point out the swirls in the work of Vincent Van Gogh's *Starry Night* that is hanging on the wall, and then they can try to paint swirls at the art easel. The teacher can model a block activity and draw the children into it, and then the teacher allows the children to continue with their own creations. As the teacher gets on the floor and builds a building, children immediately want to participate and continue planning and building. The teacher promotes a systems approach with planning, analysis, design, and implementation, just as an engineer and architect would do.

The teacher also demonstrates an aesthetic attitude or the disposition toward the love and pursuit of beauty and being open and spontaneous. The classroom teacher knows how to communicate a sense of wonder and how to express appreciation of the natural world.

Demonstration of an aesthetic attitude is further shown by having green plants that beautify the classroom, including plants native to the local geographical area (such as cacti in the Southwest). Other plants including potato or avocado plants can be grown in the classroom, alongside tops of carrots, rutabaga, or turnips. Aquariums and terrariums are also used for exhibits with rocks, stones, seeds, seedpods, gourds, shells, and blooming plants. All these exciting and stimulating exhibits provide children with the feeling that they too can demonstrate their creativity with natural objects and plants.

Demonstration can be seen in the Reggio preschools simply by the aesthetic environment. According to Vecchi (2010), the aesthetic environment is the starting point for the children's discoveries that will take place. The field trips, the workbenches in the atelier, the hands-on experiences with different media—all are places or activities for demonstrations and provocateurs of reactions.

Engagement

Leonardo da Vinci became engaged in the arts and sciences because of his strong observation skills. He expressed himself as an artist, dancer, actor, musician, scientist, engineer, and inventor in his journal as well as in his creations. His strong observational skills in nature and his artistic reproductions led to the other scientific and mathematical process skills that required further observation such as comparison and classification and, eventually, the more difficult process skills of inferring, predicting, and hypothesizing.

Children in creative classrooms can thus become the creator of their dreams and actively engaged after seeing demonstrations. Children believe they can participate in what they have seen. They think, "I can become an artist [or dancer, actor, musician, singer, scientist, engineer, or inventor]." This belief becomes so strong in an Arts–STEM classroom that their dreams become real in their creative environment. The classroom is no longer a culture of minimum compliance as the values of creative expression are demonstrated through the engagement of the children. The engagement is one of heart, mind, and spirit. They are able to transform themselves into whatever they are doing.

Children in the Reggio preschools engage in similar types of activities that occur in the ateliers (Gandini, 2002; Gandini, Hill, Cadwell, & Schwall, 2015; Vecchi, 2010). The curriculum in the Reggio preschools is neither child centered nor teacher directed; it originates in the child's interests, and is negotiated to reflect a reciprocal relation among teachers, children, and parents. According to Vecchi (2010), the verb *progettare* has a number of meanings in Italian that promote engagement: to design, to plan, to devise, to project (in a technical sense). It challenges the linear thinking of curriculum. As Rinaldi (2006) says, it means being in tune to the unpredictable results of children's investigations and research, as projects change direction. As children become actively engaged in the creative process, teachers set expectations high enough to challenge them, without the risk of failure.

Expectations

Leonardo's art teacher, Verrocchio, and his father and uncle created high expectations for the young man, and he subsequently learned to have high expectations for himself. His uncle took long walks with Leonardo, and it was through the long walks that he learned to appreciate the natural world. He learned to understand the beauty of nature, which encouraged him to become an astute observer of nature and to inspect keenly, classify, and study what he saw.

A creative teacher's beliefs in and expectations for children's abilities in the arts and sciences are critical to the development of their interests and aspirations to succeed. Teachers and families can act as role models who have high expectations for all the components of creative expression such as flexibility, uniqueness, risk taking, openness, curiosity, sensitivity, play, and humor. Children need to expect that the processes of play, drama, movement, visual art, music, science, and math are valued, and that producing a product is not a goal. They need time to explore the environment using their individual learning styles before taking responsibility for their creative expressions.

In the Reggio Schools the *atelierista* (teacher) supports connections and is a provocateur who helps children move between the worlds of the arts and sciences. The arts give a larger dimension to the building of knowledge, and according to Vecchi (2010), they are a fertilizer to the "languages" of other subjects. It is expected that the child will grow and develop from this interdisciplinary approach.

Responsibility

Leonardo took responsibility for his duties as an apprentice, and not only learned the techniques of the day but also produced new ones. The apprentices in the art studios had to take responsibility for making the paintbrushes, preparing the paints, and preparing the surfaces for use. Rather than painting on canvas, artists painted on wood that apprentices had to boil, then brush on glue, and lastly apply plaster.

Responsibility in the creative classroom of today implies that children are held accountable for their own creative, inquiry-based, and aesthetic experiences in the arts and sciences. Teachers need to provide choices for individual interests and differences. Children take the responsibility for decision making and engagement when they choose what media they will use, what character they will play, what musical instrument they will select, and how they will respond with creative movement. They take responsibility for their own creative expression and activities, based on their interests and started in their observations. These observations lead to further scientific investigations that include the use of the basic process skills of observing, comparing, classifying and grouping, measuring, and communicating. As observation skills develop, children begin to "infer" behaviors, such as seeing patterns, seeing how the patterns reoccur, and then predicting or making reasonable guesses based on observations or prior experiences. As children advance even further, they can hypothesize based on their observations, using statements such as "If I use a lever to lift objects (i.e., blocks) in the block center, then I could lift something heavier with a lever outside." They can later control variables such as what type of lever is used and what it can be used for. Teachers are responsible for interacting with children, inspiring, and encouraging them in their endeavors, as they use the available time, space, and materials to engage in the arts and sciences in a way that makes sense to them.

The Reggio preschools promote responsibility by allowing children to take responsibility for their own learning, helping them construct a deeper knowledge, and eliminating any system that compartmentalizes knowledge. For example, in building the Amusement Park for Birds, the Reggio children were introduced to the project after the adults had discussed it and written hypotheses about what directions the children's interest might take. When the children were asked how they could provide food for the birds, they talked about how they could construct a ladder for the birds and engineer pipes of a small lake at the school so the water would stay clean for the birds (Gandini, 2015). Children began to take responsibility for the project and the care of birds, and the children's input was crucial to the project.

Use

Leonardo had an environment that promoted the use of various media of the day. The artists in his time took lessons in painting on wood and painting frescoes. They learned how to make statues out of marble or bronze or design pottery out of clay. They also learned to work with silver and gold, and even construct buildings.

Teachers in creative early childhood classes must provide ample experiences and opportunities for children to use various media and employ the environment in both an individual and social setting. When children explore the creative arts and sciences, they need time and opportunities to do so in a social and individual setting. Large blocks of time need to be available for expressing creativity. The room needs to be set up in different interesting and inviting centers with many different kinds of media so that expression takes place. Much attention is given to the look and feel of the classroom. Classroom space is organized for small- and large-group projects, and small intimate centers are also provided for the use of the children.

The Reggio preschools allow children to use various media to represent the ideas that are being expressed. In the Amusement Park for Birds, for example, the children utilized drawings, paper constructions of water wheels, and then actual constructions of water wheels with construction materials. They also drew designs for bird fountains and later constructed them with clay and umbrellas on the playground. The children were taught to go beyond what they could do on paper (Gandini, 2015; Vecchi, 2010), utilizing both two- and three-dimensional shapes.

Approximation

Leonardo constantly practiced in his studios and journals to promote better and more creative ideas. His journals are filled with ideas and then changes of what he had done originally. He used approximation first, and then gradually perfected it.

Providing experiences and opportunities for children in creative classrooms to use materials to approximate what they had in mind, without fear of negative criticism, is an important part of the creative process in the arts, science, math, and engineering.

Children in creative early childhood classes that emphasize the arts and sciences are not overly concerned with how things look as they *approximate*, or create something similar to, what they intended to produce. Teachers should permit children to take risks and make approximations as they are learning skills in the creative arts and sciences. Children should be assured that they can experiment and use scientific and engineering methods and that their attempts at creative expressions are acceptable. For instance, at the early stages, young children often engage in becoming familiar with the characteristics of various media such as paint, crayons, and modeling or constructing materials before they even try to approximate making what they have in mind. With increased age and experience, however, children become more interested in receiving feedback and responses from their peers, teachers, and parents that help them self-reflect and improve their approximations.

In Reggio Emilia, approximation takes place by inferring, predicting, and trying out new ideas and possibilities. This was seen in the documentation of the Amusement Park for Birds in the Reggio preschool and how the children had to try out different possibilities in providing various opportunities for the birds to amuse themselves.

Response

The artists in the studio of Verrocchio during Leonardo's day accepted response feedback from each other as well as from the Master Verrocchio; they modified their works accordingly. The artists learned from each other and shared their scientific work of shadows and their understanding of the human forms.

Response happens in creative classrooms that emphasize the arts and sciences when children accept feedback from others, both children and adults, in order to enhance, adapt, modify, and extend their creative thinking in the arts and sciences. This responsive feedback needs to enhance the child's inner creativity in creative early childhood classrooms. A teacher may point out elements of visual art, music, or movement that are being used as the children perform, and coexplore the learning experience by taking ideas from the children and returning the ideas to them for further exploration. The teacher then relates the ideas to the physical, life, and Earth sciences. The children's responses to the feedback may provoke ideas that allow them to solve future problems.

The response feedback in Reggio preschools is critical to the learning. Children are listened to, and the pedagogy of listening takes place. The teachers and the atelier help extend the artistic endeavors, and transdisciplinary ideas take root because of questioning by the teachers. Children are able to cross fields

(Gandini et al., 2015). The Amusement Park for Birds included the arts and STEM, particularly the field of engineering in design and construction.

In summary, Cambourne's (1988) model of the Conditions of Learning can be used to explore how Leonardo da Vinci learned in a creative manner by virtue of the expressive arts and sciences, how a creative early childhood classroom can be set up to promote these conditions to develop the artist as scientist, and how the Reggio preschools use the conditions to promote creativity. Children develop aptitude and passion because they are working in their element at a given moment, just as Leonardo did (Robinson, 2009), and because they have been afforded the opportunity and conditions to promote the creative process, whether in a present-day creative class that nurtures the artist/scientist or a Reggio *atelier*.

FORCES IN THE LEARNING ENVIRONMENT: CLIMATE, SPACE, AND TIME

Another way to study a learning environment is by looking at the forces at work (Garbarino, 1989). As time passes, the reactions of people tend to conform to the environment that they are in. Ecological psychologists use the term *environmental press* to describe the force at work in settings. For instance, if the setting is designed for compliance, as Harvard educator Tony Wagner (2002, 2010) says many of our schools are, there *will* be compliant behavior. Children may initially engage in many types of behaviors, but they eventually give way to the environment. Therefore, the environment must reflect the values and research that promote the optimal development of the whole child, but particularly the child's creativity. Children come to the classroom with many experiences that need to be challenged so that they can grow into powerful human beings. Learning environments for creativity are challenging for children when they include the right combination of the basic elements. There are three basic elements of creative learning environments that researchers have studied: climate (classroom atmosphere), space, and time (Garreau & Kennedy, 1991), each of which I examine in this section.

Classroom Climate

Classroom climate refers to the emotional atmosphere created by the people in the environment, as well as the atmosphere reflected by the aesthetic arrangement of space. The climate is created by the teacher to entice or draw children into a creative and inspirational experience in the arts and by sensitivity toward beauty and nature. Although many factors, such as displaying famous works of art and listening to music, can convey the feeling of a creative classroom atmosphere to children, a most important dimension is human relationships.

Feelings of trust, self-confidence, initiative, and industry should develop progressively throughout early childhood education. These feelings, identified by Erikson (1950), provide the foundation for developing a positive classroom atmosphere in a learning environment for creativity. Children come to school with a huge range of strong emotions, and they have a right to express these feelings and receive respect in a classroom dedicated to establishing a sense of trust and a continuing development of competence in young children.

Space: Centers of Interest

If educators value creativity, this must be evident not only in the classroom climate but also in the classroom space. The space must show that teachers respect the dignity of individuals and their families and have a vision of childhood. There should be enticing materials and opportunities to investigate, change, and discover. Aesthetically pleasing art, science displays, book displays, and live plants can be in the room. Light and mirrors can be used to make the room look larger and open to the outdoor environment. For example, the environment of the Reggio preschools stimulates the creative expressions of the children and validates the belief that all children have the potential to be creative (Cadwell, 1997; C. Edwards, Gandini, & Forman, 2012; Gandini, 2002; Sturloni & Vecchi, 1999). Most recently, Vecchi (2010) and Gandini, Hill, Cadwell, and Schwall (2015) have written about the role and potential of Reggio *ateliers* in early childhood education.

Traditionally in preschools, overall classroom space is loosely divided into areas called centers of interest that children can choose to explore individually or in small groups. Center-based learning allows for decision making and problem solving as children explore their learning environments. Centers of interest provide comfortable spaces for interactions to occur among children and adults, and the relationships that "blossom" in these centers of interest can be catalysts to stimulate creative expressions.

A creative learning environment must change according to the needs, interests, and abilities of the children involved. Children's interests evolve and go through change. Centers of interest must be flexible and increased or decreased as the needs of the children change. These centers can be helpful in promoting the Arts–STEM connection and skills for the 21st century. To better understand the breadth and depth of creative expressions occurring in centers of interest, teachers often observe and identify behaviors, and as a result are able to integrate creative learning in all content areas.

Centers of interest in preschools include, but are not limited to, space for a literacy center, drama center, music and movement center, art center, block center, science center, and technology center. Interactions occur within and outside of these centers, but for the purposes of organizing a classroom, teachers usually set up specific spaces for specific content areas. Despite having specific spaces, however, the books from the literacy center are often taken and "read" in other areas.

Nevertheless, at "pick-up" time, materials are usually put back in specific areas as the children learn that everything has a place and there is a place for everything. Mathematical skills such as classification are reinforced and modeled by this type of classroom organization of space.

Literacy Center. Here young children practice speaking, reading, and writing. Many conversations take place, and these conversations allow children to practice oral language. Children choose books that are interesting to them to "read" from the classroom literacy center.

Even though preschool children may not be able to write words by themselves, they are able to draw pictures and dictate the meanings to an adult. Teachers usually do not write the dictation directly on children's work, because the artwork is the children's personal property. Preschool children generally express themselves using spoken words and pictures, whereas primary-grade children usually write stories and then illustrate their writing with pictures.

Drama Center. Children learn how to play cooperatively with each other in the space set aside for creative drama. They imagine and pretend, and when words fail them, they fall back on bodily gestures to express their meanings. As preschool children "play house" at the home living drama center, their understanding of the roles of family members become clearer to them. Children like to play house in other areas besides the drama center; they love to "move" and find other places to "live." Playing house is an activity that young children enjoy, especially at the first of the school year, possibly because it bridges the transition from home to school, and they feel more comfortable in the playhouse drama center. At the kindergarten level, children more often may be observed in the drama center playing the roles of community helpers outside the home, such as teachers, firefighters, space explorers, or train engineers. The teacher should supply appropriate materials to help enhance the play. At the primary level, "playing school" appears to be a favorite dramatic activity. Usually children are most likely to re-create situations from their home and community environments, so if teachers listen closely, they can learn about many things that are happening in a child's life.

Music and Movement Center. Children enjoy exploring the musical instruments, singing, and dancing in the music and movement center. A piano is an ideal instrument for exploration of sounds, and children enjoy improvising their own music. Young children can play familiar songs by matching color-coded musical notes with color-coded keys to learn the mathematical skill of one-to-one correspondence. Children enjoy exploring a range of key sounds, and they learn many concepts such as high and low and loud and soft as they explore the tones of a piano. There are other instruments, including xylophones, triangles, drums, rhythm sticks, and autoharps, which also stimulate the exploration of the science of sound. (See Figure 3.1.)

Figure 3.1. Listening for the Beat

An open area is necessary in the music and movement center because young children enjoy responding to music or creating movements using their whole bodies. Teachers generally do not encourage interpretations of dance from the mass media. Rather, they encourage bodily responses that are original interpretations of music or that are created by the children.

Art Center. In designated centers for art, indoors or outdoors, children enjoy painting, drawing, and sculpting. In early childhood classrooms, a media approach for exploring art allows children to experience numerous and varied media with which art can be created. Children often express their innermost feelings on paper or with clay. Some young children are able to describe what they are thinking and feeling more effectively when using art media than when they are using oral language. As they express their ideas using the various elements of art, children experiment with color, design, and proportion. By observing children in the art center, teachers can learn many interesting facts about children that may not be learned in group oral-language sessions or in one-to-one interactions.

Block Center. Children can be observed imitating architects, builders, and mathematicians in the block center. (See Figure 3.2.) Children enjoy building with large and small blocks of various shapes, colors, and materials in order to express their ideas creatively. They learn to classify by shape, size, and color as they experiment with balance and structures. It is not unusual for a building made of blocks to

Figure 3.2. Block Building Center

Image courtesy of Community Playthings (www.communityplaythings.com)

fall down because the foundation was not strong enough. It is also not unusual for children to knock down a structure they have built in order to explore the concept of gravity. There are developmental stages of block building leading up to complex structures that can be easily observed by an aspiring teacher (see Chapter 6).

Science and Discovery Center. Children can immerse themselves in the study of scientific principles in the science and discovery center. They observe, compare, classify, measure, communicate, infer, and predict. They test hypotheses, and learn to observe things very carefully. (See Figure 3.3.) The center has many implements with which to explore, such as stethoscopes, magnets, microscopes, and magnifying glasses. Children enthusiastically collect ladybugs, ants, and other insects for observations. Science materials such as "tornado tubes" filled with brightly colored liquids, nonpoisonous plants growing, butterflies hatching, fish swimming, and tadpoles hatching are available at various times for the children to observe.

The science of light can permeate the total learning environment as children interact with shadows behind a screen or put various transparent, translucent, and opaque colored materials on a light table and mix the colors to watch them change. Light tables are valuable for combining materials of different colors and textures over the light. Prisms can produce rainbows, with enough light, and flashlights located in the science center are sometimes used to provide "electric light" for block structures. Materials from any center of interest may be used in any appropriate available center.

Figure 3.3. This Child Is Sharing Her Study of Ants and What She Learned About Ants Through the Science Center

Technology Center. In the technology center there are tape recorders for children to practice their storytelling skills, digital cameras to share stories with pictures, digital video cameras to play back class activities for families on the computer, and links and fax machines to reach out to children in other schools. There are now various digital devices such as iPads and Androids that have computer access to apps that are developmentally appropriate. Recently, computer coding programs have been developed for young children. Many children do not have access to these hand-held devices and the computer applications at home, so having access to them in school gives them needed familiarity with newer forms of technology. Knowledge is constructed through the actions and experiences of the children as they explore technology.

Computer literacy and its various multiple media devices should be developed as a requirement to achieve much higher goals such as creativity, problem solving, global awareness, cooperation, communication, and interaction. The computer elicits opportunities for social interaction in the classroom. Two seats can be placed in front of a computer to encourage children to work together, and moving computers close to each other can facilitate sharing of ideas. Computer centers can help develop fine motor skills and often hold the attention of young children because they can exercise control over what happens on the screen. They are tools for learning that are becoming increasingly popular in early childhood classrooms. Although some teachers resist using computers for creative expressions, others feel that it is valuable to give children this educational experience because there are many computer programs that promote creativity and open-ended activities. Computer apps now provide more hands-on work than the computer with a child using a mouse.

The value of computers for enhancing creativity is in their open-ended use rather than in producing a product. Teachers should choose software and apps that are developmentally appropriate, are focused on how children learn, and are consistent with a child's current developmental stage. The software and apps should introduce children to a broad range of cultures and to the various diversities of the classroom children themselves. Software programs that promote equity allow for different learning styles and accommodate varying ability levels. The quality of the software motivates children to become active participants in their learning. The technology center should be a natural part of the learning environment that children can choose to solve problems, make choices, discover, and explore their world.

When children have thoroughly explored these basic areas described above, an inventor center, a manipulative center, and other centers are often introduced according to the interests and various developmental levels of the children. An inventor center allows the children to create and explore both their own inventions and the inventions of other children. This center should provide a variety of materials from the life, Earth, and physical sciences. A mathematics center can motivate children to learn about classification, measurement, numbers, and space. Other centers of interest can be developed on an as-needed basis.

Time

It takes a long time to develop and learn in an environment designed for creativity. Yet teachers are usually responsible for implementing the scheduling of time in early childhood learning environments according to prescribed instructions by curriculum developers. Teachers try to balance active and quiet times, structured and unstructured times, and spontaneous and directed times in their schedules. Generally, they have a daily routine planned that offers some consistency. The challenge is to follow a prescribed routine and to adjust the time spent according to the motivations of the children. If children are passionately involved in a specific area of learning, the time should be adjusted accordingly.

In preschool early childhood learning environments, teachers follow a less prescribed and more flexible schedule than in the primary grades, but they usually post a routine or schedule that provides a structure children soon learn. For example, one preschooler described his day in preschool as follows:

"First we come to school, then we explore our classroom. We get together in a circle or small group, and plan what we want to do today. After we do what we planned, it is time to put things back in their place and go outside to play. When we come inside, we listen to a story or sing a song together until it is time to say goodbye."

As in this child's description, usually a preschool day begins with free exploration. During this time, small groups work on various skills with others in the learning environment. Next there is a "pick-up" transition time in which learning also occurs. Classification skills are reinforced as children put things back in their place. "Pick-up" time often requires more time than teachers realize when the goal is to focus on learning skills. It is usually a happy time as children sing or chant something similar to: "Oh, yes, it's pick-up time, Oh, yes, it's pick-up time. We love to pick up toys and put them all away."

Transitions to other activities and routines are gradually established as children become comfortable in their learning environment. After some physical activity, usually outdoors, children may gather into a larger group to focus on more organized activities, such as listening to read-aloud books, or group musical and movement activities.

When children enter today's kindergarten, as well as 1st, 2nd, and 3rd grades, the schedules usually become more organized and specific, as students may have scheduled times to go to music, art, or physical education specialists. However, the main goal of any creative learning environment in early childhood is to encourage and support child-initiated learning through creative expression, not to follow a prescribed rigid time schedule. In these days of increased emphasis on accountability, however, this main goal is not always valued or feasible in a school setting. Nevertheless, time must be allowed for children to learn to think and express themselves creatively, while following the learning standards set by a prescribed curriculum.

The following vignette describes a classroom ecosystem illustrating the three elements of creative learning environments: climate (atmosphere), space, and time.

Hillary, 4 years of age, is enrolled in a preschool class in a public school, and eagerly attends regularly. As she enters, she immediately goes to the playhouse where she feels most comfortable, and begins to cook for her pretend family. As other children enter to join in the play, Hillary is in charge, and she assigns various roles to her classmates. They appear eager to play with her and follow her directions willingly. Allowing Hillary ample time in the playhouse helps her feel comfortable at school.

After establishing her comfort level in the classroom, Hillary proceeds to explore other areas of interest. She often chooses to "write" like her big sister does or to build with blocks something she knows about and has seen. She pursues her interests and continues doing what she chooses to do, giving each activity the amount of time she feels is appropriate to accomplish her individual learning goals.

BLOCKADES TO CREATIVITY

Amabile (1989) reminded teachers that children's motivation and creativity can be destroyed if evaluation, reward, and competition are misused. Unfortunately, there are some conditions in an early childhood learning environment that may prevent creativity behaviors from occurring. Too much emphasis on the product rather than on the process may discourage the creative efforts of young children.

Often outside conditions can keep creative expressions from happening in the early childhood classrooms. Some "blockades" to expressing creative behaviors in a learning environment are the presence of significant people in children's lives who do not value creativity, unfair comparisons of children's creative work and not allowing mistakes, the use of unnecessary awards for exemplary creative expressions, and a "no playing allowed" rule in the learning environment. These blockades can create a negative effect on children's creativity.

Many other things might be occurring in children's "out-of-school environment" that could have a negative effect on their creative behavior. A pending divorce, a death in the family, or other serious issues can affect a child's willingness and courage to show creative behaviors. Other times, it may be as simple as "having a bad day." It is essential that teachers be alert and observant as the children enter the classroom in order to determine how they may be feeling on any particular day.

When Mario entered the kindergarten classroom, the teacher observed that he was feeling upset, and it was obvious that he had been crying. She knew that Mario's dad had not returned from a business trip he had taken in his small airplane. The newspapers and media announced his disappearance, and search crews were sent to search for Mario's dad and the pilot. Mario's mother decided that it was best for him to carry on his regular school routine rather than stay at home worrying about his dad. At school, he did not want to talk to anyone, but went straight to the art center where he became engrossed in drawing with pencil and paper. He drew for over an hour, then he showed his paper to the teacher and said, "Teacher, tell them to look for my daddy right here." He had put a big X over the place on the mountain where he thought his dad could be found. He had drawn an intricate map using his spatial skill in the arts to show an area that expressed his unconscious fears as well as his hopes. Fortunately, Mario's dad was found alive.

His teacher's awareness of the news about Mario's father and her perception of his distress as Mario entered the kindergarten class led her to identify his needs quickly. As a result, she devoted her undivided attention to Mario and his creative expressions during this stressful time. The teacher noticed Mario's spatial skills— skills needed in STEM courses—and how he was able to represent a map in his artistic drawing. Knowledgeable, perceptive, creative teachers are the planners, organizers, expediters, counselors, implementers, goal setters, and proponents of creative expression, and they develop connections with the Arts and STEM. They must apply the many theories of creativity to early childhood, while implementing high-quality learning environments for creative expressions to occur. Teachers must act with commitment to make sure the values they hold about creativity are reflected in the learning environment, rather than erecting blockades to creative expression.

SUMMARY

Cities that attract innovation and creative endeavors in the 21st century will be producing the creative capital that will be necessary for economic growth (Florida, 2007, 2012) These cities will have to be promoting an environment that encourages creativity, just as Florence did in the 1400s during the time of Leonardo da Vinci. The early childhood classroom is a microcosm of the environment that will be needed in our cities of the future. In this chapter Cambourne's (1988) model of the Conditions of Learning was applied to encourage creativity in the learning environment with examples from the time of Leonardo, creative early childhood classrooms, and the preschools of Reggio Emilia.

Another way to look at the environment is to look at forces at work in the environment that can promote either creativity or compliance (Wagner, 2002, 2010). Classroom climate, space, and time were considered as the three basic factors in a creative learning environment that can positively or adversely influence the creative expressions of young children in the arts and sciences.

REVIEW AND REFLECT

1. How are "third spaces" in cities similar to the environment of the *atelier* in Reggio Emilia? Why was Florence, Italy, during the Rennaisance a city that was an enhancement to the creativity of Leonardo?
2. Explain Cambourne's model as it relates to a creative Arts–STEM environment using the following concepts: immersion, demonstration, engagement, expectation, responsibility, use, approximation, and response.

Part II

THE ARTS AND
THEIR RELATION TO STEM

CHAPTER 4

CREATIVE MOVEMENT AND DRAMA
Their Importance for Math and Science

The body must be allowed to express itself. Such expression is through the motions that are natural to it.

—Isadora Duncan

THE ENGAGEMENT OF LEONARDO DA VINCI IN CREATIVE MOVEMENT AND DRAMA

Leonardo da Vinci was known to be engaged in creative drama activities. Using his knowledge of simple machines, he created incredible stage sets for the Duke of Milan. For one of the Duke's banquets called the Feast of Paradise, Leonardo created a play called The Masque of the Planets, featuring a "mountain" that was split in two. Actors represented different planets. Elements of the set moved around utilizing the wheel and axle. His extensions of creative drama into the physical sciences were legendary. Leonardo drew on his keen sense of spatial awareness in creating and directing dramas.

Creative movement and creative drama are natural forms of expression, and they have been utilized by dancers, actors, and poets throughout the centuries, including in Leonardo's day. Yet in the years 2000–2010, fewer public elementary schools offered visual arts, dance, and drama classes, possibly because of the increased focus on reading and mathematics (Parsad & Spiegelman, 2012).

Creative movement is different from creative drama. *Creative movement* is an art form using movement activities that promote creative learning and exploration as expressed through the elements, categories, and types of movement. *Creative drama* is an umbrella term that covers playmaking, process drama, and improvisation. The main difference is that creative movement is expressed nonverbally whereas creative drama usually requires verbal expression. Both involve movement and awareness of space, which are necessary for math and science. Creative drama builds on the imaginative work begun in the dramatic play of young children when they express themselves verbally while pretending they are *little* and well cared for as the baby, or *big* and in command as the doctor, inventor, mother, or father. Younger children learn how it feels to be someone else as they create a dramatic role. Creative drama, an inclusive term, is an art form through which children express themselves in classroom activities such as pantomiming and narrative improvisations. Both include the expression of ideas and feelings as children simulate life experiences. The role of teachers in integrating creative movement and drama into the early childhood curriculum focuses on encouraging movement experiences through which children may come to acquire knowledge in the arts and sciences, especially through their understanding of space and objects in space. In the primary grades creative drama is often more organized than in the free spontaneous drama of the earlier years. An example of a 1st-grade movement and drama activity follows.

Ms. Knapp, a 1st-grade teacher, read the book *Swimmy* by Leo Lionni to her class. *Swimmy* is the story of a small fish that swims with his brothers and sisters in the ocean and a big fish who eats them—all except Swimmy who swam too fast. Days after hearing the story, the teacher observed children in the movement area dancing with scarves, pretending they were fish and swimming away from the large fish. The scarves in many different colors almost seemed to mimic swimming as they floated across the room. The children waved the scarves over their heads, some in front of their bodies, and others with their eyes squinted open wondered whether "the other fish" were escaping from the big fish. Children pretended they were swimming very low to the ocean floor and then very high to the surface of the water. It was a beautiful and exciting sight.

One of the children, Jimmy, suggested that the children perform a dance using the story of Swimmy for the kindergarten class. The children decided who would play the characters of Swimmy, the big tuna fish who ate Swimmy's brothers and sisters, and the fish who were Swimmy's friends. They decided to have background music and chose "The Sea, La Mer" by Debussy after listening to both that piece and "Storm at Sea" by Vivaldi. On the day of the creative drama, Jimmy told the story as the characters of Swimmy, the Tuna Fish, Medusa (jellyfish), Lobster, Eel, and Sea Anemones, as well as a school of small fish, used their scarves to dance out the story to background music. After they finished, they all enjoyed fish-shaped crackers and "sea water" as a snack. They also watched fish in the aquarium more carefully, developing observation skills that helped them notice the habits of the fish and other creatures in the aquarium. They later learned the parts of the fish: mouth, fins, scales, and tail. Their interest in marine biology grew to include many creatures of the sea.

In this chapter, research and theory in the areas of creative movement and creative drama reveal that children's creative expressions depend on their freedom to explore the environment and pay attention to the nuances of objects in the environment. This chapter will examine the theories of creative movement and exploration, with emphasis on spatial importance for the STEM courses, and the types of movement and drama and how they can be integrated into math and science. It will also emphasize how the 21st century skills of creativity, critical thinking, problem solving, communication, and collaboration can take place in selected activities.

UNDERSTANDING THE IMPORTANCE OF CREATIVE MOVEMENT

Rudolf Laban (1948), who is considered the father of movement education, recommended that educators guide children's natural urge to move spontaneously. He researched the ancient dances of North Africa and the near East, and maintained he had no particular method, but rather a spirit of inquiry, to leave as his legacy. Laban suggested the idea of natural dance for children rather than a focus on techniques of dancing, as required by classical ballet. Movement education encompasses both creative movement and dance, but it is not the same thing as physical education, which is usually a separate subject in the primary grades. Creative movement education uses a facilitative approach of instruction that is child centered, and allows the "whole child" to experience ideas in which imagination, emotions, and movement are involved. According to Rae Pica (2012), movement education is basically physical education with an emphasis on fundamental motor skills and spatial awareness. She advocates an environment free of competition, since stress inhibits rather than encourages imaginative expressions through bodily movement.

Creative movement and exploration promote learning. Maria Montessori (1949) emphasized that children's learning is related to bodily movement. For example, she wrote directions on slips of paper, such as "Run to the back of the room, water the plants, and return to the front of the room," to help children learn to read. Jean Piaget (1959) reinforced the idea that movement and learning are interrelated by describing a sensory motor stage of young children learning through moving and exploring materials in their environment. Carla Hannaford (1995), a neuroscientist, found that "creeping and crawling," or cross-lateral movements, involve all four lobes of the brain activating the brain in a balanced way. She found a neural basis of learning and concluded that bodily movement does influence learning in young children because their learning is enhanced as they become completely involved in movement activities.

For children to be free to explore their environment through their bodies, they must learn to concentrate and focus on their movement activities. Mihaly Csikszentmihalyi (1990) is known for developing the concept of a state of *flow*, in which children are completely immersed in what they are doing and temporal concerns like time are ignored. For example, if children lose themselves in creative movement, time is suspended, and there is complete absorption in the activity. He says that more than anything else, children seek happiness, and the concept of flow is the occurrence of being so actively involved in something that they are oblivious to distraction, time becomes irrelevant, the mind and body work as one, and the child is happy. Artists and scientists experience this flow when creating something new. Flow can only happen when teachers recognize learning-style differences and allow children the opportunity to learn in their preferred style.

Kinesthetic intelligence is involved in creative movement and creative drama because children's bodies are a significant part of their ability to acquire knowledge through this intelligence. Howard Gardner (1999), who developed an expansive definition of intelligence (see Chapter 2), identified kinesthetic intelligence as one type of intelligence. Learning that occurs as a result of concerted movements of muscles, tendons, and joints is labeled kinesthetic, and these movements create meaning because learning is stimulated through doing and moving. Fundamentally, kinesthetic learning involves movement, and therefore learners need to be actively engaged in their learning by hands-on manipulation and physical involvement. Kinesthetic movement involves the ability to control one's body movements and to handle objects skillfully. Individuals who have a high kinesthetic intelligence are actors, athletes, dancers, and surgeons. This intelligence allows children to use their bodies to solve problems, create, and discover as they move through space.

Another type of intelligence that Gardner emphasized was *spatial intelligence,* which is also used in creative movement. People who have a strong sense of how things are oriented in a space excel in this intelligence. Evidence has suggested that students with spatial skills are drawn into fields such as engineering, airplane design, architecture, physics, biology, industrial design, surgery, and chemistry (Humphreys, Lubinski, & Yao, 1993). Spatial development is thus related to STEM courses, and this usually begins with the body in early childhood (NRC, 2006). Body and spatial awareness have been related to what children do in a group creative movement. Marjorie Corso (1993) found that children who bump into one another and do not keep in their own personal space might also have a hard time separating spaces between words and letters. This could transfer to engineering tasks such as fitting blocks together. Her research has also shown that there is clear evidence that body and spatial awareness transfers to paper-and-pencil tasks. *Spatial orientation* involves knowledge of the body and its position in space, as well as the relative positions of other people and objects. An awareness of space outside of the body entails the following abilities:

- Comprehending directions such as left and right or up and down
- Understanding the projection of one's self in space
- Judging the distances between objects

Interpersonal intelligence (Gardner, 1999), or the ability to distinguish among moods and feelings of others by being sensitive to voice, gestures, and facial expressions, is necessary in order to work cooperatively in creative movement and creative drama. Frostig (1970) wrote about movement education helping children adjust socially and emotionally because children who are in groups of two or more learn to cooperate with each other. Children have to be aware of others and to share space with others during group creative movements.

Although children acquire knowledge using different learning styles, for many young children bodily movement is the preferred mode of learning and communication. Once these children learn certain bodily movements such as swimming or riding a bicycle, they never forget them, whereas if they learn the capitals of states, they may soon forget such facts. Reading simple words such as *who, what, when,* and *where* is difficult for many children to learn, but the word *jump* is easy for them to learn because they have an internal image of the movement. Children cannot learn optimally under stress, and requiring children who learn kinesthetically to "sit still" in a rigid school environment can cause them stress and result in their being labeled as having learning difficulties. In "whole brain" learning, imagination, emotions, and creative bodily movement all need to be involved. Ernest Boyer (1991) has said that learning to communicate, not just verbally but nonverbally as well, through movement, music, dance, and the arts, allows children to develop important expressive and receptive communication skills needed for learning subjects such as science and math.

DEFINING CREATIVE MOVEMENT

Creative movement consists of physical activity, which is a child's first means of nonverbal communication. It usually takes place as a fundamental phase of physical development that occurs between the ages of 2 and 7, the early childhood years. During this time, locomotor and nonlocomotor skills, plus stability and balance skills, become more highly developed, and are used to reflect the inner imagination and ideas of children. Children develop their motor movement skills in specific ways. They develop their large muscles such as those in the arms, legs, and trunk first. This is called *gross motor development.* Then they develop their *small motor muscles,* such as the muscles in their hands and fingers.

Generally, children develop motor skills directionally in two ways. The first way is from the head down to the toes. The infant will hold his head up and gain control of his head, then the shoulders and the torso, and finally the thighs, calves, feet, and toes. This is called *cephalocaudal* development. The second way is to gain control of the center of the body, then the shoulders, arms, hands, and fingers. This is called *proximodistal* or near-to-far development. An example of this is an infant swatting at toys in a crib by using the whole arm. Later, a child will use fingers to grasp a toy. As children grow and develop, they gain control of their bodies and become more capable of coordinating their movements. Teachers must become aware of each child's physical capabilities so that they can provide experiences that support the development of emerging abilities.

One day the kindergarten teacher, Ms. O'Brien, took the class to see the ballet *Cinderella*. Becca had never seen a ballet performed before, and her heart began to beat faster and faster, and her eyes opened wider and wider as she watched the ballerinas. Soon she got out of her seat and began to dance along with the music. After going to that ballet, Becca had a strong desire to move like a ballerina. She spontaneously and freely improvised many movements, and her classmates and teacher called her a creative ballerina dancer.

Becca's movements seemed to reflect that this early experience encouraged her to express emotions that came from within. She found her own personal, creative, and innovative ways of moving after being motivated by going to the ballet. Later in the classroom, Ms. O'Brien did not instruct Becca in specific, predetermined ways of moving, but rather provided the opportunity for her to find her own joy and satisfaction in expressing creative ideas with her body. She later transferred this creativity to her study of how animals moved and pretended she was a kangaroo, a giraffe, and an alligator after she saw these animals at the zoo, thus transferring her movement to the understanding of animals.

Creative movement may also consist of any activity in which children use their creativity and feelings in nonverbal ways. As painters use a paintbrush or musicians use an instrument, children use their bodies to express creativity. Creative movement is a way for children to know and express themselves and their relationship with the world. For the most part, creative movement activities are open-ended experiences that reflect and emphasize creativity, and most children actively seek ways to develop their physical competence.

Listening, then responding, to music is a natural way children move creatively, as the following vignette shows.

A teacher of young children said to an observer that her class did not really listen to the music she played. Her goal was to have them listen to music using their imaginations, before responding with creative movements. To encourage listening, she played a game called "Dead Dog" with her group of young children. The teacher instructed the entire class to lie on the floor with their eyes closed as the music was playing. They were told to use their imaginations rather than their bodies in response to the music. She stated that this game method of getting the children to use their imaginations worked with this particular class.

The observer found that the children appeared to enjoy the listening game. After the listening experience, they expressed what they had imagined through their individualized creative movements. Children moved anywhere they wanted to in the room, and explored various movements. They were not told how to respond to the music, and their own imaginations were the source of their creative movements. This teacher said that before she employed this game approach, the children had not really listened to the music, but had responded to different music day after day with the same movements. After playing the listening game, their movements became more and more creative, as they expressed their imagined scenes. One child even made up a story about the music and everything she saw in the woods in her head.

These fundamental sensory experiences that lead children to appreciate the beauty in everyday living can be available for children with special needs if they are encouraged to participate at their own level of ability. The following example illustrates this point:

Maria, a child who was confined to a wheel chair, used it and her imagination to pretend to be the pilot of an airplane that circled and circled the field before it landed. On another day, she pretended to be a swing, going back and forth using her wheelchair. Although limited physically, she was never limited in moving creatively by using her imagination. She enjoyed blinking her eyes in time to the music as she swayed back and forth in her wheelchair.

All children can be part of an interactive environment when they share space and explore creative movement in their own way and feel a sense of joy at being able to participate. All children need the self-confidence to express themselves through movement, but it would be difficult for children to be emotionally responsive if their nonverbal actions are not valued.

Tom was a blind child who loved to play with other children. He loved to move along with the other children, but was unable to see any obstacles he might bump into. Ms. Vallee, a volunteer who often came to school, enjoyed guiding Tom as he participated in dancing with his friends. Tom recognized Ms. Vallee by the smell of her perfume, and by hearing the high heels she wore to class. Even before she spoke to him, he would say, "Take my hand, Ms. Vallee, and let's dance." She would take his hand, to guide him as he became a galloping horse or a hopping frog, and would reassure him when it was safe to move alone when crawling like a caterpillar or spinning like a top.

Ms. Vallee focused on Tom's abilities rather than his disability, much to the delight of Tom's parents. Tom's dad said it took them a long time to accept the fact that Tom was blind. When his parents finally stopped mourning, they vowed to have Tom participate in a mainstream school culture rather than being overprotective parents. Seeing Tom dance at school often brought tears to their eyes, especially one day when Tom said, "Look, Ms. Vallee, I can see with my body."

Ms. Vallee's warm, responsive actions had cushioned Tom from many bumps and bruises that might otherwise have discouraged him from dancing. Any movement games or activities that teachers plan should be age-appropriate, individually appropriate, and culturally appropriate as well as connected to the interests of the children.

Children must be valued, motivated, and encouraged to learn through creative movement because creative movement is beneficial in the following ways:

- Increases self-awareness of the body as children learn the body parts in anatomy and how they fit together using the elements of movement
- Improves muscle development since motor-skill activities assist the child in becoming a more physically fit, active, well-coordinated individual
- Encourages social development because children are interacting with other children in space
- Improves spatial development, which is a predictor of people who go into STEM (NRC, 2006)
- Improves problem solving since spatial intelligence, as well as kinesthetic intelligence, leads to the ability to solve problems in other areas (Gardner, 1999), as for example, the ability to see the directions of gears in a drive belt requires an understanding of directions and movement
- Enhances art and music interpretation as children respond
- Develops an aesthetic sense since children are learning to appreciate nature, art, and music through creative movement and this aesthetic sense can lead to more personal relationship with nature and its movement and changes
- Enhances communication as children interact with one another in space

Elements of Creative Movement

The elements of creative movement share some similar qualities to the elements of art and music because they are used to create an original composition. Creative movement is comprised of the elements of space, shape, time, flow, and force. These elements of movement are also seen in the study of physics.

Space. During creative movement, children become aware that their bodies can move through space by using different pathways such as straight, zigzagged, around and around, up and down, or in and out. They learn spatial words used in math and science such as *high/low, near/far, forward/backward.* Children can pretend they are in a bubble so they do not touch someone else's *personal space* and protect the space immediately around them. However, most children are not content to move in a bubble and want to move more actively through the general space.

General space is the space in the room set aside for movement. When children are rapidly moving through the general space, they often accidentally bump into other children. They are focused on themselves and unaware that others are also moving through space at the same time. To avoid accidents and develop group awareness, teachers may limit the movements of children in the general space to nonlocomotor movements and recommend that rapid locomotor movements take place outside where there is more space for children to move freely.

Shape. When children move in space, they begin to understand that shapes can be formed close to or away from their bodies. As their bodies move in space, they form shapes using body parts such as their head, shoulders, arms, hands, elbows, wrists, necks, backs, hips, legs, knees, or ankles. They begin swaying, twisting, turning, gliding close to the ground or leaping high in the air and create shapes by using various body positions to communicate their ideas and feelings. As they increase their understanding and feelings of the shapes they create, the children as a group enjoy playing the game of "Freeze."

During this game, music is played as the children move with freedom, but not in a circle. When the music stops, they "freeze" into the various shapes they have created. These static shapes allow children to become aware of the shapes they and the other children have created. Some interesting shapes that have been observed are *straight* as soldiers marching in a parade, *slanted* as a slide, *bent* over as a tree in the wind, *jagged* as lion's teeth, *curved* as a dancer twirling, or *zigzag* as a child walking on a crowded street. Static shapes clearly express creativity when they are frozen in time, and look similar to stopped action frames of a video.

Time. Movement through space occurs at different speeds and time, which refers to how slowly or quickly a movement activity takes place. When time is imposed by specific fast or slow rhythm, children begin to learn the difference and respond accordingly. They may move as slow as a tortoise or a snail, or very fast, imagining they are a cheetah, a rocket, a speeding car, a fire engine, or a baseball. If the teacher plays the tambourine or a drum fast or slow, a group of children can learn to stop when the rhythm stops and begin again when the rhythm starts. The contrast between fast and slow can be experienced in this way, but teachers should not suggest specific movements. Instead they should encourage children to determine their own ways of creatively responding to fast or slow timing.

Individual children have their own internal body time, and when exploring time with a child, a teacher should follow that timing. Using a tambourine, the teacher can pick up the timing of the child's walking or running, so the child can feel the individual rhythm. Or a teacher can chant and clap a traditional rhythm such as "Let's go walking, walking, walking. Let's go walking far, far away to the forest," while following the tempo set by the child.

Flow. The element of *flow* refers to how bound or free something is. (It should not be confused with the concept of flow discussed earlier in the chapter [Csikszentmihalyi, 1990].) A statue is an example of something bound, whereas a bouncing limp rag doll is an example of something that is free flowing. Teachers often put rag dolls in the dramatic play area for children to feel their limp characteristics as compared to the relatively stiffer regular dolls. Children traditionally play a statue game where they look each other in the eye staying very tense and still; the child who blinks first is not the "real" statue.

Force. When children are relaxed, their energy flow is at a minimum. To help children feel the free flow of movement, teachers often play a relaxation game called "Sleeping Child," where the children lie on the floor with their hands at their sides and their eyes closed. The teacher tries to find each relaxed child by lifting one arm and letting it drop. The child who is truly relaxed becomes the new "teacher." The purpose of the game is to teach children how to feel free-flowing energy as their bodies relax without tension.

A strong force would be required for pulling a heavy weight on a pulley, stomping on the ground, or moving the arms like a propeller in airplane flight or the thrust of a rocket. A weak force would be required for gently tiptoeing like imaginary fairies or for using rounded ballet movements of the arms. How powerfully or lightly a movement is made is called *force*, which involves using muscle tension and refers to the qualitative aspects of movement.

The basic elements of space, shape, time, flow, and force are combined and integrated when interpersonal nonverbal communication takes place among the children. Movement communicates what words often may not express as children spontaneously apply these basic elements in order to express themselves creatively.

Categories of Creative Movement

The three major categories of movement that children use to express their creativity are locomotor, nonlocomotor, and manipulative movements.

Locomotor. Locomotor movements involve moving their whole body through space, for example, by crawling, walking, skipping, or leaping, and these skills develop in stages. While there is some overlap in the development of skills, there are also general stages during which they develop. As an example, most 3-year-old children are unable to skip, whereas by the age of 5 they are able to skip freely and with a great deal of self-control. Therefore teachers would not expect 3-year-old children to express themselves creatively using skipping skills. The following shows a basic continuum of locomotor skills from easiest to hardest (adapted from Graham, Holt/Hale, & Parker, 2004 and Nilsen, 2014): crawl, creep, walk, run, jump, hop, gallop, skip, leap.

Nonlocomotor. When children's feet or other parts of their body remain fixed on the floor and do not move, they become a base for movement of other body parts. These nonlocomotor movements are performed in place. Standing, kneeling, sitting, and lying may be the supporting base for performing nonlocomotor skills. From a stationary base, children enjoy stretching, bending, sitting, shaking, turning, dodging, or swinging. Using nonlocomotor movement, children begin to form shapes with their body, and they enjoy expressing themselves individually or in small groups. One of their favorite games is "Do what I do," where children take turns making a shape using nonlocomotor movement, and the other children mimic the shape.

Manipulative. Finally, manipulative movements are combinations that involve gross motor skills and an object such as throwing, catching, kicking, punting, dribbling, volleying, or striking a ball. Manipulative movements may also involve doing two movements at the same time, such as clapping while walking or rubbing the stomach while patting the head. Obviously, primary-age children will be more proficient using manipulative movements due to their more advanced coordination. The following shows the continuum of stages for manipulative skills from easiest to hardest (adapted from Graham, Holt/Hale, & Parker, 2004): throwing, catching, kicking, punting, dribbling, volleying, and striking. As children freely improvise their creative ideas, they use the elements and categories of movement in a coordinated approach. They use their bodies as instruments of expression as they explore and manipulate movements using motor activities that are age and developmentally appropriate.

Types of Creative Movement

Corbin and Lindsey (1996) defined six fundamental types of creative movement activities: agility, balance, coordination, power, reaction time, and speed.

Agility. When children move in an intentional way at the speed they want, they are showing agility. As they play the game of tag, a child who can stop quickly and change direction shows a well-developed kinesthetic sense of agility. However, small-muscle agility is not well-developed in early childhood, as you rarely see children proficiently play a musical instrument or knit a sweater. It takes time for their agility to develop, but yet they find a lot of pleasure in playing large muscle games that show off their emerging agility.

Balance. As young children climb up and go down a slide, hop on one foot, walk a balance beam, or do a somersault, they are showing adeptness while moving and developing their balance. Their kinesthetic sense is stimulated through running, jumping, or climbing, which in turn improves their sense of balance.

Coordination. Coordination is observed as a child moves more than one body part at a time and executes movement activities with ease and preciseness. As children are swinging, they must pull their arms and legs forward and backward in unison, and then they practice and internalize that skill, never forgetting how to swing. As they climb on the jungle gym, they move their arms and legs in opposition. They must be coordinated to use their arms and legs together in running or skipping. As they create movements using an object, such as a ball, scarf, or bat, they are controlling the interrelationships of their hands, fingers, and other body parts in a coordinated movement.

Power. The stamina and force that is needed for striking a piñata, throwing a ball, or hitting with a hammer requires *power*, the ability to turn energy into a strong force, usually with speed. Older children usually have more strength and endurance so they enjoy group games that develop their muscular strength more than younger children do. Boys can often be observed flexing their muscles to show their power.

Reaction Time. *Reaction time* is the time between stimulation and the beginning of a decision to do something. Children often incorporate reaction time in their creative movement as they make quick decisions to change from jumping up and down to twirling around to moving spontaneously whenever the mood strikes them. A good, or fast, reaction time is needed in such jobs as airplane pilots. Reaction time is an important variable in many scientific experiments.

Speed. Children like to see how fast they can move their bodies because speed is very exciting to them. It involves their ability to execute a movement in a short period of time. Primary-age children enjoy foot races to see who can run the fastest, and repeat this game over and over to increase their speed. They also enjoy having the teacher use a stopwatch to record the time it took to run a certain distance, for example, to run around the playground.

The elements, categories, and fundamental types of movement are used in concert with one another as children express themselves through open-ended, creative movement activities, which help children build on their previous motor skills and learn new skills to express their creative ideas. Imagery is used in many creative endeavors in movement education to reinforce observation skills in the arts and sciences. (For examples of how to use the elements, categories, and types of movement in Arts–STEM activity, see Table 4.1, at the end of this chapter.)

INTEGRATING CREATIVE MOVEMENT INTO THE CONTENT AREAS

Creative movement can be integrated into the science and math areas using movement and dance standards. Flaherty (1992) states that 40% of students think that they are kinesthetic learners in K–12. Many self-identified kinesthetic learners are not performing well in school. The emphasis on making connections between dance and other disciplines is meeting National Core Arts Standards in Dance (NCCAS, 2014). There is a strong emphasis in early childhood of integrating creative movement into content standards.

Science

Movement can be used to explore life cycles. Children can dramatize the life cycle of a butterfly, tornado, or even fire. For example, J. A. Danoff-Burg (2003) explains

ANNOTATED BIBLIOGRAPHY OF
CHILDREN'S BOOKS WITH CREATIVE MOVEMENT THEMES

Teachers can use the following storybooks with STEM content to engage children in creative movement:

Carle, E. (1995). *The tiny seed.* New York, NY: Simon & Schuster.

Children can act out how a seed grows.

Lionni, L. (1994). *Swimmy.* New York, NY: Knopf.

This book encourages movement as fish and other sea creatures.

Carle, E. (1997). *From head to feet.* New York, NY: HarperCollins.

This book challenges children to bend like giraffes, wave like monkeys, and so on.

Gray, L. (1995). *My mama had a dancing heart.* New York, NY: Orchard Books.

This story is about the relationship between a mother and daughter as they use dance to move across the seasons of the year. The different movement for each season and the relationship that builds between the two creates a lesson of friendship and sharing.

Jonas, A. (1989). *Color dance.* New York, NY: Greenwillow Books.

This is about mixing the basic colors of red, yellow, and blue through dance and creating other colors. The book allows for a creative way to show how different colors can be mixed and what the results are.

Kalan, R. (1981). *Jump frog jump.* New York, NY: Greenwillow Books,.

A story about a frog trying to catch a fly without catching himself, this book can help with the development of eye–hand coordination. The story can be turned into a game by making frogs and flies and using them as props. While the story is being read, the kids can enact what the frog in the story does.

Moss, M. (2004). *Jungle song.* London, United Kingdom: Frances Lincoln Children's Books.

This is a story about Little Tapir, who is led into the jungle by a spider and learns the jungle song. He is scared when he is alone, until his mom finds him. The book interacts with the reader, as 90% of the song corresponds to the beat of a drum, encouraging children to get up and tap their feet or clap their hands.

Pandell, K. (1996). *Animal action.* New York, NY: Dutton Children's Books.

This book takes the alphabet, combines it with the thrill of animal actions, and adds human motion, all in one book. It can be used to entertain kids and teach them the vocabulary that goes with the everyday animal motions they make.

Rosen, M. (1997). *We're going on a bear hunt.* New York, NY: Little Simon.

This book has the words to the familiar story and chant, "Going on a Bear Hunt." This will help children understand about the terrain outside and camping.

Dr. Seuss, & McKie, R. (1969). *My book about me.* New York, NY: Random House.

This book is interactive in the sense that it allows children to fill out information about themselves. They are asked to write down how tall they are, how much they weigh, the color of their hair and eyes, how many teeth they have, and so on. This is a perfect book for children because it allows them to explore their own physical development and write it down.

how to show the social aspects of bees in movement. Many fiction and nonfiction books illustrate the stages of the growth of plants. Children can act out the sequence of steps in the growth of plants.

Children whose second language is not English may not be able to verbally describe these life cycles, but they can use movement to describe them. In the Montessori curriculum, the child who is having a birthday witnesses what happens to Earth in one calendar year. One child is the sun, and another child is the Earth. The Earth revolves around the sun in 1 year, so if the birthday child is 10 years old, the Earth child revolves around the sun child 10 times.

Movement can also provide lessons in the sciences of anatomy and physics. What muscles are being used when Bobby jumps? Some movements of animals that may be enjoyed as a group are crawling like lizards, snakes, worms, or caterpillars; galloping like horses or zebras; or hopping like frogs, rabbits, or kangaroos.

Children need relatively little help in discovering how their bodies move, and they enjoy playing the game "Simon Says" to reinforce their knowledge of their body parts and how they move. To play this game, one child is selected to be the narrator. When the narrator says, "Simon says to move your head," the children respond by moving their heads. If the narrator only says, "Move your head," the children do not respond because Simon did not say so. If someone does respond, that child is out of the game. Some body parts the children usually name are toes, ankles, knees, legs, back, waist, neck, shoulders, arms, wrists, hands, fingers, mouth, nose, eyes, cheeks, head, and lips. Sometimes the children playing the game use their imaginations to add movements. For example, the narrator may say, "Simon says touch your nose and walk backward."

Math

Many math concepts can be taught through movement, such as lines, parallel lines, symmetry, sequencing, and patterning. Children can be taught numbers using movement. The teacher might say, "Use three bends and four shakes. How many in all?" Other examples might be: "Bend in five ways." "Swing in five directions."

Children can learn to understand direction when they move in various directions with their body. *Directionality* is an understanding of a body, laterality, in space (Seefeldt, Castle, & Falconer, 2010). As children propel themselves through space, they are constructing directionality concepts such as left and right, up and down, rotations, and flips. These skills are used in map reading and geometry, but can also be used in coding in technology and in many of the sciences, particularly physics. According to Seefeldt et al. (2010), a geography (geospatial) curriculum for young children should involve movement exploration. This movement exploration will also show children the principles of lift, gravity, thrust, and drag, which are used in aeronautics.

Literacy

Literacy is a high priority in American schools. For the most part in American schools, it is taught while students are sedentary, but for young children who are kinesthetic learners, creative movement can enhance a phonics program and still integrate science. A 1st-grade class, with encouragement from their teacher, brought different items from home whose names started with the consonant *B*. Using their dictionaries, they also made a list of words that started with the letter *B*, such as *beach ball, bagel, bananas, backpacks, beverages, basket, bike, basset hound, blanket, beach, building,* and *ballcap*. They divided into three groups, and each wrote various parts of "The Land of *B*" story, after researching what they might see at the beach. Then they put it all together with a beginning, middle, and end—that is, morning, noon, and night.

As a group, they then acted out the story using creative movements, while one child was the narrator. The children enjoyed this game because they were involved in making up the rules of the game, and because they could move in any way they wanted when the narrator read a new word. This 1st-grade class so enjoyed writing and playing the "Land of *B*" story that they wrote about other letters during the year, using the "Land of *B*" as a model and using creative movements to illustrate their stories.

This story helped the students learn about the seashore and the construction of a moat with seawater. They learned about surfboards and boats and how they could float on them as well as the importance of protecting themselves from the sun and sharks. They learned about weather and day and night at the beach. These are all concepts taught in Earth science and physics.

THE LAND OF *B*

Bounce out of bed—it's beach day! Put on your bathing suits and pick up your backpacks and fill them full of bagels, bananas, beverages, and beach balls.

Let's bundle all this up and put it in the basket on the back of our bikes. Bongo, the basset hound, bounds alongside of the bike without touching the bike. At the beach, we need to spread out our blanket. Let's build a sand castle with a moat so big no one can bounce over. The blasting sun is too hot—let's run to the blue water.

In the calm bay water we can swim the butterfly, back-, and breaststroke. Also let's balance on surfboards. Oh, no!!! There are sharks! Run! Back on the beach, we can dance to the blasting boombox, and then we can put on our ballcaps to protect us from the sun and push the boat out into the deep water. It's heavy to push the boat over the breaking waves.

While balancing on the boat, look down to see the brightly colored fish in the clear blue water. A whole afternoon out on the water? We need to go back to the beach and bag up all our equipment. Now we can walk barefoot on the boardwalk and buy hot dogs from the hot dog stand.

After dinner, we can blow bubbles and throw the boomerang.

The beeping of traffic is dying down. Wave bye-bye to the blue heron on the pier, it's time to begin biking back home to the beach bungalow. Take a nice bath and brush yourself clean.

If you have long hair, you can put it in a braid. Bend down to stretch your legs. Then bundle yourself under covers for a peaceful night's rest under the moon. Good night!

EXPLORING CREATIVE DRAMA AND CONNECTIONS TO STEM

Creative drama differs from creative movement and dance because it has a linguistic element; it is a form of imaginative expression where children use their own words rather than a written script to communicate with others. Typically, 3-, 4-, and 5-year-olds enjoy expressing themselves using puppets, whereas children 6 and older enjoy pantomime and playmaking. The older the children, the more often words are used, and some structure is provided in terms of props such as scarves, dress-up clothing, or puppets. It is improvised open-ended drama that has a great potential to develop the imagination of children. During the natural creative movement where children are moving freely to express their imaginations, there is little structure provided, whereas creative drama is more structured.

Children use their voice, body, and space to entertain others as they act out a creative story in which they have the opportunity to internalize the characters, actions, and emotions.

There are many benefits that children can gain from participating in creative drama. It offers a creative outlet, a way to playfully look at reality, and it helps children with language development and nonverbal communication. Because children can see in action the concept being developed, as they learn to interact with the audience at one level and with each other at another level, it is especially helpful for linguistically diverse students. There are specific types of drama and activities that may enhance creative drama for children, including pantomime, narrative improvisation (including storytelling), puppetry, and creating and performing plays. Creative drama is a working together of the arts because it frequently includes dancing, movement, art, music, and creative writing. It allows the transference of one art form to another art form as well as integration of STEM.

Pantomime

Gestures without words, or pantomime, help children to communicate specific ideas nonverbally. This makes pantomime different from creative movement where children are freely expressing feelings rather than trying to communicate ideas.

An easy way for children to begin learning about pantomiming is for them to act out ideas focusing on the five senses. The use of the five senses is critical in the arts and connects to the sciences.

To begin the activity, the teacher can write some examples on separate slips of paper. A child then picks one, reads it, and acts it out for the other children to guess. For examples of this activity, see Figure 4.1. To expand on this activity, primary-age children should be able to write their own examples using the five senses as a theme, and then act their ideas out without narration by using creative pantomiming.

Narrative Improvisation

Narrative improvisation, like pantomiming, is telling a story extemporaneously, but with the addition of nonscripted speech. For example, after young children

Figure 4.1. Examples of Sensory Pantomiming for Arts–STEM

Smell	Show with your face you are smelling garbage.
Sight	Show by your eyes you are seeing a robotic drone.
Taste	Show by your movements you are tasting lemons.
Touch	Show with your actions that you are touching a piece of ice.
Hearing	Show with your movements that you are waking up to an alarm clock.

have had the experience of riding a bicycle, launching a play rocket, or making a miniature clay volcano erupt using vinegar and baking soda, the teacher can ask them to describe what happened, and then ask them to make up a story—a narrative—about the experience. Storytelling is an important skill of the 21st century (Pink, 2006).

An example of a more advanced form of narrative improvisation in primary grades would be to have students research the lives of famous artists and scientists and write about why art and science are important. Then the teacher can select certain students to explain to their principal, extemporaneously, why more art and science is needed in the school. This narrative improvisation would include the following elements:

The Scene: The classroom
The Characters: Principal, selected children in the class
The Situation: A meeting to discuss why more art and science are needed in
    the school

STORIES TO PANTOMIME WITH STEM TOPICS

Sometimes books inspire children to learn to pantomime by acting out a story. The following children's books make connections to STEM:

Johnson, C. (1983). *Harold and the purple crayon*. New York, NY: Harper Collins.

In a story over 50 years old, Harold has an extraordinary imagination and creates the world around him with a purple crayon. One night he goes on an adventure led by his imagination and a crayon. The illustrations effectively capture the imagination of a child.

Keats, E. J. (1962). *The snowy day*. New York, NY: Viking.

This multicultural book shows the activities of a young boy during which he explores perhaps his first snowfall. Peter even tries to capture a bit of snow to bring home in his pocket. Imagine his surprise when it turns into water. This promotes an understanding of cause and effect and change, important in the sciences.

Small, D. (1985). *Imogene's antlers*. New York, NY: Crown.

On Thursday when she woke up, Imogene, a young girl, found she had grown a big spread of antlers. Her family tries to cope with her new adventures. Her mother collapses, but Imogene loves having the antlers, especially since she can do things like feed the birds. This promotes an understanding of form and function in an animal.

Puppetry

Puppets are dolls or figures that represent people or animals that are moved and controlled by the children or the teacher. Consider the value of puppets in the following vignette:

Luckily, Ms. Dowson's classroom had a climate of flexibility and freedom where Angelica, a child who had been afraid to talk in school, could use puppets as a "mouthpiece." She had the imaginative experience of making her puppets come alive in order to speak for her. Puppets helped Angelica feel comfortable enough to speak with her classmates. Through this form of creative drama, she became free to create whatever she wanted right then and there. Puppets allowed her to interact with her friends as they entered a world of fantasy and drama together and could share the creative fantasy together. Gradually, Angelica came up with countless other ideas for using her puppets. Her creativity, confidence, and problem solving were preparing her with 21st century skills that will carry over when she is able to talk easily in the classroom.

There are many types of puppets, but basically there are four main kinds: hand puppets, which fit on one's hand; finger puppets, in which only the fingers are manipulated; marionettes, which are separate from the manipulator; and people puppets, which consist of paper sacks or costumes large enough for the children to get inside. Children enjoy manipulating puppets and speaking for and with them. Children like retelling a story using puppets, and teachers can often use them in telling a story directly to the children, rather than reading aloud.

Many items offer the opportunity for children to create their own puppets: socks, spoons, paper bags, handkerchiefs or scarves, cereal boxes, gloves, and paper plates. Puppets can help prepare students to develop and express STEM ideas. In one classroom, the creation of puppets helped the children start to invent robots. Puppets that the children create can be incorporated into different disciplines by using them in conjunction with finger plays, poems, songs, and stories (for examples in STEM areas, see Figure 4.2).

Creating and Performing in Plays

Plays include a beginning, middle, and end through which the characters act out the main elements of a story: that is, the plot and the theme. Most primary-age children enjoy being in plays, but it may be a new and, on occasion, fearful experience for some of them. Early childhood plays should be child initiated rather than teacher directed. Children are most comfortable playing themselves and their families, so the plays they initiate are usually related to their own cultures and thus have more meaning for them. One way to give children experience in creative

Figure 4.2. Using Puppets with Poems/Songs

Following are four examples of poems/songs that teachers can use to engage children to enact with puppets to learn relevant math and science concepts:

Here is a Beehive—To be used with finger puppets

Here is a beehive, but where are the bees?
Hidden away where nobody sees.
Soon they'll come creeping
Out of the hive
One-two-three-four-five
Buzz-z-zzz

Math Concepts: Children can learn one-to-one matching, counting, addition, and subtraction. They can learn to count the legs of the bee. Teachers can ask, "If you see three legs and you know there are six legs, how many do you not see?" The children can learn how to make a hexagon, the shape of the bee hive, which is made up of thousands of six-sided cells.

Science Concepts: Using their bee puppets to engage in dramatic play, the children can decide who will be the queen bee, workers, and drones. The queen bee is the largest and lays the eggs. The workers store food and repair the comb, usually in the top. They guard the queen. The drones are male and mate with the queen. They do not work. Explain to the children that bees have ultraviolet vision and can see which flowers are full of nectar.

Eensy, Weensy Spider—To be used with a spider puppet

Eensy, weensy spider
Climbed up the waterspout.
Down came the rain
And washed the spider out.
Out came the sun
And dried up all the rain.
So the eensy, weensy, spider
Climbed up the spout again.

Math Concepts: Have the children count the legs of the spider. Ask, "If there are eight legs and you only see four legs, how many more legs do you not see?"

Science Concepts: Explain that because spiders have eight legs, they are not insects, which have six legs. Use this poem to teach about rain (condensation) and the drying of the rain from the sun (evaporation).

Humpty Dumpty—To be used with an egg puppet

Humpty Dumpty sat on a wall.
Humpty Dumpty had a great fall
All the king's horses and all the king's men
Could not put Humpty Dumpty together again.

Science and Engineering Concepts: Ask the children, "What could have helped Humpty Dumpty stay on the wall? A seat with support, a car seat, a seat belt? Why did

Humpty Dumpty have a hard time?" (He was shaped like an egg and could not balance well) "What could help him if he fell? (A padded suit, a helmet, a net.) "Why is an egg hard to put back together?"

Baa, Baa, Black Sheep—To be used with a sheep puppet

Baa, baa, black sheep,
Have you any wool?
Yes sir, yes sir,
Three bags full:
One for the master,
And one for the dame,
And one for the little boy that lives down the lane.

Science Concepts: Engage the children in discussing that wool comes from sheep.

Math Concepts: Children can learn one-to-one matching (3 bags for 3 people).

---

playmaking is to perform simple classroom plays in which children participate after writing their own imaginative stories.

Plays can also be introduced based on favorite books, preferably from stories that children are familiar with. Traditional stories such as *The Little Red Hen, The Three Little Pigs, The Tortoise and the Hare,* and *The Lion and the Mouse* are easy to use for classroom performances. The teacher can help to bring the story to life by asking the children to be the characters and act out the plot as she tells the story. Then the teacher can use the story to promote an understanding of the scientific or math concepts at work.

In the story *The Little Red Hen,* the following connections to STEM can be demonstrated:

Science

The teacher can obtain wheat seeds to show to the children. The process of planting the seeds can be shown with illustrations from a book. What needs to take place in order for the wheat seed to grow into wheat can also be shown. The children can see how wheat is cut down and how tall it is. Then they can see how it is taken to a mill and ground into flour. It is important for the children to learn and then show that in white bread the most nutritious part of the wheat grain is taken out at the mill. Whole-wheat bread includes the most nutritious part of the grain, which is the wheat germ.

The chemistry and physics of breadmaking can be explored. While making bread in the classroom, children can be introduced to yeast, a fungi. The teacher or a parent volunteer can explain: When mixed with warm water and sugar, the yeast is converted into sugar, and then the sugar is converted into carbon dioxide. The carbon dioxide causes the bubbles and then the mixture expands. It will continue to rise when the other ingredients are placed in it. If you punch in the dough, the carbon dioxide leaves it. The holes in the bread are caused by the yeast dying.

Math—Children can count the seeds, the wheat plants from a *Little Red Hen* book; see the difference in size of the bread before cooking and afterward.

Engineering—The children can design a simple machine that grinds the wheat into flour or design a machine that makes bread.

In the story *The Three Little Pigs*, children should use their own language to tell the story with puppets using science and engineering terms. Children can try making houses of various materials (toothpicks, blocks, cardboard) and retell the story. They can test to see which kind of material is the sturdiest and then tell why this is.

Children enjoy having a stage for a play, which means deciding where the play can be performed. Large blocks can be placed together to form a wooden stage. Other areas can be added for specific scenes and for children to hide offstage. Wherever the stage is set, the teacher must explain the difference of being on stage where they will act, and what it means for an actor to be off stage. Children can decide whether props, scenery, and sound effects are needed. In the play *Swimmy*, in the vignette at the beginning of the chapter, the children decided on the ocean music, colored scarves, and background scenery. Books and poems have tremendous potential for motivating young children to express themselves. Through pantomiming, narrative improvisations, puppetry, and creating plays, young children can learn the basics of creative drama, as well as STEM principles.

SUMMARY

Creative movement is a natural form of expression that supplements physical activities and helps children develop the creative imagery needed in spatial awareness, a skill necessary in the STEM courses. The elements of creative movement are space, shape, time, flow, and force. The main categories of creative movement are locomotor, nonlocomotor, and manipulative movements. The types of creative movement are agility, balance, coordination, power, reaction time, and speed. Children integrate their movements using these elements, categories, and types to express themselves creatively and scientifically.

Creative drama is a form of imaginative expression in which the children use their own words and actions to communicate with others. Pantomime, narrative improvisation (including storytelling), puppetry, and creating and performing plays are examples of creative drama in early childhood. Creative drama can enrich the 21st century skills of critical thinking, problem solving, communication, and collaboration. Creative movement and drama can be integrated into content areas such as science, engineering, and mathematics.

REVIEW AND REFLECT

1. Literature on obesity can be given to parents to promote physical activity among young children. Ask parents to chart how much time children are watching television, playing video games, and doing other sedentary activities. Then ask them how much time the child is spending in active movement and exercise. Discuss how science and math are learned through movement.
2. How is bodily spatial awareness important in STEM courses? How did Leonardo use his knowledge of the planets in a play and show knowledge of spatial understanding?
3. Identify what locomotor skills are and what nonlocomotor skills are. Place the following locomotor skills in the order they usually appear in children: gallop, leap, crawl, run, creep, hop, skip, jump, walk. Think of an animal that does each of these.
4. Choose an element of creative movement. Combine it with a locomotor movement. Develop an activity for science or math using creative imagery to go with your combination.
5. Choose an element of creative movement. Combine it with a nonlocomotor movement and a locomotor movement. Develop an activity for science creative imagery to go with the combination.

Table 4.1. Integrating Elements, Fundamentals, and Imagery into a Steam Activity

Locomotor Skill	Element of Movement	Fundamental of Movement Used	Creative Imagery Used	Activity for Earth or Life Science
Crawl	Space, Time	Agility, Coordination, Speed, Shape	Desert	Crawl through the desert looking for water.
	Force	Coordination, Power	Bear	Show how you would crawl like a bear up a tree trying to find honey.
Creep	Force, Flow	Agility, Reaction Time, Speed	Sibling	Creep up on a sibling while watching snakes at the zoo.
	Flow	Coordination, Balance	Bear hunt	Show how you would creep up to a bear cave while singing bear hunt songs.
Walk	Time, Space	Agility, Reaction time	Butterfly museum	Show how you would walk with tiny quiet steps if you were in a butterfly museum and suddenly you were startled by a butterfly.
	Force	Coordination, Power, Balance	Mountain	Show how you would walk up a steep rocky mountain.
Run	Force, Flow, Time	Balance, Reaction Time, Speed, Coordination, Power	Horse that ran away	Run to catch up with the horse that runs away.
	Force, Time, Space	Agility, Speed, Reaction Time, Coordination, Power, Balance	Cheetah	Pretend you are a cheetah running after a gazelle.
Jump	Force, Space, Shape	Power, Agility	Grasshopper	Jump in and out of tall grasses across the prairie.
	Force	Coordination, Balance, Power, Speed, Shape	Kangaroo	Jump like a kangaroo jumping across the outback.
Hop	Force, Space, Time	Coordination, Balance, Agility, Power	Bunny	Pretend you are a bunny and hop to the nearest hole.
	Flow, Space, Force	Balance, Coordination, Reaction Time	Chalk on playground	Play hopscotch.
Skip	Time, Flow	Coordination	Grandma's house	Skip on your way to Grandma's house, like Little Red Riding Hood.
	Force, Flow, Space	Coordination, Balance, Agility, Power	Yellow brick road	Skip down a yellow brick road.

Movement				
Gallop	Force, Flow, Speed, Time	Coordination, Balance, Agility, Reaction Time	Horse	Gallop like a wild horse out on the open prairie.
	Flow	Balance, Coordination, Speed, Agility	Horse	Gallop like an Arabian show horse.
Leap	Shape, Flow, Force	Agility, Power, Reaction Time	Bullfrog	Leap like a bullfrog from log to log.
	Flow, Force	Agility, Power	Squirrel	Leap like a squirrel from branch to branch.
Stretch	Force, Flow, Shape	Balance	Sky	Stretch to touch the sky and puffy white clouds.
	Flow, Shape	Balance	Rubberband	Stretch like you are a rubberband being pulled from two points.
Bend	Space, Shape, Flow	Balance, Coordination	Tree	Bend like a tree blowing in a hurricane.
	Force, Flow, Shape	Agility, Balance, Coordination	Dirt digger truck	Bend like a dirt digger truck digging dirt and putting it in the truck.
Sit	Space, Shape	Balance, Coordination	Criss-cross	Sit criss-cross, applesauce.
	Space, Shape	Balance	Rock	Sit on the ground like a rock.
Shake	Space, Force, Flow	Balance, Power	Salt shaker	Shake like a salt shaker.
	Force, Space, Time	Power, Speed, Reaction Time	Wet dog	Shake like you are a wet dog.
Turn	Space, Time, Force, Flow	Reaction Time, Speed	Merry-go-round	Pretend you are a merry-go-round and turn.
	Time, Shape, Flow	Speed, Reaction Time, Balance	Circles	Turn in a tight neat circle, like a top.
Dodge	Force, Flow	Coordination, Speed, Agility	Ram	Dodge like a ram.
	Space, Force, Flow, Time	Reaction Time, Speed, Balance, Agility	Spaceship	Pretend you are a spaceship dodging meteors in space.
Swing	Space, Shape, Flow	Coordination, Agility	Elephant trunk	Swing arms like an elephant trunk.
	Flow, Shape	Coordination, Balance	Dance	Pretend you are swing dancing.
Fall	Space, Time, Shape	Balance Reaction Time	Tree in woods	Move like a tree falling in the forest—timber!
	Space, Force, Power	Reaction Time, Speed	Apple from tree	Pretend you are an apple falling from a tree.

CHAPTER 5

COLLABORATIVE INTERACTION WITH ART MEDIA USING 21ST CENTURY SKILLS

Imagination is more important than knowledge.

—Albert Einstein

HOW LEONARDO DA VINCI AND HIS CONTEMPORARIES UNDERSTOOD THE SCIENCE AND INVENTION OF PAINTING

There were no art stores in Leonardo's day. The artists made their own brushes. They tested the furs of many animals to make brushes. The soft fur of squirrels was used to make soft brushes. If they needed a hard brush, they might use hog bristles, which were thicker and harder. The artists also had to make paints. Color making required an understanding of minerals, a part of Earth science, and bugs, a part of the life sciences. Blue came from grinding a stone called lapis lazuli. Red came from cochinal beetles and possibly cranberries. The making of a painting required a scientific study of the media. This helped artists make connections to the sciences in a way that children of today do not. Leonardo was one of the first artists to experiment with oil in his paints. He made paintings, sculptures, and some models of air machines.

Today many children do not have access to "hands-on" learning, nor do they understand how to begin a process (Silberstein-Storfer & Jones, 1997). Overemphasis on the use of TV, computers, and video games has created a feeling of apathy in children toward using tactile activities such as painting, woodworking, cooking, quilting, or weaving that in the past provided tactile, emotional, and social expression. Creating with one's own hands provides a deep identification with the material and its scientific origins. Children develop power when they develop relationships with different media (Weisman Topal & Gandini, 1999).

When children are allowed to choose their materials, they have the power to experiment with new methods, and the product becomes an outcome of experimenting and experiencing, which are needed for creativity in the arts and sciences in the 21st century. As a result of having many options available to them, children often represent the same ideas with a different medium, like making a crayon drawing of their clay sculpture of a bee. Different media will be important in the future for innovation and media interaction. It should be noted that the tools used in the early childhood arts (crayons, pencils, scissors, chalk, blocks, computers, iPads, and so on) were invented by people in the STEM fields in collaboration with artists or designers. Technology is not just advanced forms of machines such as computers and iPads; it is any tools that have been invented, including those utilized in the arts. Media are particularly important because they intersect with the crosscutting concepts from the *Next Generation Science Standards* (NGSS, 2013): patterns; cause and effect; scale, proportion, and quantity; structure and function; or how an object is shaped and its substructure determines its properties and functions.

This chapter begins with a look at how children learn using art media in the preschools of Reggio Emilia, Italy. There the children do long-term investigations of a topic utilizing various media. The chapter goes on to explore how creative teachers can support the expressive arts by providing a wide range of art materials and media, thus encouraging creative development and in many cases curiosity and investigation in science and math. The chapter concludes with a vignette about a zoo visit and how the visit can expand into an interdisciplinary, collaborative study of animal habitats, architectural design, and the use of various media to develop the habitats.

REGGIO EMILIA: OPENING NEW VISTAS
FOR COLLABORATIVE RELATIONSHIPS

Reggio Emilia's approach to early education reflects an emphasis on media representation and its importance for the development of 21st century skills. One of the most challenging aspects of the Reggio Emilia approach is the solicitation of multiple points of view regarding children's interests from the community, the parents and teachers, and the children themselves.

Teachers in Reggio persevere in collaborations, even though at times it is wearing, especially when debating, thinking critically, and coordinating different points of view through problem solving and communication become an issue (Krechevsky, 2001). Sometimes teachers find it difficult to accept hard criticism, and refuse to let go of fixed ideas when someone questions their certainties, but they must be willing to reexamine and reshape many aspects of their practice. Authentic collaboration can become a source of energy and growth for early childhood teachers as they learn together with parents and the community, because it assures that their educational approach is not static, but evolving all the time based on the needs, abilities, and interests of their children.

Loris Malaguzzi (1993), the principal founder of the Reggio preschools, emphasized that the most favorable situation for creativity seems to be interpersonal exchange, with negotiation of conflicts and comparison of ideas and actions being the decisive elements.

In the Reggio preschools careful consideration and attention is given to children's interests and thinking as they explore the "hundred languages" collaboratively using different media. Children are encouraged to depict their understandings through symbolic languages that include drawing, sculpture, dramatic play, and writing. In *The Hundred Languages of Children*, C. Edwards, Gandini, and Forman (2012) point out the many ways children represent their thinking using the arts.

The Reggio Emilia preschools have emerged as leaders in creative education for young children because of their philosophy supporting multiple experiences in the arts as extensions of thinking in other areas, such as math and science. The theoretical background of Reggio Emilia is based primarily on the work of Piaget (1952, 1974), Vygotsky (1962, 1978), and Dewey (1934, 1938).

As explained earlier, in Reggio Emilia, the children's study of long-term projects is enhanced by spaces known as *ateliers* (Vecchi, 2010). A key part of the atelier is that people with professional competencies staff an area rich in media, materials, and tools. In the atelier, children are given sufficient and sustained periods of time in which to develop creative projects and to explore their different languages. As in the Bridge Project described in Chapter 1, Reggio children are often encouraged to use drawings and sculptures as a "graphic language" to record their ideas, feelings, and observations. Children attending the Reggio preschools are introduced to as many different media as possible as they represent the many languages of childhood (Althouse, Johnson, & Mitchell, 2003; Slavin, 1994; Vygotsky, 1962).

The Reggio preschools stress interaction with peers and others on long-term projects to develop children's understanding of the relationships among people and things in the world. Piaget (1952, 1974) similarly theorized that children are learning to see another viewpoint as they construct their own knowledge interacting with objects and with their peers. This exchange of viewpoints is important in the Reggio preschools, and error and conflict are regarded as a way of moving forward, because children assimilate and accommodate knowledge in the process of creating their plans to produce an artifact (Walling, 2000). Current research shows how young children have the capacity for conceptual growth as they investigate how the world works (NRC 2007, 2012). An example of the ways collaborative interactions can take place with children and materials in unique ways is displayed in Figure 5.1.

The preschools in Reggio Emilia foster collaboration and co-construction of knowledge and adhere to the idea that children develop while interacting with others. Vygotsky (1962, 1978) similarly emphasized that children learn from more competent peers and teachers using the concept of scaffolding, the temporary support of learning experiences. The major ideas of Vygotsky are based on children watching and interacting with adults or more advanced peers to help them understand thought and concepts. He stated that children learn by making discoveries

Figure 5.1. Collaborative Interaction Web

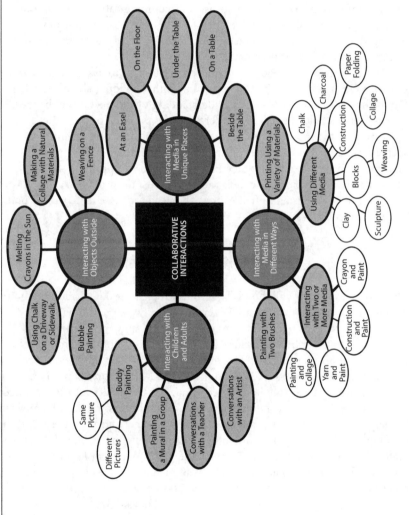

on their own, as well as from the experience of others, and that they will express themselves, through the arts, at a higher level when interacting with a more skilled peer or adult.

The creative Reggio teachers are comfortable providing an unspecified amount of information about a subject, as long as it includes and respects the child as a cocreator. By making the effort at observation, a child and a teacher collaborate. The more they experiment using the science process skills of observation, comparison, classification, measuring, communication, and hypothesizing with the media, the more they are open to new ideas on their journeys of learning together. According to Vygotsky, most learning takes place when children are challenged to reach their potential developmental level.

In the Reggio preschools the children are invited to ask questions and engage in a discussion with the teacher and the other children about the science of the media. In this way the child's understanding of the media is enhanced, and the discussions help the teacher understand the thinking of the child. It should be noted that the inquiry-based discussions can also include scientific concepts such as "What makes the water disappear while painting?" (This process is evaporation.) Additionally, this inquiry-based approach can promote the intellectual skills that are needed in our schools rather than just the academic skills. Inspired children notice details and often express the need for these details to be pointed out through collaboration.

ORIGINS AND USE OF MEDIA

Materials used in early childhood classrooms to enhance young children's ability to communicate and express themselves creatively in two-dimensional and three-dimensional forms are referred to as art media or simply media. The term *media* is also used to describe the various forms of artistic communication; for example, computer art is an electronic form of media for artistic expression. According to Copple and Bredekamp (2009), adults should help children, ages 3–5, explore and work with various media and techniques as the adults introduce concepts and vocabulary to extend children's experiences in the arts. As children move into kindergarten and primary grades, they revise and expand their ideas with new techniques. Children explore unfamiliar art media by first asking, "What is this material?" and "What does it do?" *before* they ask, "What can *I* do with the material?" Teachers should make connections of media to life science, Earth science, and physics. It is important for children to know about the scientific study of the media as they use it. To help children understand the similarities or differences in media, it should be displayed with different materials in a variety of combinations of colors, textures, lines, and shapes. Children need to explore and find out the origins of the media and how they are made.

As children explore and experiment with various media, they begin to develop their ability to express themselves creatively using the visual arts. When art media is used in many processes, children begin to see a variety of possibilities for their creative expressions. Before discussing in detail two- and three-dimensional forms of children's artistic expressions, we review two important topics: safety measures for art activities and general guidelines regarding creativity.

Maintain a Physically Safe Art Environment

There are certain safety measures that must be met in order to keep young artists safe in their studios. An understanding of chemistry can help adult artists prevent illnesses from use of materials, while helping children understand the chemistry of art safety can introduce them to the importance of this field. The following suggestions are important safety measures regarding art materials and activities:

- Keep a record of the allergies of children; families are generally happy to share this information with the teacher. Check to see if children may have medical conditions such as asthma or allergies that may prevent them from using certain materials, such as shaving cream.
- Beware of children inhaling such things as powdered and aerosol paints. If you must mix any powdered tempera paint, use a protective mask to keep yourself from inhaling the harmful particles in the paint, and do not mix it when children are present. Preferably use liquid tempera paint. Do not use aerosol paints or solvent-based products such as rubber cement, paint thinners, or turpentine because they give off fumes, which children may inhale. Do not use any toxic materials in schools; instead use water-based, nontoxic paints, glues, and markers.
- Do not use loose glitter because it has glass in it, and sometimes glitter may be ingested into a membrane, mouth, or eyes. Instead use glues that contain glitter, thus eliminating the risk.
- Some crayons may contain asbestos, especially those manufactured in foreign countries, so read the label carefully.
- Do not use commercial fabric dyes for activities such as tie-dyeing because they may be poisonous. Instead use food or vegetable dyes.
- Never use Styrofoam meat trays that have been used before because of the bacterial danger to children's health. Also never use popsicle sticks that have been used before because of the potential spread of germs.
- Children should not point any sharp edge toward others, or toward themselves, and safety rules need to be quickly enforced, especially when using scissors or other sharp objects.
- If children have cuts or sores that could be vulnerable to infections, ask the school nurse to cover them.
- Purchase washable paints. Children may wear smocks or other kinds of clothing to protect their clothing from paints or other art materials, but preferably they should wear clothing to school that can easily be washed.
- Children should be taught to wash their hands after participating in any art project.

Enhance Creativity

Teachers should give careful thought to planning experiences that promote creativity. Children should be allowed to see their work in a portfolio over time so that they can appreciate the advances they have made in their own developmental changes in art. However, teachers should be aware of certain art activities that stifle creativity such as the following:

- Lowenfeld and Brittain (1987) have said that coloring books stifle creativity because they are limiting. Children do not benefit from filling in someone else's drawing with color. Some people contend that children are learning motor control by coloring in a coloring book; however, the same purpose can be achieved by coloring in their own artwork.   .
- Precut forms, such as shapes and forms for a collage, do not tap into the child's self-expression, and children need to create their own forms because this is part of the inventive nature needed in the arts and sciences. Precut forms may have a place in understanding spatial relationships, but they do not help in promoting the creativity of children. Children should not be given models of any type of work, and then told to do one just like the model.
- Teaching children to use stick figures hinders them from their own development of the figure.
- Children who are shown how to draw a bird or a tree in a certain way may never create their own bird or tree again. One teacher encouraged her art class to make trees in as many different ways as possible in the media of their choice. Acceptance of all types of trees was important.
- Never tear up a child's picture since it is not your property. Let the children make the decision as to whether they want to tear it up.
- Never openly prefer one child's art to another's because all art is representative of the creative child within.

With appropriate teacher guidance, young children can express their creativity in two- and three-dimensional forms, as discussed in the next two sections.

TWO-DIMENSIONAL FORMS OF ARTISTIC EXPRESSION AND CONNECTIONS TO SCIENCE AND TECHNOLOGY

There are five main methods of artistic expression with two-dimensional forms in early childhood: drawing, pasting, painting, printing, and weaving. The term *two-dimensional form* refers to any art form that has length and width. This section will show the scientific and technological origins of the materials used in this form.

Drawing

Some of the earliest evidence of drawing was produced by cavemen on their walls, indicating that drawing is not just a medium or technique but a human way to communicate. Drawing can serve as a powerful way to develop children's perception and thought, so in broad terms young children should be allowed to work with various drawing tools often enough to practice improving their skills and to represent what they see in nature. Drawing is the main medium for representing the life science of nature. This connection has been strong since the days of Leonardo da Vinci and his journals. As children become proficient in drawing, they are motivated to use their imagination in expressing their ideas, feelings, and observations through this medium.

Pencils, both regular and colored; crayons, both large and small; and felt-tipped markers are commonly used for everyday drawings. The most common and accessible tools for drawing are pencils, as evidenced by the fact you often see children drawing with them in school, at home, on airplanes, and many other places. A pencil usually consists of graphite and a gray binder inside a protective casing—typically wood. Many of the protective casings are circular or hexagonal in shape. Graphite rocks can be shown to the children so that there is a connection to the Earth sciences, and they can even be allowed to write with the rocks, to show the uniqueness of the invention of the pencil.

Since children often use many sheets of paper at a time, inexpensive or free paper can be found in the scrap bins of photocopying or printing shops. The paper can include a variety of colors, and using paper already printed on one side for their everyday practice drawing does not trouble young children. Recycled paper offers children the opportunity to use as much as they feel they need to progress from the scribbling stage to making recognizable shapes to pictorial representations. The connection to the science and technology of papermaking and where paper comes from (trees) is important for the young artist to know and experience, as well as the connection to recycling for the natural environment. They should also learn that paper was invented by the Chinese. There are now papermaking machines for young children so they can see the actual process of making paper.

Children should not be expected or encouraged to be drawing "something," but rather they should be given the chance to practice their drawing, much like a musician practices scales. For young children the product—what a drawing looks like—is less important than the content—the thoughts, feelings, and ideas that children put into their drawings. Sometimes children will tell stories about their drawings. There should be no coloring in predrawn worksheets because these do not give children a chance to be creative, which is the focus for all expressive art experiences. Children need to be exposed to drawing of human anatomy and animal anatomy. When drawing the human figure, children should be made aware of the main body parts (head, body, legs, and arms) and then the more technical parts of the head (eyes, ears, nose, mouth), arms (hands, fingers), and legs (feet and toes). When drawing a bee, children should see that it has three parts: head, thorax, and abdomen. It also has antennae and six legs. When drawing fish, they should be able to identify the eyes, fins, tail, and scales. In primary grades the position of the fins can be identified. The wings of the bird and the directions of the wings can be pointed out. Wings are not always in the same place. The dragonfly wings can be emphasized because they can act like a helicopter as well as an airplane. Drawing connects to life and physics standards in science.

The use of chalk leads to further understanding of Earth and its constitution. There are three major types of chalk-like materials used for drawing: colored and white chalk consisting of a soft limestone made up of fossils or seashells; oil pastels made out of oil and chalk; and charcoal, made out of charred wood. Children should be shown how chalk can be made from seashells. It is important for children to know the scientific origin of the media so that they can grasp the technology involved in the products. Because chalk is a softer media than crayons, it is somewhat easier for young children to explore. Young children often prefer chalk for their drawings, because it is pliable, and they are often more able to express their feelings and imaginations in the visual arts using a softer medium. Colored chalk, generally called "sidewalk" chalk, comes in large sizes that are easy to grasp. Children enjoy drawing on the sidewalk using colored chalk of various colors. However, some multicolored sidewalk chalks contain high levels of lead that could pose a risk of poisoning for young children, so teachers must be sure to purchase sidewalk chalk that does not contain lead. It's easy and preferable for teachers to make their own colored chalk using molds of various sizes and shapes, plaster of Paris, and tempera paint so that the scientific process can be witnessed and the properties of chalk can be seen.

For young children, using chalk outdoors is preferable to using it indoors due to the danger of inhaling chalk dust. Children can paint the sidewalk with water and then draw with the dry chalk, which makes the colors brighter and cuts down on the chalk dust. This helps the children learn cause and effect. Often children enjoy having art shows that display their chalk drawings outdoors, similar to that of artists in Paris along the River Seine. Assure children that it is all right to draw on sidewalks with colored chalk because it washes off easily with water. (Using paint on outdoor surfaces requires permission.) Children need experiences with all kinds of media to discover what works for them. For example, consider in the following vignette how important expressing himself with sidewalk chalk was to Pheng, a victim of many negative situations in his young life.

Pheng, a Hmong boy from Laos, loved to draw outside with colored chalk. In Laos, his family had lived outside in the forest, and he had been free to explore his environment. As a primary student, Pheng felt free to express himself in the outdoors at school. He had seen so much violence and shooting in his early years that those experiences were still appearing in his drawings. He did not speak English, and since the Hmong had no written language, his means of communication was through drawing. He drew airplanes landing and people shooting at the planes. He used red chalk to represent bloody people. Pheng spent many hours drawing war scenes with chalk and then erasing the sidewalk production forcibly with his shoes. Only toward the end of the year did the mountains and trees of his native country begin to appear in his drawings.

For some reason Pheng felt free to express his feelings of displacement from his own country in an outside environment using sidewalk chalk. Not speaking English, Pheng was unable to tell his classmates at school anything about his past experiences, but he was able to express his innermost fears and feelings through drawings using this medium. At first he felt like an outsider, then like a visitor, but after expressing himself to others using sidewalk chalk, he soon felt himself to be one of the class.

As his classmates began to understand the feelings of confusion and anxiety Pheng experienced when he found himself in an unfamiliar cultural environment that used a language he did not understand, Pheng appeared to let go of his anger at being displaced by a war, and was able to communicate the beautiful things about his culture and customs to his friends. The experiences of the class were enriched, especially since Pheng was willing and able to communicate things about the traditions and games of Hmong children from another part of the world using the medium of sidewalk chalk.

Since oil pastels are more expensive and do not last as long, they are not as widely used as the other chalks. An oil pastel is a medium consisting of chalk and oil produced in a crayon-like form. Oil pastels are somewhat messier for young children to use, but primary-grade children enjoy mixing the colors since oil pastels are easier to blend than crayons. When exploring oil pastels, children can blend several colors together, build up layers of colors, and smear the colors to get various effects. Children learn not to press too hard on the pastels or they will break, not to sharpen them in a pencil sharpener, and not to wipe them on their clothing because the oil pastels will stain cloth.

Pieces of charred wood were used for drawing in prehistoric times, but today charcoal is a drawing stick or pencil made from charred wood and comes in a variety of widths and hardness. Charcoal, or black chalk, which looks like a crayon or a piece of chalk can be used for rubbings on anything with a rough edge, for sketching, and for free and expressive drawing. It is a medium that is not recommended for young children, but primary-age children are excited to draw with charcoal because in an instant they can create rich black colors, and the lines they draw can be blended easily with their fingers. For rubbings, they place shapes or textures under paper and rub over the surface.

However, charcoal has a serious drawback for children, and that disadvantage is charcoal dust. Charcoal is definitely considered to be inappropriate for younger children since if dust from the charcoal is aspirated into their lungs, they could need immediate medical attention. Charcoal as a drawing medium should never be used indoors with young children.

Another reason charcoal is not often used with young children is that it gets under their nails, on their faces, in their hair, and everywhere except on the paper. For primary-age children, teachers can purchase charcoal in pencil form because the dust is easier to control, and fewer fingers become blackened. Charcoal pencils were invented in France in response to the shortage of graphite that resulted from the Napoleonic wars. However since charcoal pencils are made of compressed charcoal, they lose many of the qualities of natural charcoal when they are used.

Teachers in primary grades may purchase "laid paper," which has a texture that helps hold the charcoal on the paper as children shade or blend their drawing, but it is expensive. If primary-grade children work with charcoal, they should work outdoors in the fresh air, use the charcoal on laid paper to explore shading by pressing lightly and heavily, and experiment with dark and light effects. They can use all the surfaces of the charcoal pencil, as well as the point, to make different shades and lines. When compared to other media used for drawing, charcoal ranks last as an appropriate medium for young children to explore.

Pasting

Creating a *collage* (French for "pasting") allows children the opportunity to touch and manipulate materials of various colors and textures and then select, arrange, and paste them on a flat surface. Unlike painting or drawing, which has limits to the different textures available at once, building a collage or pasting involves children working directly with varied textures. Furthermore, this tactile experience need not be limited by the boundaries of paper. There are no "rules" or patterns for making a collage, so children must focus upon creating their own artistic designs. Although most collages are two dimensional, they also can be three dimensional, depending on the materials used.

Collage making encourages children to recycle and reuse paper. Children are always using their sense of touch because it is one of their tools for exploring, so during a "nature walk" they might collect and sort materials such as leaves or pinecones that would be appropriate for a texture collage. Many household materials such as leftover yarn, bits of fabric, or sponge pieces can be used for a collage, but be sure not to provide things like beads or small buttons that young children might put in their mouths.

In early childhood, a typical collage is a picture containing glued-on objects or paper. There are many techniques for manipulating paper for collages, such as tearing, cutting, and layering; however, it is important to remember that children should experience paper tearing first because it is easy to handle and does not require as much eye–hand coordination as scissor cutting. Paper-tear collages encourage children to do the following things:

- Choose from lots of colors and types of paper
- Try out different textures
- Tear paper toward themselves as opposed to tearing away
- Tear paper apart using their hands, not their teeth
- Tear along the edges and learn about the difficulties of tearing along the edges

Gather resource materials, develop ideas, and think about how to mix materials to help children develop their compositions. Teachers might explain to children that they can reposition their shapes for different effects. Children can make new discoveries this way by looking at something from a different point of view.

Be aware of the effects of the choice of papers by considering the thickness of the paper, whether the paper is transparent, and whether it is durable. For a dramatic effect, heavy, textured paper works well, and for a lighter, more layered effect, opt for transparent papers. Tissue-paper collages can be constructed with liquid laundry starch instead of glue on translucent waxed paper with overlapping colors.

When making a collage, children often want to use a great deal of glue. The teacher must demonstrate that a little dab will do. However, if they are exploring the consistency and the effects of the gluing process, it is acceptable for them to use a larger amount of glue. Some children prefer to brush glue on their paper and then add collage materials, while some choose to use self-stick clear shelf paper with the back removed as a surface and put miscellaneous art materials on the sticky side. Collage is a versatile method of presentation, and it cannot be emphasized enough that there is no right or wrong way for a child to produce one.

Collage making is a process that helps children appreciate form, shapes, colors, and textures. Children regularly use paper, mixed media, pieces of fabric, and many other items to create their collages. The process affords them the opportunity to look at and touch many kinds of materials, and to make choices about how to arrange them and paste them on an infinite supply of surfaces. Collages are fun and inexpensive, and allow children the chance to practice creative problem-solving skills. If scissors are used, it should be pointed out that that the scissors are a lever, or simple machine, with the connecting point as the fulcrum. The wedges or sharp edges are simple machines too. This promotes the mechanical engineering STEM connection.

Painting

Painting centers can be offered both indoors and outdoors. Paint is a solution, suspension, or colloid, made up of a colored pigment and a binder, a material that evenly disperses the pigment and adheres to a surface when the paint is applied and dries. As explained in the chapter's opening vignette, early artists made their own paints and therefore were scientists, as well as artists, who were constantly experimenting. When selecting paints, as emphasized earlier, the teacher must be sure to choose *nontoxic* and *washable* versions so that children do not need to wear paint smocks to protect their clothing from inevitable drips and spills. It is easier for young children to manipulate short-handled brushes, but a variety of brush sizes should be available for children to choose.

There are two major types of paint that are appropriate for young children to use: tempera and watercolor paints. Tempera painting in particular is an exceptionally versatile art media that offers children many opportunities to experiment and explore. *Tempera paint* is an opaque, water-soluble paint available in nontoxic liquid or powder form. In egg tempera, powdered pigment is bound with egg and water. Liquid starch may be added to tempera paint to make it thicker. Teachers should introduce children to tempera paint before watercolor, because tempera paints dry opaque and blend well with other colors. Allow children to freely mix and explore colors in their own way and on their own time schedule. Children advance in mixing colors by mixing them on their paper, not by seeing them mixed in cups. Tempera paint dries relatively fast, allowing children to change their minds and paint one color over another. Using tempera paints to enhance and develop the imaginative and artistic powers of young children is a common practice in early childhood centers.

Sets of watercolor paint used in early childhood programs are actually dehydrated tempera paint in cakes of various colors, yet they lack the visual appeal of the regular tempera paint's vivid colors. Young children can use watercolor sets by putting a few drops of water on a cake to moisten the paint. Most often when they mix the colors together, they form a brownish color. Watercolors can be mixed on a palette, but it is difficult to blend them on a painting surface since colors run together. Watercolor can be more effective when used to make lines, shapes, or abstract designs rather than detailed pictures. Watercolor painted on wet paper will bleed into very attractive designs. Teachers often display famous watercolor pictures in the classroom to inspire children to paint with watercolors.

Instead of using the brush provided with a watercolor set, some children enjoy wetting their fingers with water, pressing them into the cakes, and then pressing their fingers onto paper to make oval designs or fingerprint pictures. As children use watercolors, they soon learn to use thick paper to prevent having a soggy picture. However, watercolor paper is very expensive, and recycled good bond typing paper will work just as well in early childhood. Since there is only one brush for several colors, it is necessary to clean the paintbrush with water in between using colors. Children should soak up excess paint in the watercolor set when finished painting using a sponge. If this does not occur, the paint will dry into a muddy color, which will not inspire children to use the watercolor set again. Today, nontoxic liquid watercolors are available in intense colors, and they are less expensive than watercolor sets. Although children enjoy the "traditional" means of working with tempera and watercolor paint, it is also important to vary the experience to challenge the children, so they do not become bored with the activity and so they can experiment like an artist and a scientist.

Children may also be asked to paint in response to a story or to allow their imaginations free range as they paint to music or even blindfolded. Children need time to experiment with painting, and teachers should not interrupt their painting by asking too many questions about their picture or the color they are using. Painting is an aesthetic experience, not an academic one. Colors are only as important as how they are used in the artwork. Painting is visual thinking, and teachers should not ask children to tell what they plan to paint, because this interrupts and inhibits their visual thinking processes. In addition to varying the medium, children can be presented with other ways to apply or manipulate the different types of paint.

Other Methods and Variations of Painting

Children can be scientists and create a pallet of natural paints. They can find colored rocks or black coal. They can grind each rock and add a binder of glue, starch, paste, or egg yolk. Then they can use the paints and identify the combination of elements.

Many materials including sand, dirt, and leaves can be added to tempera paint to give a textured look. Enhancing the smell of the paints can add another dimension to the children's experience, but it is not advisable to add smells that could be associated with food like lemon, orange, or peppermint extract, for example, since young children may be tempted to taste the paint. Instead, try adding equally pleasant, nonfood smells like floral essential oils.

Teachers can also vary the painting surface. For example, the children could paint on cardboard, grocery bags, newspaper, wrapping paper, newsprint, or butcher paper. For more alternative surfaces for children to paint and experience textures, see Figure 5.2. Very young children often like to experiment by painting on the walls, but children can be encouraged to find more appropriate surfaces on which to paint. Painting outdoors allows children to have more freedom, *and* the clean-up process does not present a problem. Outdoors, teachers often allow children to paint the bricks of the building using water. Painting a fence, sidewalk, or wall with water, when the sun is brightly shining, is very enjoyable for young children. Images they paint using water will only last until the water dries, which encourages the practice of living in the moment and constantly exploring new shapes and designs. It also teaches the physical change of evaporation.

Finger painting is still the most popular painting activity in early childhood classrooms. Children enjoy finger painting as much for the feel of the paint as for the cause-and-effect designs they make. The expression need not be limited to the fingers; using hands, arms, and elbows, as well as feet or toes, and sometimes even the face to create images with nontoxic paints helps children discover all kinds of effects they can make when they use different parts of their body as paint brushes. Because of the potential massive clean-up, it is an activity that is seldom done at home.

"Finger paint" is used on glossy, smooth paper. Special "paper" can be purchased at art stores, but is relatively expensive. Waxed paper and other smooth

**Figure 5.2. Alternative Surfaces on Which Children Can Paint and
    Experience Textures**

In the Kitchen	In the Garage or Yard
Aluminum	Sand paper
Cellophane	Wood
Plastic wrap	Cardboard
Paper plates	Linoleum
Egg cartons	Ceramic tiles
Metal juice lids	Clay or wood sculptures
Wax paper	Rocks
Styrofoam	Flower pots
Plastic from milk jugs	Cardboard tubes
Coffee filters	Corrugated cardboard
Paper towels	Bricks
Juice cans	Pinecones
Corks	Leaves
Sponges	Flowers (big petals)
Baskets	Cement
Paper bags	Driveway

papers work just as well. Formica tabletops are often used for finger painting, and if the children want a copy of their work, a piece of paper can be placed on top of the painting to get a print. Finger painting is messy, but it is an activity in which children make direct contact with the medium without a brush or other object to separate them from the paint. It is important for children to be allowed to finger paint and get messy without fear of reprimands.

Another novel and experimental painting activity is blow or *straw painting*. To produce designs, children blow through a straw filled with paint onto a paper. Blow painting is *only* for primary-age children who can blow out. Young children often don't blow out, and they suck in paint. A better approach to blow painting for young children is to put small amounts of different colors of thin paint on a paper with plastic eye droppers and then use the straw to blow the paint off the paper or to create new color combinations.

A paint technique that provides a mysterious process for young artists is *spatter painting*, using a special stand. It can be purchased or made and looks like a small table with a piece of window screen framed in the middle. Children use it by putting a piece of construction paper under the stand and then creatively arranging various shapes or natural items such as leaves on top of the paper. Then they dip an old toothbrush or other small brush into the paint, and rub the brush back and forth across the screen. After the paint has dried, they carefully remove the shapes or natural items to find an image has been produced with paint specks around it. The creativity of this activity comes from the arrangement of objects to be spattered.

Sand painting can be enjoyed by primary-age children. Sand of various colors can be purchased or made by mixing dry tempera paint with white play sand. The Navajo people paint with sand by letting colored sands flow through their fingers onto the ground. Using the same technique, children can make beautiful sand paintings on the ground using the four colors of the Navajo paintings: purple, yellow, blue, and green. The teacher can explain to the children that these colors represent the mountains, sun, sky, and grass, as they use their hand and fingers to drop the sand onto the ground. It is preferable to sand paint outdoors since the dust from the sand and paint is too easily inhaled indoors. An adaptation of sand painting is to fill a clear plastic glass with layers of different colors to make a vertical sand painting.

Printing

Along with painting, another favorite art medium of young children is printing. *Printing* is a process that involves making impressions over and over again by stamping on a surface after an object has been dipped in paint. The prints can be shapes or patterns of things in nature, pictures, or words. Some outstanding prints have been made in Japan. Hokusai, a master Japanese woodblock printer, used as many as 90 separate wood blocks to paint his detailed prints (Harden, 1995). Aside from the work of masters, printmaking is easy for children to do, and they enjoy making designs with a variety of materials. In fact, many household items can be used for printing.

In addition, water-soluble, large circular ink pads with assorted colors are readily available for printing by young children. Small rolling pins with various shapes glued on them can be used with inkpads, but wood blocks or rollers used for printing ink onto objects are preferably used with primary-age children. They are more complicated to use since they involve rolling a thin film of printing ink onto the object they are using for stamping, and then making designs by stamping the inked surface onto the surface of absorbent paper.

Children are fascinated with making prints such as paw prints from their dogs, fish scales from fish purchased at the store, and leaves of various types and sizes. During printing activities, children focus on making patterns, and teachers often point out patterns used in woven baskets from different cultures or display patterns captured on colorful woven tapestries, both of which can stimulate an interest in weaving.

Weaving

According to archaeologists, weaving is a very ancient technique that dates back over 5,000 years (O'Reilly, 1993). A craft using interlacing strands of material, weaving was one of the occupations in the Froebelian kindergarten. In the United States we have modified Froebel's approach by enlarging his materials for weaving in the belief we are guarding children's eyesight and because of our greater knowledge of motor development. Weaving helps with the development of small-muscle coordination and thus the fine-motor skills necessary to complete such tasks as drawing, sculpting, and writing. Weaving involves small-muscle movements that control the hand, fingers, and thumb, and develop over time with practice. Weaving also contributes to vocabulary development as children come to understand the meaning of words such as *over* and *under.*

Although there are many different types of weaving materials, the one most frequently used in classrooms for beginning weavers is construction paper. Before children can embark on creative activities with weaving, they must first master paper weaving, a basic early childhood activity in which the outcome is specified in advance. Generally the teacher prepares most of the paper for this activity. After folding a piece of construction paper lengthwise, the teacher cuts several evenly spaced slits, extending from the folded edge to about an inch from the open edge. The cuts can be straight, curvy, or zigzagged. Children must be first taught to use an under and then an over motion to weave. Later, the teacher can prepare other media to include different textures like wallpaper, ribbon, or yarn. After children have experienced weaving according to directions from the teacher, they soon learn to cut their own papers and other materials.

Children should not be limited to solid-color construction paper; a picture from a magazine, for example, may be cut in strips and then used for a paper-weaving activity. They will certainly come up with many unique ideas for weaving, such as using a paper plate with slits cut in it for weaving across. They may use various weaving patterns including, but not limited to, "over and under," "over two and under one," or "over one and under two." This helps with patterning, spatial understandings, and number in mathematics. Children may also choose to use contrasting colors or else just one color. They also may use different types of paper or cloth for weaving. More advanced weaving apparatuses can be introduced later.

A loom is a device that will hold twisted yarns under tension to make it easier for the weaver to interlace the threads. Having a weaver visit the classroom for children to observe the process can be a valuable experience and helps them learn some of the unique vocabulary associated with weaving. For example, weaving uses two kinds of thread or paper, the *warp* and the *weft.* The warp is the lengthwise thread in weaving, and the weft is the name for the crosswise thread in weaving. Other vocabulary words that can be learned are *space, rough, smooth, pattern, texture, design,* and *thread.* A spider is nature's weaver, and children can observe this weaving process if a nonpoisonous spider is captured and put in a plastic jar in the science center.

When working with children, allow them to use their creativity in designs, once they have mastered the over-and-under process. Children can find creative spaces to weave such as weaving yarn over and under the holes in plastic strawberry containers, or weaving strips of colored crepe paper in and out through the chain-link fence around the school's playground to create a festive atmosphere for a school party. Give the children time to finish their work, and never take the children's work apart. If there is a problem, discuss it with the children, and let them proceed to correct the problem, that is, if they perceive it as a problem. Children often enjoy taking a cloth weaving apart, and burlap is ideal for this because of its loose weave. From this activity, children can visually experience how the burlap was previously woven.

Stringing items is a precursor often used to introduce and reinforce children's understanding and practice of the over-and-under process used in weaving. Young children learn the concept by stringing large colored beads, straws cut into small pieces, or other materials. Plain weaving is weaving in and out, and as such it is closely related to stringing and sewing. Also, needles for stringing should be large and made of plastic to avoid injuries, but wrapping transparent tape around one end of the string is safer to use than a needle. For young children, a bead tied to the end of the yarn will keep the other beads from falling off the end. Children need an endless supply of beads for stringing since they enjoy wearing them for jewelry and want to take them home.

Creativity is expressed as children use their imaginations to form various designs when weaving. The most important attribute for children involved in two-dimensional art activities such as drawing, pasting, painting, printing, or weaving is ingenuity, for only by fully exploring the possibility of a medium can something original and exciting be created.

THREE-DIMENSIONAL FORMS OF ARTISTIC EXPRESSION AND CONNECTIONS TO SCIENCE AND MATH

The term *three-dimensional form* refers to any art form that has depth, as well as length and width, and the artwork can be viewed from all sides. Some examples of young children engaging in creating three-dimensional forms include, but are not limited to, constructing with blocks and wood, and sculpting with clay, paper, and pipe cleaners. Although blocks are not usually thought of as an expressive art medium for creativity, children often use their imaginations and feelings more readily when making block structures.

Constructing with Blocks

Block building is an aspect of constructing that is associated with the arts, math, architecture, and engineering. Children generate new responses and expressions while constructing. Sharing their creative ideas extends their ability to appreciate the work of others, and develops in them an awareness of the creative opportunities offered by block building. This activity is a powerful and effective means of communicating and sharing ideas and feelings. When small groups of children work together to build a creation, blocks are perhaps the best material for integrating the 21st century skills of creativity, critical thinking, problem solving, communication, and collaboration. It has the most potential for making an Arts–STEM connection because of its connection to the fields of engineering, industrial design, airplane design, architecture, and physics, and the trade fields of drafting and construction. Children who play with blocks are able to gain a great deal from block building, as MacDonald (2001) lists 29 mathematics and 20 science concepts and skills that children can develop through blockplaying. The Common Core State Standards (NGA & CCSSO, 2010) and the Next Generation Science Standards (NGSS, 2013) use blocks as a basis for many standards. Wolfgang, Stannard, and Jones (2001) found that children's block play performance in preschool is a predictor of mathematics scores in middle school and high school. Seo and Ginsburg (2004) and Park, Chae, and Boyd (2008) have found that preschool children use many sophisticated geometric concepts in block playing that are usually taught in elementary school and that block play prompts the use of mathematical skills. (See Figure 5.3.)

Although block building is important because of the role-playing that generally accompanies block play, it also is a visual art form with aesthetic values. Since playing with blocks is open-ended, children's creative development is enhanced. In fact, many facets of a child's creative development, including imaginative thinking, are served by block play, as children communicate and solve problems

Figure 5.3. What Art, Math, and Science Skills Can Be Taught by Using These Building Blocks?

together. A wide variety of types of blocks and other manipulative materials can be used in the block area to help children represent geometric forms (Clements & McMillen, 1996). Harriet Johnson (1966/1933) has described seven developmental stages of block playing that progress from a 2-year-old carrying blocks, through beginning building, bridging, enclosing, making decorative patterns, and naming, to the symbolizing stage of a 5-year-old.

Like artwork, block building with 2-year-old children emphasizes the process, not the product. Children cannot use the blocks for building a house until they have explored the various physical properties of the medium. They start by carrying them around.

Ms. Steiner, a teacher of 2-year-olds, saw how John was carrying around the unit blocks. She wanted to help him with his vocabulary, so she started identifying the little or small blocks he was taking. Later, he started using larger blocks, so she used the words bigger and larger. She later made him feel them to see if they were smooth or rough. He later started to discover if the blocks were heavy or light by putting them on the scale nearby.

As children grow in their understanding of what they can and cannot do with blocks, they enter a stage of beginning block-building during which they use blocks in ways that seem more appropriate to adults. Instead of asking a child, "What are you building?" which is a product-oriented statement, hand this child a block and ask, "Where will you use this one?" In this way you are encouraging the child to continue the process of building that begins in this stage. Children begin by making mostly rows, either horizontal or vertical, with a great deal of repetition.

Jan, a 3-year-old, started stacking blocks in a vertical way. To encourage Jan, the teacher started using the words on, on top of, over, above, and later the words off, under, and below. Jan made another tall vertical construction, and the teacher used the words next and beside to describe the other tower. Later the teacher saw the other children laying the blocks horizontally on the floor. She started to describe them using next to, close to, and far from. In a few days, the children made a long line with various sizes of blocks, and the teacher introduced vocabulary to compare the sizes.

Bridging is when a third block to form a roof or a bridge connects two blocks with a space between them. Teachers sometimes model this next stage by putting up two vertical blocks and asking children to put another on top.

Once Joey saw his teacher make a bridge, he decided to make one higher so boats could go under it. Then he tried more blocks to make it go higher. Finally, it collapsed. He later experimented with many other kinds of bridges that were wider and longer. His teacher taught him about balance and how much weight it could carry before falling. He later tested his bridges to see if they could support cars.

Enclosures begin to predominate in blocks around the age of 4. Since the concept of *enclosure* is important in understanding space, teachers often intervene by giving directions and asking open-ended questions.

After a class trip to a farm in pre-K, the teacher encouraged the children to make a farm with their blocks. They made enclosed areas for the farm animals. The horses were in one area, the pigs were in another enclosed area, and the cattle were in a third enclosed area. The teacher asked the children to describe the gates to the different animal areas. She also asked them to take the animals out of the enclosure and put them in. The girls in the room later made enclosures for houses and placed furniture in them. They made house enclosures that were the same size, as well as different sizes. They were experimenting with walls that were high and low.

Once facility with building with blocks is acquired, children begin making decorative patterns. This is the stage when the children learn names of shapes such as square, rectangle, triangle, pentagon, and octagon, and they learn the names of the three-dimensional blocks such as cube, rectangular prism, and cylinder. Teachers can encourage children to make patterns, both horizontally and vertically, and to talk about long, short, or curves. Teachers may help children see how a cube can be made into two triangular prisms. Various sizes and colors of blocks may be used to encourage patterning of AB, ABA, ABBA. Children often create their own patterns especially when using parquetry blocks. Spatial words the teacher may introduce are *forward, backward, around, through, sideways, across, back and forth,* and *straight.*

Naming of structures for dramatic play begins after the children have experimented with building patterns. This stage appears when children are thinking of a structure that they would like to build. If children ask for suggestions, teachers could suggest a grocery store, house, or park. To expand this stage, teachers may ask, "Do you want to add anything to your building? Perhaps people, signs, or cars? What else can you use?" Before this stage, children may have named their structures, but the names were not necessarily related to the purpose of the building.

Beginning around age 5, children often reproduce or symbolize actual structures that they know, and this reproduction sets the stage for dramatic group play. All of the skills for the 21st century are developed through block playing at this stage: creativity, critical thinking, problem solving, as well as communication and collaboration. The group negotiates on what they are going to build, perhaps a tall building, stadium, or store. Children collaborate in problem solving and ask themselves questions such as the following:

- What jobs do people have?
- Who is the leader?
- What design do you want to make?
- Can someone think of a better idea?
- Can we listen to the idea?
- Can we change things to accommodate new ideas?
- What patterns and shapes do we need?
- What things do what in our building?
- Do we need to make a map or blueprint of our building?
- Can we tell another group about our structure?
- Can we write a story about our structure?

This is the time when children explore the language of building with such words as *curves, column, arch, blueprint, tunnel, bridge, ramp, tower, buttress,* and *steeple.* They use these words in their creative writing in primary grades.

One teacher had an open house to show off the new building the children had made. She invited families, and the children shared what they had constructed. In one kindergarten room, where there was a morning and afternoon class, a display of children's work in the morning class was left up for the afternoon class to see and vice versa.

The block area should be in an open space and accessible from other play areas to encourage interaction from one play area to another. Block constructions should not be placed in doorways or traffic patterns because someone may fall and stumble. Shelving for blocks should be low and easily reached by children. Shapes of blocks can be traced on construction paper, and then covered with contact paper. When placed on the back of the shelves and/or the bottom of the shelves, children can easily sort and stack the blocks in an orderly fashion. However, some teachers prefer to mix all the unit blocks together in a block cart for problem solving. Then the children get daily practice in finding and arranging the shapes using the criteria they choose, such as all the blocks they need to build a garage. Many different accessories can be used to add variety to block play, and children often make accessories such as cars in the woodworking center.

Woodworking

Woodworking, like block building, is another medium that lends itself to an Arts–STEM connection because of its relationship to the fields of engineering, industrial design, airplane design, architecture, and physics, and the trade fields of drafting or construction. Woodworking also has the potential for using the 21st century skills of creativity, critical thinking, problem solving, communication, and collaboration.

The woodworking area in early childhood is presented differently from other areas where the materials are put out and children explore them. Children must learn how to properly use the necessary tools for safety reasons. Although it can be quite beneficial for primary-age students, woodworking is not recommended for younger children because they usually don't have the coordination to use the tools without injuries. Saws that slip and cut hands, and hammers that hit fingers are not pleasant experiences, and young children have even been known to throw claw hammers when they are frustrated. If woodworking tools are to be used in preschools, teachers must discuss what to do and what not to do when using them. Some preschools have dangerous tools, such as hammers, secured to the workbench with a chain so they can be used only for hammering in one place. Preschoolers can explore the functions of tools in simple ways such as pounding golf tees into Styrofoam using a wooden hammer, whereas older primary-grade children learn to use tools to implement creative ideas they have for building.

Children learn about different trees and tree products as they build a wood sculpture. As children make decisions about what shape and types of wood to use, they are learning to solve problems. They also are learning social skills if they are collaborating on a large project. It requires both small and large motor movement to work with wood. Hammering requires large motor movement, and a screwdriver requires small motor movement. Woodworking requires eye–hand coordination and balancing, and children can use the tools from the woodworking area to combine wood, cardboard boxes, and junk in order to create beautiful structures. It is important to know that there are tools that move things like a screwdriver, pliers, adjustable wrench; tools that shape things like scissors, saw, or drill; and tools that measure things like a tape measure or builder's square. Tools have different purposes that are related to their form and function, which are part of the art and science standards.

Tools can be extended to a study of simple machines, part of the study of the physical sciences. The simple machines include the wheel, which helps things move; the drive belt, which helps another wheel move; a pulley, which can make lifting easier; a wedge, which drives things apart; a screw, which helps convert a force that goes around and around into a force that goes up and down, making it easier to hold things together or lift things; a ramp, which makes it easier to move up or down; and a lever, which reduces the amount of effort to move something.

Sculpting

Sculpture is a three-dimensional artwork that comes in many different shapes and sizes. One reason children like three-dimensional forms is that they are able to see the artwork's presence in space. Clay, paper sculpting, and pipe cleaner sculpture are three types of sculpting that will be discussed.

Clay, by far the most frequently used sculpting material in preschool and kindergarten classrooms, is an amorphous, malleable material that can be used to express shape. Degas and Rodin have created many fine sculptures of people, and Michelangelo's work provides excellent sculptures of people and animals. Children enjoy looking at postcards from museums of famous sculptured works.

There are three types of clay used in early childhood: clay from the earth, commercially produced "play dough" (e.g., Play-Doh), and homemade play dough. Modeling materials such as clay from the earth, a moist natural substance, are used in every culture and should be used regularly in early childhood, though in practice today that is not always the case. Many educators appear to be unaware of the multidimensional aspects of clay from the earth. Children enjoy playing with this clay because it is a natural material with the tactile appeal of sand and water. Although some children may find it difficult to work with clay from the earth at first, it is preferable not to give them something like a wooden tongue depressor for a tool at this time, because this can encourage cutting the clay rather than expressing their ideas using this medium. Children like to talk about what it feels like and what they are making, so conversations between the teacher and the child should focus on describing these sensations and actions. Children should be encouraged to use their senses when playing with clay—see the color, smell the odor, feel the texture—and then imagine the creation. Children feel in control of the clay when they can change or destroy what they make very easily. It is important that they first make direct physical contact with clay before other objects are brought in between them and the medium.

When clay from the earth is introduced as a center of interest, children often rush over to the rolling pins and cookie cutters. Because it is important for children to respond to this clay in creative ways, it is not a good idea to offer any gadgets or tools that limit this possibility. Young children usually make figures by sticking pieces of clay together for bodies, legs, tails, or heads. However, primary-age children who have never made three-dimensional artwork can benefit by making a simple structure that can be formed in their hands without setting the clay on the table as they work. Using a small-sized lump of soft clay, they can be encouraged to keep turning it in their hands so they can see it from every direction as they work. Three-dimensional quality comes naturally for these children as they turn the piece around, turn it upside down, and so on. Teachers should avoid doing demonstrations, because that will limit their creative options by making them dependent on copying work. Children should be encouraged to experiment on their own in order to become self-sufficient in visual thinking and problem solving using their clay-sculpting skills. Although many items can be used while working with clay, such as toothpicks, corrugated paper strips, plastic shapes, foam for packing, pipe cleaners, plastic mesh, applicator sticks, plastic forks, or bottle caps, children themselves must decide if and when to choose these items for use with their creative sculpture.

To be able to connect with the level of creativity a child is displaying, a teacher should be aware of the stages of working with clay. According to Schirrmacher (2002), there are four stages of working with clay:

1. What is clay?
2. What can I do with clay?
3. Look what I made.
4. I know what I'm going to make out of my clay.

Very young children do not start out to make something with their clay, but explore the qualities of clay to find out what it feels like and what it can do. They use their sense of touch to explore the medium by touching, pushing, tearing, and pounding, and their sense of smell by smelling the clay. Kneading clay is often very enjoyable for children, satisfying a kinesthetic desire. As they manipulate the clay with their fingers and hands, they begin to explore things they can do with the clay such as poke holes in it, squeeze it like a rubber ball, roll it like a ball, or stretch it into a snake. Even though they did not have anything in mind to make, they often end up making snakes, balls, and hamburgers. Children are interested in how they can shape the clay as they begin to roll the coils and balls either between their hands or on the table. Teachers can encourage exploration by asking questions such as

- How can a round shape become a long one?
- How can a shape stand up?
- How can a shape sit down?
- How can a shape lie down?

As with any appropriate art activity for young children, certain educational benchmarks or stages can be observed. Once children have mastered rolling coils and balls, they will begin to line them up, often creating designs by sticking objects such as feathers into the clay. They also explore creating textures by pressing various fabrics or objects into the clay to express their design ability.

When children become aware they can make "something" out of the clay, they begin to do this naturally but very informally. Using basic shapes such as coils and balls, children will begin to create people, animals, and objects in their immediate environment. Often three balls stacked on top of each other will become a snowman, or a ball of clay with a pipe cleaner sticking out of both sides will become a person. One boy, whose family was grieving over the death of his mother, made figures of all the members of his family out of clay, and he used them to "talk together" about the family tragedy and to express his deep feelings.

Finally, when children choose the clay area, they usually have in mind just what they intend to make. The malleable nature of clay gives children the power to change any part of the form they have made using pressure from their fingers. They have their own ideas, and they finish the product according to their own specifications. At this stage a visit to the zoo is a great stimulus for children to produce clay sculptures of elephants, giraffes, horses, birds, cats, and dogs. One teacher read aloud *Leonardo's Horse* by Fritz (2001) to serve as a stimulus for a clay-sculpting lesson. A study of bees was an impetus to create a bee showing the three parts of the body—the head, thorax, and abdomen.

Commercial and homemade play dough are used more frequently in early childhood classrooms for sculpting and experimentation because they are not so "messy" and the areas used for sculpting can be cleaned up more easily. Sadly, this is a fact of life today in classrooms, where there is relatively little time available for sculpting activities. Children may enjoy working with play dough on individual vinyl placemats, and some teachers do not encourage sharing play dough due to the spread of germs. Children who participate in making homemade play dough can learn many other skills, including measuring in math and blending. Children enjoy using play dough because it is soft and pliable and has many beautiful colors available for mixing to make new colors.

In some cultures the art of paper sculpting, or folding paper into shapes, has been passed down from parents to children for many generations. Simple paper folds can be used with children as young as 4 years of age. Froebel (1887/2001) emphasized paper folding as an "occupation" that furnishes materials for practice in learning about surfaces (see also Chapter 6). Children can be taught basic folds such as the triangular fold, the rectangular fold called the "hamburger way," the long rectangular fold called the "hot dog way," and the arrow fold, which helps children see three precise triangles. By far, the most popular paper-folding activity for primary-age children is making paper airplanes.

Most teachers "pull their hair out" when the children fold their homework into flying aircraft. Ms. Crawford, however, used this interest to reinforce reading and following directions for her primary-age students. She began to teach them about basic skills in paper folding such as the valley fold, mountain fold, and pleat fold, but she did not capture their attention and enthusiasm until she showed them the airplane fold. The children all wanted her to fold airplanes for them, but instead she decided to help them develop their reading skills by preparing a chart from which they had to read and apply directions. In a folding area, she provided rectangular pieces of paper and colored pencils for decorating the paper. She explained to the children that they must fold with precision since uneven folding results in a lopsided airplane. They soon learned the value of being able to read accurately as they folded their airplanes.

The children had the added reward of being able to fly their airplanes outdoors to see if movements of air really carried them along. Ms. Crawford, who had a pilot's license, decided to make this a science lesson where she introduced the children to the study of aerodynamics through paper airplanes. They discussed lift, gravity, thrust, and drag. They also labeled the parts of the airplane. Throughout the year she wrote out instructions for making jets and other designs. They later had an air show and tried to figure out which plane flew the greatest distance. The children measured the differences, recorded them, and tried to figure out which type of wing made the plane go greater distances. This later led to a study of helicopters and rockets.

Another sculpting activity for primary-age children uses pipe cleaners found in a craft store. They come in many different colors and can be twisted, bent, and braided and made into a sculpture. The children enjoy twisting and turning the pipe cleaners into unusual shapes, and then gluing their creative sculpture to a base made of wood or another sturdy material.

ELECTRONIC FORMS OF ARTISTIC EXPRESSION

While computers have enriched our lives, they do not replace the tactile experiences and important interactions that can take place with media. Computer art supplements early childhood activities but does not replace highly valued childhood activities such as the traditional expressive arts with a STEM connection. Computers are tools that can be used in developmentally appropriate ways, but they can also be misused, just as any tool can. They are beneficial if the software programs encourage collaborative play and opportunities for children to express themselves creatively, but they are misused when they offer software that has a similar approach to worksheets that "drill and kill." The teacher's role is critical in selecting software that supports creative expressions as well as software that develops sensitivities to children from other cultures and children with disabilities. When teachers critically evaluate educational software, they should make sure there is no stereotyping or violence in the software. They need to make judgments about what is age appropriate, individually appropriate, and culturally appropriate.

Computer programs can be used to reinforce the media, the elements of art, and other art concepts. Nevertheless, they should never replace children feeling and experimenting with real art media. Critics of computers have stated that computers hinder creativity. However, when used along with manipulatives and as a tool in the curriculum, they can enhance creativity (Haugland, 1999, 2000).

Recently, there are apps or applications out on Android (Google's Operating System) and IOS (Apple's Operating System) that run on smartphones and tablet devices. Apps can be downloaded at a minimum price, and they can be used as an art medium. Apps need to be evaluated for developmentally appropriate practice, just as software and websites have been evaluated in the past. The App Store, a creation of Apple, spawned a new content-creation industry, and applications can be bought for reasonable prices. There are now art apps such as Drawing for Kids, Drawing Desk, Draw Sketch and Doodle, and Drawing Pad that can be downloaded for smartphones and tablets.

It should be noted that early childhood is now using interactive art, and some companies are selling interactive art tables for child-care centers. This is similar to the whiteboard except children use them at a table. Interactive art is now in many museums and schools, and it requires the child to interact with objects in different ways. Children can use their hands, tools, and even bodies to produce art and scientific experimentation. Individuals in the fields of art, design, science, and architecture have created designs for full audience participation to promote curiosity and discovery.

Software is becoming less and less a form of creativity and innovation because it is restricted to hardware on the computer and the mouse as an instrument of creativity. A more hands-on approach are the mobile devices listed above that lend themselves better to creativity and tactile expression because they take advantage of natural human interactions and gestural interfaces.

Many teachers believe that certain software programs not only help children learn language, but become a form of language (Clements & Sarama, 2003). Similarly, the children in Reggio Emilia use it *as* a form of language (C. Edwards et al., 2012). Art software can promote very creative behaviors but also very mechanical behaviors. Good questions to ask before buying both software and apps are the following:

- Is there a way for children to experiment?
- Are children able to expand their knowledge of the elements of line, color, shape, and texture, and the principles of design?
- Is the quality of marks unique or unusual so that personal and not stereotypic figures can be drawn or painted?
- Are children able to elaborate or extend the visual representations into something of visual complexity or artistically unique productions?
- Are children able to problem-solve?

Animation, graphics, and music may distract from the objectives that the teacher has in mind. It should be noted that if the purpose is to promote creative art, children should be creating with the different media, lines, shapes, and textures. Just because software says paint or color does not mean that it is helpful in producing creative behaviors in the child. Each piece of software must be reviewed individually. The software must offer something for creative growth in the child rather than make something that just looks great to an adult. Computer interactions with color cannot replace working with the real paint; they can, however, enhance children's learning experiences.

Children enjoy being in charge of their own learning, and for this reason computers are intrinsically compelling for young children. They can repeat an activity and control the pacing of most software. When given a choice, most children will choose to express their creativity using a computer or application software in which they are in charge of their learning, although at other times they seem to prefer working with their peers at the computer. In early childhood classrooms there must be equitable access to the computers, including for children whose first language is not English and children who have special needs. Often in low-income areas of a city, children attending early childhood classes do not have access to a computer at home. This can put them at a definite disadvantage in the long run since technology today plays a significant role in most children's lives.

INTEGRATING THE ELEMENTS OF ART INTO STEM AND OTHER AREAS: A FIELD TRIP TO THE ZOO

The following vignette describes a study of animal habitats with a variety of different art media. Children studied the habitats, visited the zoo, and later developed habitats using box art and block play. Children made their habitats in small groups so that collaborative interactions took place.

The children in Ms. Moore's kindergarten class had been studying animals and their habitats. They had learned about the desert and its sandy soil and how camels lived in the desert. They learned that the camel's fat is converted to water in the humps. They learned about bighorn sheep, which lived in mountainous regions and were very sure-footed. They could climb and jump with grace and did not fall. They learned about the rainforest and the many animals that lived there such as colorful birds, monkeys, frogs, snakes, and alligators. They learned about the polar region and the polar bears, seals, and cod fish.

Then Ms. Moore took them on a field trip to the local zoo, which was divided into four habitats for animals. At the zoo the children saw desert terrain, mountainous terrain, rainforest terrain in a giant geodesic dome, and the polar ice area. They saw many of the animals they had learned about in school. When they got back to school, the teacher divided them into four groups to build the four different terrains in shoe boxes. The teacher had gathered many books for the children to look at, and she had taken photos of the habitats at the zoo. The children had free choice of many media such as construction paper, tempera paint, crayons, chalk, pastels, blocks, and clay to design the habitats in the shoeboxes.

The children were amazed at the many different interpretations of landscapes that their classmates drew or built. They soon realized that there is not one way of representing any object, but many different ways. The work of each child and group was unique and valued, and provided stimulation for a more in-depth and long-term study of the zoo habitats. The children studied the best way to design habitats by defining the problem, developing possible solutions, and comparing solutions, as recommended by the Next Generation Science Standards (NGSS, 2013). They used their shoe box exhibits in the block-playing area. They later created a map of the zoo and made a zoo enclosed with a five-sided (pentagon) wall of blocks: Four of the sides represented the four terrains the children had observed on their field trip, and one side was an archway entrance. In the center they designed a pond with construction paper.

After the kindergarten field trip to the zoo, the children utilized various media to develop habitats for the animals they had seen, connecting the Earth and life sciences with engineering and artistic design. The teacher guided the children to make the following extensions:

Math
Children made a five-sided enclosure wall with blocks to learn the concepts of length, width, depth, and shape and to measure whether the exhibits would

fit within the zoo walls. They learned the term *arch*, which they had seen at the entrance to the zoo, and that an arch consists of two weaknesses which, leaning on each other, become a strength by the force of compression. They could also transfer this learning to the clay area. Children discovered more about arch bridges in the block-playing area, where they started to pay attention to the beauty of the graceful curves of the arches.

Children designed different types of bridges within the walls of the zoo to go over the water in the center of the zoo.

Children learned about spatial development by seeing another viewpoint in mapping the zoo.

Technology—Children were able to create a bridge using different media in Kidpix Deluxe. Kids Doodle by Bejoy Mobile is an App that allows children to use different colors and paint materials to make designs of bridges with their fingers.

Science/Engineering

A process skill in science is observation. Children keenly observed many types of habitats and figured out how to design them. They learned that the shape and stability of structures of natural and designed objects are related to their function. (NGSS: K-2-ETS1-1)

The children followed science and engineering practices when they made habitats and when they made the bridge: asking questons (which one would be stronger, longer, wider), developing a model, understanding the problem, developing solutions, communicating ideas to other people, and trying to optimize the design solution. (NGSS: K-2-ETS1-2, 1-3)

Social Development—The children decided what kind of bridges and walls to make. They made a blueprint and decided which materials to use (blocks). Through negotiation and cooperation, they worked together to construct the walls and bridges.

SUMMARY

This chapter began with a survey of how the preschools of Reggio Emilia help children develop an understanding of media through a collaborative approach that connects Arts–STEM with 21st century skills. Teachers in the United States play the primary role in integrating art media into STEM by providing developmentally appropriate practices, challenging cognitive experiences, safety in the art environment, activities that do not stifle creativity, and by understanding and collaborating with the young artists. Art media refers to materials provided in early childhood classrooms to enhance young children's ability to communicate and express themselves creatively in two-dimensional or three-dimensional forms. They learn more about the science of the materials by finding out how the materials are made and appreciating the inventive nature of the materials, as illustrated by the chapter's closing vignette.

REVIEW AND REFLECT

1. How do collaborations using media promote the 21st century skills of critical thinking, problem solving, creativity, and communication?
2. How would knowing more about the inventive nature of the materials children use and their composition transfer to science?
3. What would you cite to defend the use of blocks in a kindergarten room using Arts–STEM ideas?
4. Find out the scientific origin of an art material and how it was invented. Share your ideas with the class.
5. Try an Arts–STEM activity such as making paints from natural materials. Grind the rocks using a mortar and pestle. Add a binder such as glue, starch, or egg yolk. Use these paints.

CHAPTER 6

The Elements of Art and the Principles of Design
Their Importance to STEM

Every child is an artist. The problem is how to remain an artist.

—Pablo Picasso

Before he can create, man must have a deep awareness of the world about him—he must be able to really see, hear, feel, touch, and move.

—Harold A. Rothbart

HOW LEONARDO DA VINCI THOUGHT ABOUT ART AND DESIGN

Leonardo's eyes were so sharp that he could see the details of a reflection in a drop of water. He watched carefully the shapes the drop made as it splashed and recorded them. He paid very close attention to shapes and forms. He did drawings of waves and currents and performed many experiments with water. He also had an intense interest in the study of light, including how the eye works, which he applied to his art.

An individualized composition reflects the artist's organization in space of the elements of art and the principles of design. The elements are visual properties, such as line, form, color, shape, texture, and light, which should be taught to young children by using examples from nature, as well as from mathematics and the life, Earth, physical, and space sciences. The principles of design, such as balance, patterns, scale, emphasis, and unity, are ways of using, combining, and arranging the elements. A composition is created by weaving the elements of art and the principles of design into a whole work that represents the "artist within." Famous works of art can be used to illustrate how the elements and principles of design are used in a composition, and they can serve as an introduction to the world of art appreciation, but they should not be used as a model for children to copy. The early years, when children are so fascinated with famous works of art, is an ideal time to increase their sensitivity to the elements and principles of design. Design is a deceptively common word for artists, but in certain STEM fields like engineering it is an approach to solving problems that involves collaboration and communication with all those involved, producing designs that are shaped with specifications and constraints.

From studying this chapter, teachers will become familiar with one of the original early childhood educators, Friedrich Froebel, and gain the necessary knowledge to enhance the use of the elements of art and the principles of design with young children in the science and math curriculum.

OPENING CHANNELS TO SUPPORT DESIGN–STEM CONNECTION

With regard to exploring the elements and principles of design and their relationship to 21st century needs in the STEM workplace of the future, it is important to consider the early childhood theorist Friedrich Froebel. A German educator born in 1782, Froebel is considered to be the "father of kindergarten." Froebel's curriculum specified using principles of nature and design in combination with mathematical concepts, and in a unique way he influenced the interrelationships of nature, art, mathematics, and science more than other theorists. The arts are a methodology for the study of geometry and nature, according to Froebel (1887/2001), and this unified connection is very similar to the Arts–STEM movement of today. It is also evident in the Bauhaus movement of the early 20th century, where artists, architects, and engineers studied together to design inventions. Teachers often use Froebel's materials in a way that integrates mathematical and artistic designs. In 1840 Froebel was exploring and developing the concept of the relationships of nature and mathematics to art, and was ahead of his time in integrating curriculum of expressive arts into science and math.

Froebel designed educational materials he called "gifts," which included geometric building blocks, points, lines, and pattern shapes that provided children with hands-on active learning in two-dimensional and three-dimensional work. He believed that all children were creative and that they could learn art, design, and mathematics by discovering how these elements were integrated into nature. Educators of today rarely review his pedagogy, although Froebel—naturalist, architect, and mathematician—carefully chose materials that allowed young children to explore the properties of geometry in relation to design. He incorporated the geometric design of minerals he had studied. His work may be more important today than ever before because the understanding of the three-dimensional spatial perspective in a two-dimensional plane using wireless technology is evident in many of the inventions of today.

Research has suggested that young thinkers are advanced as mathematical and spatial thinkers (Geary, 1994), and yet the National Mathematics Advisory Panel of the U.S. Department of Education (2008) and the National Research Council (2009) report that young children usually receive minimal mathematics instruction before they enter elementary school. Consistently on the TIMSS American students score the lowest in the area of spatial development (Gonzales et al., 2009). Spatial development promotes innovation, and it converges with many fields such as art, math, science, geography, technology, and architecture. According to these studies, primary and elementary students in the United States are failing to learn basic geometric concepts and geometric problem solving. (For a more in-depth understanding of these concepts, see Pollman, 2010.)

Our present-day philosophy of minimalist teaching of geometry and spatial development is unlike the times of Froebel (and Leonardo) when geometry was a subject taught with great importance. Years ago Froebel created a complex pedagogy that was based on the use of geometric forms and the manipulation of symmetry (Balfanz, 1999; Pollman, 2010). In-depth research by Brosterman (2014), an architect and collector of antique blocks, documented that the architect Frank Lloyd Wright and more than likely artists Piet Mondrian and Wassily Kandinsky and mathematician and architect Buckminster Fuller have all been influenced by a Froebelian system. This system allows for a profoundly deep exploration of spatial reasoning, analytical thinking, and creative design. Given the knowledge that children from other countries score higher than the United States in spatial development, it appears to be time to use this knowledge of art and mathematics and incorporate it into the early childhood curriculum.

Incorporating Froebelian Gifts

Froebelian materials, or gifts, are objects that most early childhood educators already have in their room, such as eight cubes, that can be used to promote artistic and mathematical concepts. For example, the children might be given the gift of eight cubes (Gift 3) and asked to form something they see in everyday life or in nature. They may also create what they saw on the way to school. Then they can tell the story about what they saw in a small group. They will be exploring "eightness" in many different shapes and transformations.

During another session, the gift of eight blocks can be used to create what Froebel called the Forms of Beauty, using patterns in many different formations. His Forms of Beauty incorporate many of the elements and principles of design. The principles of design such as balance, patterning, emphasis, and unity were used to reinforce the Forms of Beauty.

The same gift of eight blocks can also be used to create a mathematical and scientific exploration, or Forms of Knowledge, by using the process skills of observation, comparison, classification, measurement, and communication and thereby learning many things about mathematics, such as addition, subtraction, multiplication, division, composing, decomposing, using only these blocks. Children will observe how symmetrical patterns, made with eight cubes, can be manipulated using geometry in many different ways. (See Figure 6.1.)

Extensions of the knowledge about geometry, gained through small-group interactions, can be utilized at the block area, the light table, and the art area, so

Figure 6.1. Forms of Eight Using Froebel's Gift 3—Unit Blocks

that the connections of forms and space can be explored. Froebel's curriculum specified using blocks, beads, rings, shapes, and curves. He also utilized work with paper such as cutting and origami folding, and tangrams for creations of art.

Exploring Geometric Forms

In early childhood classrooms some teachers only have children identify the basic shapes of triangle, circle, and square. Naming shapes is not an adequate way to teach about shapes in the area of spatial development, and manipulation of shapes and spatial development is usually neglected, according to Juanita Copley (2001). Because geometry requires more specific types of manipulatives than any other content area, she recommends attribute blocks, which are nine shapes of different colors of various sizes and thickness; pattern blocks including red trapezoids, orange squares, green triangles, yellow hexagons, and blue and white rhombuses; and tangrams. Young children, Copley reports, are limited in their use of plane figures, so she recommends using plane figures and making them into three-dimensional figures. Based on research on young children's developmental levels of math (Clements & Sarama, 2009; Sarama & Clements, 2009), the Common Core State Standards (NGA & CCSSO, 2010) have been developed to promote trajectories in geometric and spatial thinking.

Tangrams, a Chinese puzzle consisting of seven shapes, help children understand relationships among various geometric forms. Through the use of tangrams children are able to experience many transformations and flips of shapes into other shapes. In Asian schools spatial development is emphasized, and tangrams are used with young children.

Four-year-old Ba appeared very adept at putting together three-dimensional puzzles at school. His teacher, Ms. Gina, decided to make a home visit to discuss Ba's unusual spatial development. Ba's family had recently immigrated to the United States from Vietnam, so Ms. Gina asked Mr. Vovan, a colleague who spoke Vietnamese, to accompany her to help bridge any language barriers. Mr. Vovan explained to her that teachers are highly regarded in Vietnamese culture. He said the teacher actually had a higher standing than the parents in terms of a child's education!

When they arrived at Ba's home, not only his immediate family but also his extended family was present to visit with Ms. Gina and Mr. Vovan. First they offered the two teachers refreshment. Then they sat and listened as Ms. Gina explained Ba's proficiency at working with three-dimensional puzzles. No one seemed surprised when she opened a complicated three-dimensional puzzle of a dinosaur, and within a short time Ba had organized the structure in space. As Ba was working on the puzzle, he received tremendous encouragement from all his relatives. They applauded and cheered as he rapidly put it together.

Mr. Vovan said it was not unusual for Vietnamese children to be encouraged to develop their spatial abilities. Ms. Gina replied that her other 4-year-old students would rarely, if ever, be able to visualize this form in space; cultures appear to reward what they value. Froebel's ideas were understood and implemented by this Vietnamese culture, since they too focused on a visualization of forms in space and developing the spatial reasoning and analytical thinking that is required for spatial development in young children.

As one can see from the discussion of Froebel, he integrated geometry with art. Today geoboards help children explore geometry along with the elements of art. Geoboards have arrays of pins on them, usually five pins by five pins; colored rubber bands are used to create different shapes. The pins are useful in helping children identify the sides and angles of shapes, and visualize ways to measure and compare the length and areas of the shapes. Using a geoboard can be open-ended. For example, a teacher can ask a child to make a place where people live or make a shape and change it by moving the rubber bands. The children "draw" on the geoboards with rubber bands.

Froebel's philosophy of education is worth reexamining, especially because of its relationship to the creative expressive arts, the elements of art, and the principles of design. He also had children create and share their work with the group. This is similar to the way the Bauhaus artists shared and the way Frank Lloyd Wright had his students share at Taliesen, his school for architects. This sharing and explaining a piece of art is similar to the 21st century skills of communicating the story and the design—a part of selling a product in the STEM fields.

DEFINING THE ELEMENTS OF ART

A work of art includes many elements, the fundamental visual properties of art. As children develop their understanding of the elements, they learn to use them to express and communicate their feelings, thoughts, and ideas. To enhance and encourage children's experiences with art, teachers need a primary knowledge of what makes art "art" so they can express it to children in words appropriate to their level of understanding. The next sections will define the elements of line, color, shape, texture, and light separately by giving examples from nature and famous works of art. However, elements of art do not work independently of each other, but like letters in the alphabet, they work together to create a composition that contains many of the elements of art. Therefore, the various elements defined below should be presented to children within appropriate contexts rather than in isolation.

Lines

"A line is a dot out for a walk."—*Paul Klee*

Lines in Science. Lines have only one dimension, can be straight or curved, and have names that describe their place in space. Lines are in every area of science. For example, in the life sciences, as a tree grows, it makes a vertical line to the sky; when it is falling, it makes a diagonal line; and when on the ground, it makes a horizontal line. Lines are found in the Earth sciences, such as in the layers of rocks in the Grand Canyon. Lines are in space sciences in the curvature of the moon. Lines are in the physical sciences in the design of simple machines such as the saw that has jagged lines or the lever such as a knife that has smooth, slanted lines. When two lines are next to each other with equal space between them, they become parallel lines in math. Lines can be bent into curves or broken into angles, and can be used to outline shapes. Lines can be thick or thin, blurry or clear.

Curved lines may express softness because they are associated with natural materials in the world such as hills and the weeping willow tree. Curved lines can also be seen on the banana, the cat's tail, the elephant's trunk, the sprouts of a plant, tree rings, and the curves of an orange section. Pointed lines appear on thorns, a woodpecker's beak, or a thistle, and they represent danger. Form can follow function as some lines help identify their function. The shape and stability of structures of natural and designed objects are related to their function, and this scientific fact can be pointed out as children draw. When teachers identify the lines as children draw them, they will become aware of the types of lines they have created, and their functions. This helps children understand how form follows function in science and engineering.

Lines in Paintings by Famous Artists. Wassily Kandinsky painted from his imagination and feelings. He used straight lines, wavy ones, zigzags, dots, and

WHAT CAN HAPPEN WHEN THERE ARE INCREASED INTERACTIONS BETWEEN ART AND MATH?

When more in-depth interactions between art and math take place, children will more than likely develop increased understanding in the following areas:

1. Geometric forms, as experienced at various centers of interest
2. Rotations and flips in geometric forms
3. Shapes using different combinations of triangles
4. Geometric figures, as seen in children's artwork
5. Paper-folding methods
6. Basic concepts
   - Location words—on, under, over, front, in, out, into, out of
   - Movement words—up, down, forward, backward, around
   - Distance words—near, far, close to, shortest/longest path
7. Number, size, shape differentiation, part-whole relationships, and patterns
8. Motion

stripes to make patterns in *Improvisation Klamm*. His work lines show excitement and perhaps a carnival. His whirling lines seem like a gush of wind. His *Panel for Edwin R. Campbell No. 3* expressed his thoughts on how his paintings should be heard and sounds should be seen. It fills the observer with the feeling of wanting to dance fast.

Georgia O'Keeffe in *Evening Star, No. III* painted her fascination with a star. She used thick, curvy, and straight lines to show her abstract feelings of it. It should be noted that she painted many versions of the evening star, and children need to know that they can paint many versions of the same thing. In one classroom, children started observing the stars closely, and began to paint many versions. They asked the teacher to show them how to make a star and learned to make a five-pointed star and a star out of two triangles. This demonstration helped the children see how stars can be designed in different ways.

Jackson Pollock made lines with wiggles and splats in his painting entitled *Convergence Number 10*. His drip paintings came from squirts, and drips from a brush or other objects he held while he danced or walked around the picture. Children enjoy following the lines and identifying the thick, thin, curved, straight, or wiggly lines in his pictures.

Paul Klee, a Swiss painter, uses many lines and shapes and was heavily influenced by the Bauhaus movement, which in turn was influenced by the work of Friedrich Froebel. In the painting, *Farbtafel*, Klee uses horizontal and vertical lines in a grid to create squares full of various vibrant colors. He utilizes the lines and shapes similar to Froebel's gifts in his forms of nature and forms of design, and in *Landscape with the Setting Sun, 1919,* Klee used lines to represent enclosed space. Matisse used curvy lines in all of his forms of art. Albrecht Dürer in *Rhinoceros, 1515,* showed on his engraving of a rhinoceros thousands of lines and shapes. The patterns of the skin make the rhinoceros look like it is wearing armor.

Famous works such as these can be studied by children, and the lines can be used to promote the understanding of natural phenomena in the life and physical sciences as well as the geometric forms.

Color

Generally, young children in the scribbling stage of drawing do not pay attention to color. Color awareness comes later, and by kindergarten, most children are able to recognize colors. However, teachers should not interrupt children's work by asking, "What color are you using?" With this, the focus of their composition changes from an expression of feelings to one of naming colors. In the primary grades, children enhance their perception of colors beyond the eight colors in the crayon box. They are fascinated to learn about the colors in paints, crayons, and markers, and they enjoy making new colors by mixing colors. This mixing satisfies their curiosity and inventiveness, which are skills needed in the arts and sciences.

Categories and Concepts of Color. The *primary colors* of red, yellow, and blue are the colors of pigments used in tempera paints. These colors are called primary colors because they can be mixed to create all the colors of the rainbow, and are the foundation of the color wheel.

The primary tempera colors can be mixed to create the *secondary colors* of orange, violet, and green. As children discover secondary colors by mixing them, it is as if they are playing hide and seek, because they see the new secondary color approaching as the primary colors are leaving. Children enjoy mixing secondary colors to match the colors they see in nature.

Pairs of colors, such as orange and blue, that are directly opposite each other on the color wheel are *complementary colors.* There is usually a great contrast between the two colors. For instance, the Denver Broncos football team chose orange and blue as their colors since this combination makes each color stand out on their uniforms. In nature you see blue butterflies with orange markings. Clay pots full of violet and yellow pansies or red apples on green trees are examples of complementary colors in nature.

Mixing a primary color and the secondary color next to it on the color wheel makes a *tertiary color.* Since the primary colors of red and yellow make orange, the tertiary colors become red-orange and yellow-orange. Mixing helps the child see primary, secondary, complementary, and tertiary colors as well as their relationships to each other, and also to visualize that any color on the color wheel may have an infinite number of values and other properties.

Properties of Color. When colors are used at full value, they appear to be strong and bright, and when colors are mixed with water or white they appear as lighter tones. *Value* refers to the darkness or lightness of a color. Children enjoy mixing black and white to make various shades of gray because black is the darkest value and white is the lightest value so there is a wide array of grays between the two. However, the concept of value is not limited to blacks, whites, and grays. Color also has value, and a light-valued painting has a lot of light colors, and a dark-valued painting has a lot of dark colors. Most famous paintings have a combination of light and dark values to add interest and contrast.

Adding white to a color makes a tint that is lighter and clearer. For example, if children keep adding a drop of white paint to red and mix them together, they eventually get the color pink. Adding black to a color makes a tone that is more obscure, since black makes a color darker.

Artists use darker colors to show the shadows that are cast, and light colors to show which side the light is shining on. A teacher can use students' observation of these effects to develop a whole science unit on shadows and how shadows are caused in our universe. Colors help create the mood of a painting, and bright warm colors express enthusiasm, whereas cool colors can give a feeling of calmness, and very dark colors may give a feeling of sadness. Yet color is relative, and how a color looks depends on the colors around it, the colors it is mixed with, or the amount of light on it. Nevertheless, colors can have a strong emotional effect on children, and this is why care is taken to paint the walls of a classroom a warm color.

Colors in Nature and Their Impact on the Viewer. Almost all colors are the result of various combinations of the primary colors, except white, which is considered to be all colors of light—that is, all the colors mixed together. Black is considered to have no color of light, that is, it is the absence of color. Colors can signify various things in different cultures; for example, in some cultures white signifies purity, whereas in some Asian cultures white signifies death. In any culture, color in art is used for expression and communication. The impact of colors may be divided into three categories:

- Warm colors—red, orange, yellow, and brown. These colors are usually associated with the sun and fire, and they make pictures appear closer. For example, if warm colors are used in a painting, the viewer's eye will be drawn to these bold, warm colors.
- Cool colors—green, blue, and violet. These more subdued colors are usually associated with greenery outdoors, the sky, or water. When used in a painting, they generally give the viewer a feeling of distance by inducing the associations we have with the outdoors. They might make the viewer think of ice and glaciers.
- Neutral colors—gray, white, and black. Note that you do not find these colors in a rainbow. Scientists do not call black and white true colors. Artists, particularly Chinese and Japanese artists, use shades of black and white in their paintings.

Colors in Paintings by Famous Artists. Georgia O'Keeffe was known for her bold colors that filled the whole page. She painted flowers using bold colors in the paintings *Red Cannas, Petunia,* and *Oriental Poppies.* These pictures are wonderful for encouraging children to use a few bold colors.

In Monet's *Japanese Footbridge,* he used different shades of color in painting the water. *Japanese Footbridge* was one of the many bridges he painted in Giverny, his home in France. Even though many of Monet's paintings appear dark in color, there are also many lighter colors in them. Primary children can use their own creativity as they decide to make a piece of art using Monet's techniques of smudged lines and blending of colors. A variety of media such as paints, pastels, watercolors, finger paints, or other media can be explored to create effects of color similar to the works of Monet. If there is a bridge nearby with water flowing under it, take the class to view the bridge and the water reflections of light and color. This experience may inspire them to use various media to create their own paintings.

Another master, Matisse, was known for his use of bold colors. He spent long hours selecting and mixing the colors he wanted to use in his collages; he then cut the colors into shapes and arranged them as he preferred. Children can be encouraged to paint and cut out shapes from their own bright, bold colors, or cut shapes from magazines or colored paper, and arrange the pieces to make a collage.

Shape

> "I dipped the paintbrush in the red and swirled the paintbrush around
> and around like a circle." —A child at the easel

When lines come together, they form a shape. Some geometric shapes, such as a triangle, circle, square, and rectangle, are easily recognized by most kindergartners. Other shapes can be more complicated, such as an oval, diamond, star, semicircle, heart, spiral, crescent, pentagon, hexagon, and octagon, but children can also learn to recognize them. Rotations of these shapes should be taught because children may not be able to identify them if the shapes are turned another way. Third-graders can recognize the different shapes of triangles, such as equilateral, isosceles, scalene, right angle, obtuse, and acute, and the different rotations of them. The Common Core State Standards (NGA & CCSSO, 2010) emphasize the importance of learning the precise names of two- and three-dimensional figures, which children can be taught through art.

Types of Shapes. In math and science, shapes are classified as two-dimensional forms—circle, triangle, rectangle, square, oval, pentagon, hexagon, and octagon—and as three-dimensional forms—pyramid, cube, rectangular prism, sphere, cylinder, and cone. (See Figures 6.2 and 6.3.) These shapes can increase in complexity with geodesic dome shapes such as the tetrahedron, a pyramid with four triangles; a square pyramid with four triangles and a square base; a hexagonal dome with four triangles and three squares and a hexagonal base.

Figure 6.2. Two-Dimensional Shape Designs

Figure 6.3. Three-Dimensional Shape Designs

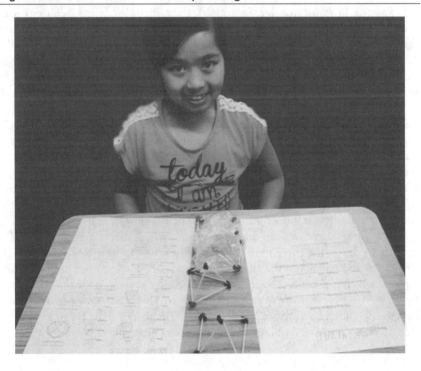

Shapes in Science and Math. To guide children in learning about shapes, a teacher first can allow children to explore on their own in the garden, in the woods, and at the seashore. Secondly, she can support what they saw by enhancing the exploration and discovery of artistic design. This was similar to how Leonardo's uncle supported him. Flower shapes, found in a garden, such as the sunflower or daisy represent a radial or round shape, and the snapdragon and daffodil represent different shapes as well as shapes within shapes. Children can see the number of blooms that have five petals: buttercups, pansies, violets, hibiscus, geraniums, primroses, apples, and pears. The bracts on artichokes, pineapples, and pine cones spiral in two different directions, and the leaves on corn stalks are arranged in a spiral around the stem so they do not overlap. These marvels of nature can be pointed out to the children. Children can observe the growth of the shapes of the flowers, and their teacher can guide them to collect, record, and share information from the natural world to integrate science, math, and artistic design.

In nature children can see and discover what Fibonacci (c. 1175–1250), an Italian mathematician, discovered about the snail and the coiling shape that helps it survive. They can compare the curves in the snail to the walrus tusks, the elephant tusks, and the parrot beak to see how they are similar and how that particular curve helps each survive. Older children might even be able to determine the mathematical code in the spiral, according to Fibonacci, using books such as *Wild Fibonacci: Nature's Secret Code Revealed* by Hulme (2005) or *Blockhead: The Life of Fibonacci* by D'Agnese (2010).

Shapes in Paintings by Famous Artists. Piet Mondrian's paintings with geometric abstractions mirror the paper weaving that was sometimes seen in the Froebel-inspired kindergartens. Mondrian's *New York City,* as well as the *Composition in Blue and Yellow*, showed shapes and forms that were rectangular and square. In the Bauhaus museums in Berlin and Weimer, there are many objects using geometric forms, probably originating from the grid work of Froebel. Josef Albers, Bart van der Leck, and others used a geometric framework originating from a grid, similar to Froebel's work.

Matisse's *The Snail* showed what a snail could look like in a spiral of rectangular shapes. His *Vegetables,* a paper-cut design, features an assortment of vegetables of various shapes. Picasso and, to a lesser degree, Georges Braque, transpose shapes in their work. Looking at Picasso's rearrangement of shapes is instructive for children who have difficulty in seeing shapes from a perspective other than the front. A profile view is more difficult to draw than a view from the front. Studying Picasso's *Three Musicians,* children can see how shapes were arranged very differently to depict the three musicians. Children can examine Roy Lichtenstein's *The Violin* and talk about the shapes, specifically the circles, used in the picture. Op Art, which is short for "optical," can be seen in *Composition with Red Squares* by Victor Vasarely. His use of repeated geometric shapes, contrasting colors, and perspective shows how shapes are intertwined. His shapes show bulging or something coming closer or flashing, which produces a flickering effect.

Texture

Texture in art is the appearance and feel of the art. It can be taught to children by feeling objects from nature. Later, they can see implied texture in pictures. Materials a young artist might incorporate into their art are wood, string, stone, and metal. Some artists design their artwork to be touched or felt. Many modern, contemporary artists incorporate three-dimensional objects into their paintings and sculptures and in computer work. Encaustic artwork has been painted with heated, colored beeswax to produce a layered and textured appearance. Children can be introduced to many vocabulary words associated with texture, such as *sharp, spongy, slippery, rubbery, dull, shiny, wet, sticky, rough,* and *bumpy.* Touching the textures is an easy way to learn the meanings of the various qualities of a surface.

Texture in Sciences. Texture in nature is all around in the life and Earth sciences. The surface of every object has its unique look and feel. For example, pine cones and fish scales are rough, feathers are smooth, metal is hard, and sand is grainy. The eye can be trained to recognize that something is rough or smooth, hard or soft, without touching it. Young children must see and feel the texture of materials before they can express the textures in their artwork. Children can express rough and smooth textures on paper by using tempera paint without much water and then using tempera paint with much more water, which becomes smoother.

Texture in Paintings by Famous Artists. Artists have made objects look more realistic through the use of texture. A famous work of art known for its texture is *Mother and Child* by Mary Cassatt. Many artists actually add real objects to produce texture, but most just utilize the paint they have to imply the texture they create. Oil paints easily produce texture because of certain materials artists mix in with the paint; for instance, if they mix lacquer thinner with oils, it thins the paint out, making it smooth, but if they leave the paints alone they are thick and seem to jump off the page. Artists create textures because they give a painting movement and dimension. Van Gogh often utilized texture as, for example, in the painting *Crows in the Wheatfields.* In this painting he layered the paints of the wheat diagonally, thereby giving the wheat the dimension it needed to stand out from the sky that was flowing horizontally above. Young children obviously are not going to be creating three-dimensional art with oil paint, but a teacher can introduce texture by showing them an oil painting, and allowing them to touch and feel the texture that was created with the paint.

Light

Isaac Newton experimented with color by putting the colors of the rainbow on a metal circle, and when spinning the circle, he noticed that the colors reflected light. Thus he concluded, "Color is light." Light has been introduced as an element of art in early childhood settings primarily because of the emphasis of the Reggio Emilia preschools on the uses of light and secondarily because of its connection to science.

Throughout the history of art, artists have used light in their paintings. Light can be described as dappled in Renoir's paintings, stormy in seascapes, calm in pastoral scenes or reflected in ponds, textured in Van Gogh's paintings, or patterned when coming through the patterns of windows.

During the Italian Renaissance Leonardo da Vinci began an art movement known as *Chiaroscuro,* the Italian word for "light and shade." He was the first to use light and shade in high contrast in his paintings, creating a modeling of volume. Since light and shade are important elements of the real world, the use of *chiaroscuro* in painting allowed for a more realistic depiction of the world and its inhabitants.

Light has aesthetic, psychological, and educational value in a school. The Reggio preschools have emphasized the value of light throughout their curriculum. They have used many transparent and translucent items in their centers to produce varying types of light. They use windows to let light enter the classrooms, shadow puppets to reflect light, and light tables to emphasize light under objects. Their interest in light and shadow has been documented in *Everything Has a Shadow Except Ants* (Sturloni & Vecci, 1999). Light tables have recently begun to appear in early childhood centers, although many teachers still do not take advantage of the opportunities to study the element of light. Of all the elements of art, the study of light leads into science the most.

Light Terminologies: Physical Science Concepts. Light is studied in art and physical science, and it is found in the Next Generation Science Standards (NCSS 1-PSA-3). Light is the kind of energy that helps things grow. There are manmade sources of light such as candles, light bulbs, and lamps, as well as natural sources of light such as light from the sun, lightning, and stars. When these sources of light hit certain objects, different things happen. Objects can be seen if light is available to illuminate them or if they give off their own light. Light travels in straight lines. Straws may be used to demonstrate various concepts; light will shine down a straw. However, if the straw is bent, then the light bends. Although it travels in straight lines, when it hits certain objects, it bounces off them. An example of this can be found by observing how light bounces off a mirror. Light can also bounce off silver foil or a silver spoon.

White light is made up of all colors. Rainbows happen because all the colors in the white light spread out. When the sun shines through the rain, the raindrops split the sun's white light into the many colors of the rainbow. Experiments on how to make a rainbow and sunset in the classroom can be found in Ardley (1991). The concept of white light spreading out can be observed by using a prism.

Transparent materials are materials through which light flows easily. They do not leave a shadow. A clear piece of transparency paper is an example. Air, water, and clear glass are other examples. Translucent materials are materials in which some light goes through, and the light gets scattered. Waxed paper, white notebook paper, colors of stained glass, and tissue paper are examples of translucent materials. Opaque materials are those in which no light goes through. Silver foil and black construction paper are examples of opaque materials. Children enjoy using these types of materials at the light table to see what happens (NCSS 1-PSA-3).

SOURCES FOR THE STUDY OF LIGHT AND COLOR WITH CHILDREN

Ardley, N. (1991). *The science book of color.* San Diego, CA: Harcourt Brace Jovanovich

This wonder book about color describes about 10 color experiments. Many of these experiments can be used at the light table.

Cole, A. (1993). *Color.* Washington, DC: The National Gallery of Art.

This "Eyewitness Art" book describes color from artistic, scientific, and historical perspectives. This is an adult book with many fine art prints.

Gordon, M., & Gordon, M. (1995). *Simple science: Fun with lights.* New York, NY: Thomson Learning.

This children's book has many experiments and explanations of light, reflection, and shadows.

Rowe, J., & Perham, M. (1993). *Colorful light.* Danbury, CT: Children's Press.

This book contains simple experiments about light.

Spero, D. J. (1994). *Light: Reflection and refraction.* Monterey, CA: Evan-Meer Corp.

This is an excellent source for studying light. There are many experiments that are reproducible for your class.

Zubrowski, B. (1995). *Shadow play.* New York, NY: A Beech Tree Paperback.

This is a fascinating book about shadows. It shows the reader how to use everyday materials to carry out an exploration of shadows. (Boston Children's Museum Activity Book).

Zubrowski, B. (1992). *Mirrors: Finding out about the properties of light.* New York: Beech Tree Books.

This book gives children an understanding of reflection.

Shadows are formed because light travels in straight lines. If an opaque material is placed in the line of light, it creates a shadow. Children enjoy experimenting with their shadows when they place themselves in and out of the line of light from the sun.

Light in Paintings by Famous Artists. Famous movements of art have been started because of the way artists have used light. For instance, Monet, one of the leaders in the Impressionist Period, was amazed by the way light changed a scene. He tried to capture the changes in light in the same places. He loved the dancing interchange of light and shadow, and he tried to paint the impressions this play of light made on him. Renoir, in *The Swing*, showed the effect of sunlight on the dress of the woman hanging onto the swing and at the same time showed how the sunlight darts between the leaves. Light splashes and flickers throughout the picture.

UNDERSTANDING THE PRINCIPLES OF DESIGN

When making a work of art, artists use line, color, shape, texture, and light in accordance with certain principles of design, such as balance, pattern, scale, emphasis, and unity. A composition is created by weaving the elements of art and the principles of design into a whole work that represents the "artist within." Design is a part of every invention in science also.

There are many principles of design, but in thinking about how to teach young children to create compositions, our focus will be on only the terms *balance, pattern, scale, emphasis,* and *unity* because of their developmental levels. All of the above artistic concepts are emphasized in the Common Core State Standards (2010) and the Next Generation Science Standards (NGSS, 2013).

Balance can be one of three types. *Symmetrical balance*, the first type of design, is where both sides are designed to appear equal. A child who says, "I have one house on one side of my paper and another house on the other side of my paper with a tall tree" shows that this child is learning about symmetrical balance. A child who folds his paper in half is learning symmetry. A child who folds a paper to make a heart and observes that both sides are equal understands symmetry. A child that folds a hexagon into two equal trapezoids understands symmetry.

A second type of balance is *asymmetrical balance*, where one side is not equivalent to the other side. Capital letters such as F, G, and J are asymmetrical. A third type of balance is *radial balance*, where everything spreads out from a common center. A child placing his flower in the center of the page and drawing petals coming out from it is expressing radial symmetry.

A *pattern* is a shape or design that is repeated. Patterns are a crosscutting concept of the Next Generation Science Standards (NGSS, 2013). There are examples of patterns in many places. Patterns in the natural world can be observed and used to describe phenomena as evidence in science. Georgia O'Keeffe used patterns of nature in her painting *Out Back of Marie's*. She repeated lines and curves. Patterns can be repetitive, alternating, progressive, or flowing. A beehive has repetitive designs of the hexagon shape. A zebra has black and white alternating stripes. The use of alternating patterns adds interest to artwork. Progressive patterns are those that keep adding a little bit more to the picture. A different kind of pattern is a flowing pattern. Examples in paintings are a flowing tree, such as a weeping willow, or flowing hair.

Scale is seeing relationships in size. This art concept is now one of the crosscutting concepts in science, and it is critical to recognize because changes in size can affect a system's structure and performance. Usually children draw the father larger because he is taller, but they may not be aware of this. When primary-age children are working with clay, the size proportions of a clay man may be discussed with them. For instance, the legs are larger than the arms, and the head is smaller than the body. If the body is too big, the legs might not be able to carry it.

Emphasis is the way an artist creates a special forcefulness to keep your attention. Children like to talk about the most important thing in their pictures. More often than not, this focus will be large and vibrant in color so that it stands out more. In nature there are certain distinct features of forms that are prominent and relate to a function of the animal. The emphasis of the beaks of birds is related to the function and what it eats. For instance, the beak of the woodpecker is long and narrow. It taps into logs to find beetle larvae. A beak of a cardinal is short, strong, and thick so it can open seeds.

Unity is what makes a composition a whole picture. Unity might be achieved by repeating designs and completing the designs of the composition so it makes sense to the artist. To a young child, unity means that the composition is complete; it is not left unfinished.

In summary, the elements of art and the principles of design are used to create a composition. Children should be exposed to all the elements and principles of design by the teacher, thus fostering experiences for the arts and a gateway to STEM.

INTEGRATING THE ELEMENTS OF ART
AND THE PRINCIPLES OF DESIGN INTO STEM

Children's experiences with the various elements of art must be related to their previous experiences, interests, and stages of development. When integrating the principles of design into the early childhood curriculum, teachers should not present each principle in isolation. The role of the teacher is to help all children appreciate the qualities of their work and to connect them to events in their world by using the elements of art and the principles of design.

Ms. Chang had many famous works of art displayed in her kindergarten, but she never encouraged children to copy the famous works of art. Instead, she used them as springboards for teaching the elements of art.

One day Jamison was painting at the easel. She always painted just a little bit of the paper. Ms. Chang pointed out that Georgia O'Keeffe painted by covering the whole piece of canvas when she painted a flower. In the painting *Red Poppy* she used all of the space on the paper to paint a giant poppy. Jamison observed the painting and gradually began making larger designs on her paper. Later Ms. Chang pointed out the swirls of paint in Van Gogh's *Starry Night*. Gradually, Jamison's work reflected swirls and curves in a more colorful and deeper way, using the whole paper.

Some teachers suggest that children who paint very few items on a paper are experimenting, or these children may feel that they themselves are very small and unimportant so this feeling is reflected in their art product. Displaying famous works of art may inspire children to visualize ways to become more flexible in their artwork, yet the children must not perceive them as models to copy. Paintings should not look the same, because everyone has the right to create the ways they choose. Painting should come from the soul, and be recorded on the paper as an expression of one's self and imagination.

Judy, a preschool child, was intently observing poppy flowers on a table. Nearby, Mr. Holmstead had displayed Georgia O'Keeffe postcards and several books depicting her work. Judy said, "I'm looking at this flower through a magnifying glass." Her classmate, Carol, responded, "What do you see?" Judy said, "It's a big flower with a long string in it. I don't know what the string is, but this flower looks just like tissue paper." "Let me see," said Carol, and she looked, too. Later in the day, Mr. Holmstead observed the two girls painting big flowers full of strings. They were painting from their previous visual experiencing of the flowers. Mr. Holmstead commented on just what was in their paintings, not what was missing or looked odd.

Mr. Holmstead sensed the interest of the children in the art of Georgia O'Keeffe and integrated it into the arts curriculum as follows:

Art—Georgia O'Keeffe liked to fill up the whole canvas with her art, such as her painting *Red Poppy*. Children were asked to examine the striking black stamens of some actual red poppies. They were also asked to look at the petals to see if they were reminded of something else. They looked at the base and saw the deep purple and noticed that the foliage was hairy.

Music—The children sang the folk song, "I Love the Flowers." They listened to Tchaikovsky's "Waltz of the Flowers."

Creative Movement—The children pretended they were bees going into a flower for nectar. They moved around to smell the flower, twirled around like a bee, and twirled low and high. They demonstrated feeling the curves of the leaf and the curves of the petals. They were in the world of a flower. Then they pretended they were butterflies. They flew into the flower and flapped their wings.

Dramatic Play—They played "art museum" and featured Georgia O'Keeffe's work. Georgia O'Keeffe's pictures that showed strong reds, velvety purples, and pure, gleaming whites were displayed alongside children's work. They organized their museum for others to visit, and assigned jobs to each other, including curator, ticket taker, and guide.

As the interest in the Georgia O'Keeffe project continued, Mr. Holmstead also wrote out his ideas and plans to integrate Georgia O'Keeffe's work into STEM:

Math—Children can begin to experience perspective. What would a flower look like to a bee or a butterfly? What shapes are in some of the flowers? Can they see the shapes within the shape of the flower? Count the petals, the leaves, and the flowers.

Technology—Children can create a flower using different media in Kidpix. Then they can create a digital Cyber Gallery. Beautiful pictures deserve a beautiful gallery. Have an opening night in which the collection is displayed to friends and family. Primary-age children can create their own presentation in HyperStudio as a compilation of their own work and be allowed to display it creatively. After presentations are finished, they can be put on a disc and sent home to the families, where children can present their own work and the class's other work.

Science—A process skill in science is observation. Children can keenly observe many flowers under the magnifying glass. They can observe the flower from all sides. Is the whole poppy orange? Do some parts appear to be different colors? What is inside the poppy? Can you find the stamens and the pollen? What does the poppy feel like? These flowers are perennials. This means that they grow year after year. If plants die after a year, they are called annuals. Plant flowers from seeds and watch them grow. Help children identify the names of flowers. Where do poppies grow? In which season do they grow? How is the Oriental poppy like a bowl?

SUMMARY

As this chapter demonstrates, the elements of art and the principles of design help enlighten children's understanding of art and support thinking creatively. There was a review of the elements of art, and an enhancement of them by using examples from nature, famous works of art, and STEM to inspire the true artist in the child. Teachers are challenged to use materials in a way that integrates artistic, mathematical, and scientific understandings in the early childhood curriculum. In the 19th century, Froebel implemented the concept of integrating mathematics and science with artistic design and nature, and this integration is needed for the present time.

REVIEW AND REFLECT

1. Leonardo da Vinci studied in depth in many areas including optics, anatomy, geology, hydrology, flight, and astronomy. He thought that scientific knowledge was useful to him. He blended his understanding of the universe with the skills of the artist. Discuss why Leonardo's keen observation skills of an artist can help scientists and inventors of today think more deeply about their subject matter. For more information, read his biography by Michael White (2000).
2. Show how the following three crosscutting concepts from the *Next Generation Science Standards* are used in art: patterns; scale, proportion, and quantity; structure and function.
3. Create designs or use ready-made designs in the following shapes: rectangle, triangle, square, oval, diamond, semicircle, heart, spiral, crescent, pentagon, hexagon, or octagon. Combine these to make other shapes.

CHAPTER 7

MUSIC

A Catalyst for Math and the Science of Sound

In music one must think with the heart and feel with the brain.

—George Szell

THE IMPORTANCE OF MUSIC IN THE LIFE OF LEONARDO DA VINCI

Leonardo played the flute. He was invited by the Duke of Milan to play the flute at the court. Leonardo loved music, and the Duke did too. Leonardo even made a lute and gave it to the Duke. He had a strong interest in the design of musical instruments, as evidenced by his journals. He understood musical notation, and there is some evidence that he may have composed music and designed musical instruments with an understanding of the science of sound.

Music is such a wondrous part of life, and when we introduce it to young children, we are laying the groundwork for a lifetime of music enjoyment, communication, collaboration, and creativity. At the same time, there are other reasons music and movement activities are important to promote 21st century skills. Van der Linde (1999) has pointed out the following reasons:

- Mental capacity and intellect are affected because there is a connection between music and mathematical thinking.
- Children's mastery of the physical self is used to develop problem solving with their bodies. This can be done through learning to play an instrument and through movement activities with music.
- Children learn ways to express themselves affectively, which can relieve tension.
- Children develop creativity because they make musical instruments out of objects in the environment, create scenes inspired by classical music, and add new words to old songs for pure enjoyment.

Understanding the science of sound is a byproduct of investigating music.

Musical experiences have a major effect on learning in math (Burrack, 2005). Particularly noteworthy are how the patterns of music in beat, rhythm, and melody are related to the patterning for the Common Core State Standards (NGA & CCSSO, 2010), preschool and primary math learning standards of mathematics (NAEYC & NCTM, 2010; NCTM, 2006), and most recently, the Next Generation Science Standards (NGSS, 2013). Early exposure to patterns is especially important to mathematics (Geist, Geist, & Kuznik, 2012). Children should be able to recognize, describe, extend, and create patterns. Further, children who do not sufficiently develop musical skills during the early years risk having these skills remain underdeveloped throughout their lifetime. Children gain musical knowledge and skill by actively taking part in musical experiences, and at this stage they should be enjoying participation without being concerned with perfection. As with other areas of early childhood, musical activities must be developmentally appropriate, as illustrated by the following vignette.

Ms. Waters taught 1st grade and sang all day long with the children. She was known as the "Singing Teacher." She sang the "Good Morning Song" when the children arrived, the "Clean-up Song" when they cleaned up, and the "Good-Bye Song" when they were ready to go home. She knew numerous songs and fingerplays about farm animals, animals in the woods, pets, bugs, flowers, mountains, water, and every other topic of interest to children. When a child brought in a book about or an actual animal, bug, flower, or other form of nature, she would discuss the animal or plant or read the book and break into a song about the topic. She used hand movements with the fingerplays and action movements with many of the songs. Rhythm-band instruments were used for rhythm at the end of the day to enhance the songs she sang, and she taught her math that way. She taught the science of sound while using the rhythm instruments and determining what made a sound high or low, long or short. Children learned to count and dance to the beat of the music, and therefore learned number sense. Children were taught the elements of music in a very informal way. The children in her class thought they were in a symphony orchestra, and to some degree they were. Even though she knew the songs by heart and sang them spontaneously, she made sure each song was written on the Promethean Board or paper by the end of the day, and she neatly drew rebus pictures on chart paper to represent some of the words to reinforce literacy through lyrics. Ms. Waters used a Musical Arts–STEM approach, which led to a high level of literacy in the areas of science and math.

Teachers of early childhood education have an obligation and responsibility to provide the best possible musical experiences for young children so development of the whole child will take place. For preschool years, teachers provide developmentally appropriate activities by giving children an opportunity to explore sound through music centers, and allowing children to spontaneously sing and explore their music potential. As children develop language skills, they produce rhythmic speech and begin to experiment with vocal chants and sing favorite songs. Children use their ears, hands, voice, brains, and bodies to develop the musical intelligence that lays the foundation on which all later music learning is based. This chapter introduces and discusses research related to music education, methodologies, the elements of music, experiences that children should have in music, and the integration of music into STEM.

OPENING VISTAS OF SUPPORT FOR MUSIC–STEM CONNECTIONS

Music Education Research

Teachers should proceed with caution when approaching the tremendous amount of research on developmentally appropriate musical experiences for the young child. Yet, as a result of competent research, there is increased belief that music education should be a central component of the curriculum, particularly in early childhood (Ellis & Fouts, 2001). One of the many hypotheses offered by Eric Jensen (2001) is that music activates and develops the areas of our brains most involved in facilitating mood, social skills, motivational development, cultural awareness, self-discipline and personal management, and aesthetic appreciation. He emphasizes that we hear with our ears and listen with our brain. Daniel Alfaro, my late husband and former member of the Denver Symphony, said that as a small immigrant child he could hear a piece of music played once on the radio and the language of that music stayed in his thoughts indefinitely. There have been many leaders in the field of music education who have emphasized positive effects from early listening to and study of music.

K. L.Wolff (1979) studied the effect of music instruction on 1st-graders. He found that the music students exhibited significant increases in creativity. Children who were given music lessons scored higher on spatial-temporal skills than those who did not receive training (Rauscher et al., 1997; Rauscher & Zupan, 2000). Howard Gardner (1993) identified musical intelligence as a separate intelligence worthy of development and theorized that if the experiences of listening, moving, singing, playing instruments, and creating music are explored in early childhood, musical intelligence can be improved. It appears logical that if children's natural musical instincts are stimulated early in life through listening and responding to music, they will begin to develop musical aptitudes. Silberg (1998) thought that musical experiences had the potential to use many more of the intelligences identified by Gardner (1993) than just musical intelligence. The other intelligences potentially used in musical experiences are listed below:

Linguistic Intelligence. Singing is related to language. Linguistic
intelligence refers to producing language with sensitivity to the rhythm
and the very slight differences in the meanings of words.

Logical Intelligence. Rhythm is based on sensible reasoning. Logical
intelligence refers to recognizing and manipulating abstract connections,
using reasoning.

Kinesthetic Intelligence. Manipulation of instruments and dance is
kinesthetic. Kinesthetic intelligence refers to the physical movement of
using the body to convey ideas and emotions.

Interpersonal Intelligence. Musical interpretations are interpersonal.
Interpersonal intelligence refers to person-to-person communications
and working effectively with others.

Intrapersonal Intelligence. Connections between the musician and
the instruments are forms of intrapersonal intelligence. Intrapersonal
intelligence refers to understanding and reflecting on one's own emotions.

Music Instruction

Over the centuries, many educators have stressed the value of music education for
young children. Jean Jacques Rousseau around 1758 imagined a child whom he
named Emile. He wrote about the importance of music education for Emile in the
book *Emile or On Education* (1764/1979). He recommended that mothers sing to
their children and that the songs should be simple, interesting, and appropriate.
Friedrich Froebel, originator of kindergarten in the early 1800s (see Chapter 6),
wrote a book of songs (1895) that mothers could sing to their children to promote
their musical skills. He too emphasized the importance of early musical experiences. A criterion he used when selecting teachers for his kindergarten was that
they could sing and play an instrument. Maria Montessori (1965) developed a set
of bells that helped children explore sound and develop other musical concepts
in her "prepared environment," thus emphasizing the importance of instructional
methodologies in music education.

There are four major instructional methodologies that music educators use
to stimulate the musical development of children, and they stem from educational philosophies on how children learn best. The Suzuki Method recommends a
nurturing environment, and the Kodaly Method emphasizes the importance of
cultural folk songs in developing quality music education for all children—not
just the gifted. The Dalcroze Method stresses rhythmic movement as the basis for
stimulating musical development, and the Orff approach gives special emphasis
to improvisational responses to stimulate creative thinking. All approaches agree
that music education should begin in the early years, and that it is an essential
catalyst for learning in all content areas. These philosophers from Japan, Hungary,
Switzerland, and Germany disagree only on how best to stimulate and encourage
musical development of young children. Another method used by many teachers
today was developed by the legendary Ella Jenkins, who employed a combination

of the methodologies that preceded her along with her facility with various instruments and rhythm techniques.

Suzuki Method. Sometimes called the "mother-tongue approach," the Suzuki method is based on an educational philosophy with the goal of creating high-ability students through a nurturing environment, using music education as the vehicle for achieving this goal. The "nurture" involved is based on some of the same factors present in native-language acquisition such as immersion, small steps, and an unforced timetable based on each child's individual readiness.

Shinichi Suzuki (1898–1998), a Japanese educator, recognized the importance of parent involvement, and used a process of rote learning and imitation in his program. He said that any properly trained child can develop musical ability, just as all children can develop the ability to speak their native language. From this belief he developed the Suzuki method, which requires that parents become heavily involved in their children's learning. This method mimics a mother's natural way of teaching a child to speak, which is informal and includes a lot of imitation, repetition, and practice as the child develops in proficiency (Suzuki, 1969). Before children can enter the program, parents must first receive several months of instruction on how to model playing simple compositions on the violin or piano.

The Suzuki approach builds on *parents as teachers* to strengthen their program, although parents and families assume various roles such as parent as an observer, parent as a volunteer, parent as a resource person, and parent as a teacher of his or her own children. Although the most important role of the parent is to become supplementary teachers, Suzuki involves parents in many roles because they are the one continuous force in the music development of their children throughout the years. Festivals in which children have the opportunity to perform for an audience are an important aspect of the Suzuki method, and today many music teachers also use recitals as a way to assess the progress of their students. The Suzuki approach was originally developed for teaching the violin, but it is now also available for the viola, cello, bass, piano, flute, harp, and guitar.

Kodaly Method. Like Suzuki, Zoltan Kodaly (1882–1967) recommended a child-development approach to music education and introducing skills according to the abilities of the child, even though he used singing rather than a musical instrument as a vehicle for music education. The Kodaly Method is a developmentally appropriate approach to music education stemming from his philosophy of education. A Hungarian music educator, Kodaly became appalled at the music he heard in the schools and wrote numerous articles designed to improve the methods used. He insisted that any child who is capable of reading language is also capable of reading music. He felt that no education could be complete without music and stressed that music be taught daily as part of the core curriculum and given importance equal to language and mathematics (Kodaly, 1974).

Kodaly had the primary goals of teaching children to read and write musical notation, but he focused on a sequenced progression of folk songs to accommodate the developmental levels of children. The first level begins with two-syllable chants and builds up to simple folk songs. The tone direction is emphasized, and children are taught to match the progression they hear with body and then with hand movements, and thus the progressions are represented visually. The Kodaly schools develop a method of singing in perfect pitch, starting with folk songs. Later, students can read any piece of music and sing, in perfect pitch, something that was composed for an instrument (Jensen, 2001).

Dalcroze Method. Emile Jacques-Dalcroze (1865–1950), a Swiss educator, agreed with Kodaly that movement is important for the internalization of music, and his method also includes rhythmic hand movements. The Dalcroze Method was based on a philosophy that emphasized body movement, ear training, and improvisation to awaken children's awareness of musical elements (Jacques-Dalcroze, 1921/2013). A rhythmic approach to music, called "eurhythmics," is basic to the Dalcroze Method. He taught music entirely through movement, beginning with the heartbeat and extending to even and uneven walking patterns, and timed periods of "rests" that helped children develop an inner sense of timing. His teachings have been adopted by music educators throughout the world and are the basis for folk dancing as well as interpretive dance emphasizing creativity and improvisations.

Orff Method. Like the Suzuki Method, the Orff approach is based on a philosophy of education that treats music as a basic system that, like language, can be learned using a gentle and friendly informal approach without formal instruction (Rozmajzl & Boyer-White, 1990). Carl Orff (1895–1982), a German educator, stressed that the music children create is improvisational and builds a foundation for creative thinking. He emphasized spontaneity, originality, and creative improvisation, and encouraged children to create their own music,

He designed Orff instruments with only 5 steps of the scale. The tones produced are the same as playing only the black keys on the piano. The five tones of a pentatonic scale are: do-re-mi-so-la. These scales are used all over the world and were used in traditional music in many societies.

Teachers who know how to play chords on the piano or keyboard can play the following chords in order while the children play any black keys they choose. The chords are E-flat for four times, A-flat for two times, E-flat again for two times, B-flat for one time, A-flat for one time, and E-flat for two times. For classroom teachers who do not play the piano, the autoharp can be substituted while children play any black keys on the piano. The resultant music is pleasant in sound, and children love exploring the black keys as they create music along with their teacher. According to some music teachers, using the five pentatonic tones of do, re, mi, so, and la for a melody makes for a beautiful and creative musical expression. Children can explore sounds on the Orff instruments; for example, the xylophone has removable bars that can be rearranged to develop various tonal patterns. The instruments Orff developed are of high quality and produce beautiful tones. They include a metallophone that produces alto and bass tones, and a glockenspiel that is high-pitched and produces a soprano tone.

The Orff approach was designed to be passed on through interactions, and teachers trained in the Orff approach would, for example, play the beat of a drum according to the child's movements rather than expect a child to march to the beat of a drum. As children realize that their steps dictate the beat of the drum, it becomes a game where they will walk faster and then slower to set the pace. This rhythmic activity reinforces the concept that musical responses should come from within the student not from within the teacher. The Orff approach combines movement and singing with the use of instruments, but creative improvisation is particularly emphasized

Jenkins Approach. A prominent U.S. educator, Ella Jenkins has incorporated parts of all four of the preceding methods, including improvisation, nurturing, folk songs, and rhythm, and she focuses as well on a global perspective for music education (Jenkins, 1995). Known as the "First Lady of Children's Music," Jenkins is well known for her ability to stimulate children through listening and responding to music. Born in 1924 in St. Louis, Missouri, her "call and response" method is focused on engaging children for both entertainment and education. Her best-known record title is "You Sing a Song and I'll Sing a Song." Jenkins has been described as speaking to—not *down* to—children, and she has taught children over seven continents to celebrate the beauty and value of diverse cultures. Internationally, she has been recognized for her ability to captivate, teach, and entertain young children, and her recordings have helped many teachers involve their children in learning about the environment, sharing various cultures, and participating in rhythms found in nature, dance, and traditional West African chants. Her legacy spans more than 50 years, during which time she has focused on group vocalizing and rhythm building with traditional rhythm instruments like sticks or drums. She and other educators are well known for valuing and integrating music into content areas such as science and social studies.

All of the music educators reviewed above, even though they were from different cultures, agreed that music should be incorporated into the daily activities of young children. They also agreed that children should be active participants in a variety of musical experiences, even when a specialist supplements music education for a specific time period each day. The main way their opinions vary is on their selection of the best possible vehicle to learn music. The significant finding from a review of these philosophers is that music should be part of the core curriculum starting with the early years.

Although the vehicles of music education vary, they have a common goal: to develop high-quality students who are more likely to succeed in all content areas because of their involvement in musical experiences. In Hungary, math and science scores top those of the United States by a wide margin. Some educators think that this may in part be due to the Kodaly method that is used in their schools. According to the brain researcher Eric Jensen (2001), music may be the foundation for later math and science excellence. In Japan, where children regularly outscore the United States in math and science, music is required, and children learn to play two instruments in order to develop their creative-thinking skills. In Japan, Hungary, and the Netherlands, music is mandatory, and students' math and science scores are near the top in the world. Jensen theorizes that it all starts in early music education.

DEFINING THE ELEMENTS OF MUSIC

Music, an expressive art form, is created and communicated by using sound and silence as a medium of expression (Wright, 2003). Musical experiences should be integrated within the daily play of young children, forming a natural part of their growth and development. Children should be provided the opportunity to listen and respond to various types of music. The music elements of rhythm, melody, pitch, dynamics, form, and mood are of particular interest to young children, although they should not be taught in isolation, but through musical experiences.

Rhythm. Listening to the rhythm of the wind blowing or the sound of ocean waves can provide an opportunity for children to experience a connection between nature and the rhythm found in the musical expressive arts. Children can also listen to their heartbeats and hear rhythm since it often refers to any recurring pattern of activity, such as the cycle of the seasons or repeated functions of their body. In music, *rhythm* refers to a regular pattern of emphasis and beats found in a piece of music and to the time-based aspects of music that include the groupings of sounds and silences of varying durations.

"Name That Tune" is a game in which children can experience rhythm merely by clapping the rhythm of the words of a song. Try clapping the "ABC Song" without thinking the words and you find it's not possible. You are not clapping the beat but the rhythm of the words of the melody. Teachers often give children the opportunity to feel the rhythm of words when they encourage them to clap as they say the words of a fingerplay or favorite chant.

Melody. Students singing their favorite songs or experimenting on the piano or keyboard can experience the element of *melody*, which refers to a series of musical notes that form a distinct unit. Some teachers in preschool and kindergarten use color-coding on a simple song their students know, such as the "ABC Song," to reinforce the element of melody. The keys on the piano are labeled with colored dots from middle C up an octave. The colors on the song sheet match the colored dots on the piano keys, and students play the melody by matching the colors. As an added benefit, this activity also promotes the mathematical concept of one-to-one correspondences.

The piano-key colors beginning with middle C stay constant, so other songs may be written using the same color-coding. The piano-key colored dots basically include red (middle C), orange (D), yellow (E), green (F), blue (G), purple (A),

COMPONENTS OF RHYTHM

Rhythm is the characteristic of music that includes tempo, beat, accent, and meter:

- The *tempo* is the rate or speed of the music.
- The *beat* is the underlying pulse that is unchanging, constant, and steady. You tap your foot to the beat of the music.
- *Accent* refers to the stress placed on particular notes in a piece of music. The waltz is a group of three beats with the accent on the first beat.
- *Meter* refers to the pattern of beats that combines to form musical rhythm. The meter is the regular accenting of pulses. It provides an emphasis on the first beat, causing the pulses to be grouped in twos or threes. The meter is the basic recurrent rhythmical pattern of note values, accents, and beats per measure in music.

brown (B), and black (C), in the same order as on the color wheel. For the "ABC Song," the colored dots on the song sheet are red red, blue blue, purple purple blue, and so on throughout the song. Using one-to-one correspondences, students match the colors and experience playing the melody.

Pitch. A beginning step in teaching the element of melody is for children to hear the *pitch*, the difference between high and low notes in their favorite songs. It is sometimes hard for children to understand the semantics of *high* and *low* in music because they are more familiar with something high on the shelf or low on the shelf. It is taught by letting children listen to familiar songs as a teacher sings them with a high-pitched voice and then with a low-pitched voice. The next step is to teach them the contour of the melody as going up, going down, or going straight. Children can play high notes on the piano by going up and low notes by going down the keyboard. They can later learn to identify the direction of high or low melodic tones and soon learn that a melody is based on a set of pitches that move up or down making various vibrations and sounds. Notes that are in the ideal range for young children's voices go from middle C, up to high F.

Dynamics. The element of *dynamics* refers to variations in the loudness of sounds. Vibrations traveling through air that can be heard by the human ear produce sounds. Some sounds of nature like thunder are very loud, and some sounds like the chirping of birds are very quiet. Some sounds get gradually louder or quieter, such as a train coming toward you and leaving you. At home, children may experience the element of dynamics when someone says, "Whisper, you are talking too loud and it might wake the baby" or "Turn down the TV because it's too loud for my ears."

Primary-age children can experience the element of dynamics while participating in movement dramatizations. For example, they can pretend they are sleeping flowers, and as the music gets louder, they can stretch and grow very tall as they face the morning sun. As the music becomes quieter, they can fold their petals and sleep through the night. As children listen to the music, they respond to the contrast of loud and quiet that they hear.

Form. A form of musical expression that is sometimes directly taught to primary-age children is a round. *Form* is the element of music that includes beginnings and endings, patterns as in phrases, and repetitions as in the chorus or *rounds* of a song. A *round* refers to the exact imitation of a given melody sung one or two measures later. To sing a round, one must learn the tune, and then divide into groups and begin singing at different times. When the first group reaches the end of the first phrase, the second group starts singing from the beginning of the song. Some rounds can be in two parts, and some in three or four parts.

When singing rounds, children must listen carefully to the other voices and should not sing louder or quieter than the other children's voices. It should be noted that rarely are young children able to sing rounds, and their beginning introduction to harmony is the late primary grades. The traditional English song "Row Row Row Your Boat," the traditional French song "Frere Jacques," and the Australian song "Kookaburra," by Marion Sinclair, are examples of simple rounds that primary-age children enjoy singing.

Mood. A combination of musical elements that cause an emotional response refers to the *mood* or feeling picked up from a musical composition. Often it is through an emotional response to music that children develop a lasting interest in music. They respond by singing or moving according to the mood of the music. Listen to the composition *Mood Indigo* by Duke Ellington. How does it make you feel? Then listen to the jazz song *In the Mood* by Glenn Miller. How do the two moods differ?

MUSICAL EXPERIENCES IN EARLY CHILDHOOD

In early childhood education, musical experiences should be play-based and include many kinds of musical interactions in one-on-one situations and in small and large groups. A formal position statement on music in early childhood education was developed by the National Association for Music Education (NAfME, 1991) as a guide to the teaching profession in order to promote developmentally and individually appropriate music activities for young children. The musical experiences of listening, movement, singing, playing instruments, and creating can be integrated within various content areas. It is through musical experience with rhythm, melody, dynamics, form, and mood that children learn about the elemental components of music.

As young children listen to music, they generally respond with their bodies, and in early childhood they begin to discriminate among sounds as they explore simple musical instruments such as the xylophone. Later on in the primary grades, musical notations are introduced to them through music books with pictures to help children understand the meanings of the words of a song. Children also enjoy singing, chanting, and playing musical games they learn from these books.

Listening

Developmentally and individually appropriate music experiences for young children begin with the experience of listening. There are three main types of listening skills that are needed as children refine their knowledge: auditory awareness, auditory discrimination, and auditory sequencing.

Teachers should guide children to be alert to sounds that help them develop *auditory awareness*. What did they hear on the way to school? What sounds do they hear inside their bodies? Children can practice the patterns of in and out breathing. Some teachers have placed stethoscopes in the science and health areas so children can listen to their hearts beat. Students are often scared by sounds, and they move very close to the teacher when the thunder roars outside. They are fascinated by the sounds they hear on listening walks such as the wind rustling in the trees, the birds singing, the dogs barking, the sirens screaming, or brakes screeching. When they return to the classroom, they often "draw" the sounds they have heard. After a trip to the zoo, they can be observed crawling and roaring like the lions or chattering like the monkeys. The tinkle of the bell as the ice cream man drives up their street is an especially enjoyable sound for young children to hear. Once children are aware of the sounds around them, they then begin to identify some differences and characteristics of the various sounds, a skill in both science and music.

Being able to identify sounds in terms of loud and quiet and high and low is called *auditory discrimination*. During Orff studies, aspiring teachers are reminded that the opposite of loud is quiet, not soft, because soft is the feel of materials. Children need to hear the difference in tones on various instruments, as well as with voices. As students listen to sounds, they also begin to hear the sounds in letters, and most 4-year-olds can identify the sound of the letters s as in "snake," i as in "ice cream," m as in "M&M's," and t as in "tea." They begin to show signs of reading readiness using auditory discrimination.

The final and most complicated of the listening skills is *auditory sequencing*, which is the ability to sequence sounds. Echo clapping is a technique where the teacher claps a pattern and the child imitates the clap. Children especially enjoy clapping the beat of their name, that is, clapping once for each syllable in their name: 1 beat for Ann, 2 beats for Ma-ry, 3 beats for Jac-que-lyn, and 4 beats for Al-ex-an-der. As they respond to the beat, they begin to understand that names are made up of syllables, syllables make words, and words make sentences. There appears to be musical rhythm in language as young students chant "Evelyn, Evelyn, Evelyn, Evelyn," as they cheer her on to win in an exciting game of "Skip and Stoop."

Teachers should help children become aware of their listening skills, which involve the ability to analyze and respond to sounds they hear. In the Hollywood movie *Amadeus*, his rival Antonio Salieri was amazed that Wolfgang Amadeus Mozart could play a composition by Salieri after hearing it only once. Mozart was composing at the age of 4, and it was stated that he would sometimes write down an entire composition without changing a note (Shaw, 2004). It is in the sequential use of the music patterns that the real genius of Mozart is most evident. These musical patterns and their sequences in Mozart's works represent, in some highest and purest form, the internal neural language of the brain and its patterns and sequences of patterns (Shaw, 2004).

Children should have the opportunity to listen to all appropriate types of music, including current popular music. Teachers definitely must preview any music, music videos, or CDs to determine whether the content is suitable for young children. Listening to music with various themes increases their understanding of the many sounds of the orchestra and develops a deeper understanding of many musical compositions. Listening to Sergei Prokofiev's tale, *Peter and the Wolf*, which has been set to music, can provide an introduction to the musical instruments of the orchestra for primary-grade children. Each character in the story is introduced by one of the instruments of the orchestra: Peter is the violin, grandfather is the bassoon, the duck is the oboe, the cat is the clarinet, the wolf is the French horn, the hunters are the kettle drums, and the bird is the flute. It is the story of how Peter, the bird Sonya, the courageous duck, and other friends of Peter outwit the malicious wolf. Recently *Peter and the Wolf* has been composed in a jazz version called *Peter and the Wolf Play Jazz* by Dave Van Ronk. The context of listening to classical music or jazz in early childhood may include having the music playing as background during center time or responding to the music with movement. In the primary grades, a drawing created when classical music or jazz is playing usually expresses and follows the rhythm of the music.

Children who are hearing impaired do not listen to music in the same way that the other children do. For those with some ability to hear, headphones can be provided, and the music on their player can be turned up loud enough for them to feel the vibrations. Wireless headphones are best so the children can respond with their body to the vibrations they feel. All musical instruments vibrate; for example, when you hit the top of a drum, the head or top bounces back and forth and vibrates. When children who are hearing impaired pluck a guitar string, they make it vibrate, and the harder the strings are plucked the bigger the vibrations are. For this reason teachers should not be disturbed by the loud sounds coming from the music center of interest. Hearing-impaired children "listen" to the sound of a musical instrument like a guitar or a drum through their fingers by feeling

---

LISTEN AND RESPOND: NATURE AND SCIENCE

Children can be asked to listen and respond to the following kinds of sounds in certain classical compositions:

Sounds of Nature

- The *Grand Canyon Suite* by Ferde Grofé
- *6th Symphony* by Ludwig van Beethoven
- *The Blue Danube* by Johann Strauss

Animal Sounds

- *Flight of the Bumblebee* by Nikolay Rimsky-Korsakov
- *Carnival of the Animals* by Camille Saint-Saëns
- *Peter and the Wolf* by Sergei Prokofiev

Rodeo Sounds

- *Rodeo* by Aaron Copland

Water Sounds

- *The Sea* (La Mer) by Debussy
- Storm at Sea by Vivaldi
- Water Games (Jeux d'Eau) by Maurice Ravel

---

the vibrations. They also can feel vibrations through their bare feet when a drum is played on wooden floorboards. Many of the musical instruments in the sound center of interest such as a xylophone, maracas, or wood blocks have the capability of making vibrations that children with hearing impairments can "hear" as they respond to "their music" with movement.

Movement and Music

Movement in young babies is largely a subconscious experience, but as they develop, their rhythmic experiences with movement become a great source of pleasure to them. Music, with its rhythmic beats, encourages natural aspirations for them to move along with the music. Young children first use arm and leg movements to move rhythmically with the music. They then move to fine motor movements with fingerplays and playing musical instruments. There are many traditional musical games that children like to play such as: "Did You Ever See a Lassie?" "Mulberry Bush," "Looby Loo," and "Bluebird, Bluebird." The African Swahili Game song "Kye-Kye Kola" uses the development of rhythmic coordination while matching the words to the chant. (See also Chapter 4 for a full discussion of creative movement.)

Singing and Chanting

Singing is a favorite musical experience that involves melody and pitch, and making up original songs is quite natural for young children when they are given numerous opportunities to sing in the classroom. Teaching songs is a natural part of the early childhood program. One way for a teacher to teach an especially long song to children is to break the song into manageable chunks or phrases that the teacher sings first and then the children repeat. Gradually, the song is put together and sung as a whole song. Be sure not to encourage children to compete with one another during a group singing time to avoid their trying to outshout one another. Teachers may also teach a song by singing the whole song, and the children gradually learn it. This approach is similar to how children learn to sing songs from listening to TV singing commercials.

A strategy to encourage creative singing is to substitute words in a song to make it more personal for the children. For example, teachers may substitute different names of children or things in nature when chanting the words of fingerplays or songs. In the fingerplay that begins "Two little blackbirds, sitting on a hill. One named Jack and one named Jill," substitute names of the children in the class and other birds they have seen (blue jays, robins, hawks).

Playing traditional singing games can encourage children to create singing games of their own. A traditional favorite is "Farmer in the Dell," used in preschool. Another traditional singing game is "Skip to My Lou." For primary-age children, old favorites, such as "Oh Susanna" by Stephen Foster and "I've Been Working on the Railroad" by Calumet Music, can be sung to carry on the traditional songs of American culture.

Be sure to distinguish between singing and chanting. Chants are words uttered rhythmically, the pitch usually lies within a small range, and they are not considered a form of singing. For example, when chanting names such as Daniel Al-far-o that has five syllables, the chanting is rhythmic speech, not singing. Examples of three favorite chants of children are the traditional "Pease Porridge Hot," "Engine, Engine Number Nine," and "Miss Mary Mack." Chanting can promote successful language experiences since the goal of a chant is not memorization but the opportunity to share rhythmic speech. Fingerplays are rhythmic words, spoken, chanted, or sung, that have gestures to help with the meaning. Many chants and fingerplays can be found in books or on the Internet. There is also music written for many of the chanted nursery rhymes such as "Hickory Dickory Dock" from Mother Goose and the traditional "Eensy Weensy Spider."

One of children's favorite musical experiences in early childhood is singing and clapping to rhythmic music, and then spontaneously creating their own songs. Spontaneous music naturally leads to improvising with rhythm instruments.

Playing Instruments

Young children enjoy the experience of playing a rhythm instrument as they explore musical sounds. As children experiment with various rhythm instruments, they become sensitive to patterns, and the possibilities of rhythm instruments help them become creative musicians. Some real musical instruments should also be available for exploration in the music center, which helps with understanding the science of sound (NGSS, 2013).

The classroom piano or a keyboard can be available for one child at a time to explore many of the sounds made by striking the keys. Although for years a classroom piano was standard equipment for a kindergarten, today they do not appear to be available in most classrooms. A piano is ideal for children to hear and produce sounds using loud tones, quiet tones, long tones, and short tones. However, if a piano is unavailable, there are keyboards and many different types of musical instruments such as string instruments, wind instruments, and percussion instruments (such as the xylophone pictured in Figure 7.1) that primary-age children enjoy exploring.

String instruments contain one or more strings that are made to vibrate and produce musical sounds. Some strings are stroked or rubbed, and some strings are plucked. When exploring some string instruments, children discover that the

Figure 7.1. Playing the Xylophone

longest strings create the lowest notes and the shortest strings create the highest notes. With regard to the pitch, the looser the string, the lower the pitch, and the tighter the string, the higher the pitch. A thicker string has a lower pitch, and a thinner string has a higher pitch. To help children learn about string instruments, they can bring different sizes of rubber bands to school and put them around small boxes to experiment with the concept of sound. Take a rubber band and stretch it tight over the box, and then put a pencil between the box and the rubber band. Pluck it to determine whether the sound gets louder when it is plucked harder, and whether the sound gets higher or lower when the pencil is moved. Children are happy and enthusiastic to make simple instruments to explore sound.

Wind instruments such as a trumpet or a clarinet contain a column of air that can be made to vibrate and produce musical sounds by blowing into it. Wind instruments are divided into two classifications, woodwind and brass. Making the air column longer or shorter can change the pitch or frequency of the vibrating air column. Pressing or releasing the keys of an instrument will open or close the holes in the instrument, making the length of the air columns longer or shorter. The longer the air column is, the lower the pitch will be, and the shorter the air column is, the higher the pitch will be. Children can make a wind instrument by blowing across the top of an empty plastic water bottle to make a sound, and when they blow harder the sound changes to a higher pitch. When children change the size of the bottle, they get different sounds from their homemade instrument.

Although children cannot control the sound of drum notes, as they can with their bottle wind instrument, they will also take pleasure in making and playing their own percussion instruments. Teachers often model how to make percussion instruments out of creatively decorated hollow cardboard cylinder boxes. Percussion instruments are either made of solid materials, like wood and metal, or of materials stretched over a hollow container.

In addition to the traditional instruments, there should be instruments from different cultures for children to explore. At some schools in Hawaii, many children carry their ukuleles to and from school, and they can be observed strumming their "ukes" on the playground, before and after school. A ukulele that is tuned to a basic cord can have a pleasant sound. Some other examples of instruments from other cultures are the bongo drums of Cuba, peyote drum and tom-toms of Native Americans, glockenspiels from Germany, maracas from South America, rain sticks from Brazil, wooden flutes from Africa, and bells from Tibet. Children enjoy making instruments similar to those of other cultures, using their own ingenuity such as filling a long mailing tube with sand and closing the ends of the tube with tape. By moving the tube, they can create the sounds of the rain sticks from Brazil.

Teachers sometimes contact musicians and invite them to play their instruments at school for families and children. Many musicians will allow children to touch and feel the vibrations of the instruments. Field trips with the children and their families to "Tiny Tot Concerts," during which musicians model songs and then encourage children to create their own music, are exciting musical experiences.

Creating Music

Children usually create their own music after actively listening to many kinds of music. They hear the music, and they respond with their bodies by moving to the music. They respond with their voices by improvising their own tunes as they move around the classroom. Children enjoy improvising and making up songs, and often they make up songs similar to a song that they already know well. Usually the songs they create include chants about things they have experienced in their own environment. For example, they might sing, "First you put the flour in, then the salt, then the water, and you mix, mix, mix it all up together." Children like to create their own music when playing musical instruments. Some children are even capable of creating emergent compositions (Ohman-Rodrigu, 2004).

The early experiences of listening, singing, and movement in response to music form a strong foundation for children to create their own music, as well as seeing patterns and counting. However, whether it is through dancing, singing, playing with simple musical instruments, or experimenting, we want children to feel the desire to respond rhythmically and to translate their ideas into creative musical expressions. The music used in the classroom should incorporate the best of the old and the best of the new so children can learn to enjoy and respond to all types of music.

EXPLORING AND INTEGRATING
MUSIC INTO THE STEM CURRICULUM

The following vignette of a "concert hall performance" occurred during the dramatic play of a preschool class. It serves as an example of how music can be integrated within the dramatic play area.

Child One: Come on, it's time for a show.
> (Child One grabs shoes to wear with her long pink dress and sparkling headband.)

Child Two: Okay, let me get dressed first.

Child One: Who'll be our audience?

Teacher: I'll watch the show.

Child Two: You have to buy tickets. They're $1.00.

Teacher: Okay, I'll buy one ticket.
> (Teacher hands Child Two a dollar, and Child Two gives the teacher a ticket.)

Child One: Let me get the seats.
> (Child One counts three people in the play area, and grabs three seats. She sets them in a row in front of the stage area.)

Child Two: You guys can play the music.
Child One: Look at my pretty dress!
Child Two: We're starting.
   (Child One has the microphone, and Child Two has the maracas. They
   begin singing an improvised tune.)
Child One: Now it is my turn to use the maracas. Don't forget to dance.
Child Two: Okay, let me sing and dance too.
   (They swap the microphone for the maracas, and then sing and dance
   for their audience.)
Child Two: It's my turn next.
Child One: No, the song is over, now someone has to clap.
   (Teacher and audience clap.)
Child Two: We have to take a rest, good-bye, and thanks for coming.

The children in this dramatic play are learning what goes into a performance and how to create one. They are hypothesizing that in order to give a concert hall performance, they need to be dressed up, have an audience, have an instrument, and sing and dance. The children also know that if the teacher gives them a dollar, they need to give her a ticket. They show an understanding of one-to-one correspondence, because of the size of the audience and the number of chairs needed. In such a dramatic play episode a teacher can promote the children's learning through questioning:

- Why do people come to performances?
- How does the audience pay for their tickets?
- Where does the money come from?
- Why would you get all dressed up to perform?
- What other instruments could you use?
- What other things can you do in a performance?
- Was your performance successful?

Early childhood teachers are motivators, planners, collaborators, and observers as they integrate music throughout the school day across various subject areas. The children's concert hall performance offers a perfect opportunity to incorporate the experiences of listening, singing, moving, playing, and creating. Such a performance also incorporates the elements of music into the total curriculum. Note that the children who planned this concert hall performance lived in an environment that valued concerts, and children from another culture or different socioeconomic group might have created a different type of musical project. There are many opportunities for young children to learn concepts in various content areas through music (see Kemple, Batey, & Hartle, 2004, for other ideas for integrating music into the total curriculum).

CURRICULUM BASED ON THE
CHILDREN'S INTEREST

The following ideas for an emerging curriculum in music, STEM, and other subjects are based on the dramatic play described in the book text in which the children demonstrated their interest in this particular type of concert hall performance:

Music. Teach young children to sing a song together, and sing it for other classes in the school. The songs students like to learn are those that have a personal meaning to them, such as songs about their birthdays. Just as children quickly learn the lyrics and melodies listening to a radio or TV commercial, they will easily learn songs in the classroom after they have heard them a few times. Older students enjoy learning a new song in a group taught directly by the teacher. They also enjoy incorporating dance, instruments, and singing into one song.

Literacy. Make brochures advertising the performance and programs with the names of the performers and which songs they sing. Make a songbook with the songs in it.

Mathematics. The children can plan for a large performance by setting up seats for a specific number of audience members. The children can also count the money collected, and determine how many people are present based on the number of tickets sold. They can count the beats to the music.

Science. Display rhythm instruments in a place where students can easily choose them. Children appear to prefer selecting an instrument to hear its sound. They learn about vibration as they tap a triangle suspended by a string, as compared to tapping it when they are holding it in their hands. They enjoy exploring the "science of sound" for their concert hall performance.

Social Studies. Children in early childhood environments have diverse backgrounds, and their home languages and cultures should be valued by the teacher. Music of various cultures can be a practical and motivating way for teaching literacy skills. They can learn a song in another language or a dance from another country. Some games appear to be universal. Although musical games are exciting and fun for children, they are usually teacher initiated and lack student input, and they should not be considered to be the only musical games appropriate for students. It is the initiation of games by the students that inspires creativity.

Mathematics

Mathematical concepts such as patterning, counting, classification, seriation, estimating, one-to-one correspondence, space, and time concepts can all be developed through the use of music. These concepts are part of the math Common Core State Standards (NGA & CCSSO, 2010).

A regular or repetitive form or arrangement refers to the mathematical concept of *patterning* that young children learn as they use rhythm instruments or body movements to make up simple patterns like AB or ABA. They can recognize, describe, and extend a pattern with music. As children develop these patterns, the teacher can relate this to the National Council of Teachers of Mathematics Standards (NCTM, 2006) and the newer Common Core State Standards (NGA & CCSSO, 2010). Primary-age children use different musical notes to make up simple musical patterns as they listen to different patterns in songs and write down the patterns they hear. The mathematical concept of *counting* is closely related to patterning because the children can count the beat as they recognize a pattern in a song. Counting how many notes are in a song, how many beats each note gets in a measure according to whether it is a half note, quarter note, or a whole note, or how many times one strikes a key or plays an instrument can provide support for their counting proficiency.

Geometric forms such as a square, triangle, cone, or cube refer to the mathematical concept of *shape*. Children can compare the shapes of rhythm instruments, and respond to the shapes or patterns in a song by drawing the shape that is called out; for example, in "Twinkle, Twinkle Little Star" children can draw a high arc when they hear a high pattern. (See also Chapter 6 for a discussion of shapes.)

Children can also learn to make an *estimation*, which is a judgment about something, by exploring this mathematical concept. They can estimate such things as which musical instrument produces the louder or quieter sound, how many beats are in a song, or the volume of water needed in a glass to produce a high or low sound.

Using the mathematical concept of *volume*, the children can fill several drinking glasses with various amounts of water and discuss which has more or less water, as they tap the glasses with a pencil or spoon so they ring like bells. After listening to the different sounds, the children can practice the mathematical concept of *seriation* by arranging the glasses according to the volume of water in each glass. Closely related to mathematical concepts are scientific concepts.

Science

The scientific concept of *sound* and its properties is part of physical science in the Next Generation Science Standards (NGSS, 2013) and can be studied informally through music. Using the scientific and mathematical concept of *classification*, children can use rhythm instruments and categorize them by the sounds they make, for example, as high or low, click or ring, or scrape. The instruments can be classified as string, wind, or percussion, or as purchased or homemade. When studying the mathematical concept of *patterns*, children can compare songs or patterns according to how fast or slow they are or how high-pitched or low-pitched they are. They can also compare musical instruments according to the sound they make such as clinging, ringing, swishing, or booming. For example, sounds caused by vibrations occur when children are plucking a guitar, stroking an autoharp, blowing a bassoon, or hitting a drum.

Exploration of sound is not the same thing as just making noise, so teachers should encourage children to listen to the sounds they produce. Some inexpensive metal tambourines definitely produce a tinny noisy sound, so be sure tambourines and other instruments are of the highest quality possible because then the children can enjoy the beautiful sounds they produce. In order to help children understand more about vibrations, pass an unwound music box among the children. Ask children if they feel anything. Then wind it up and play it. Is the music box making sounds? Can children feel the vibrations?

A group response to sounds is another way to explore the concept. When a teacher plays a drum fast or slow, then loudly or quietly, these sounds provide the impetus for response through movement. When the drum stops, the students stop,

DEMONSTRATING THE SCIENTIFIC CONCEPTS OF PITCH AND INTENSITY

Place an autoharp or a guitar on an empty box that is standing on end. As the teacher strokes a chord on the strings, children can experiment in several ways. They can put their head inside the box to listen, they can touch the side of the box with their fingertips, or touch the side of the box with their ear in order to feel the vibrations. Sounds differ in pitch and intensity.

As defined earlier in the chapter, *pitch* is the highness or lowness of a sound as defined by the frequency of its vibrations. The faster an instrument vibrates, that is, the more vibrations it produces in a second, the higher the sound or pitch. The slower an instrument vibrates, that is, the fewer vibrations it produces in a second, the lower the pitch.

Intensity, or the strength of a sound, is reflected in its loudness or quietness. The loudness or quietness of a sound depends on how strongly the object is vibrating. The stronger the vibrations, the more energy the sound wave has, thus the greater the size of the sound wave. The harder a string is bowed or plucked, the more strongly it vibrates, and the louder the sound that is produced. The more gently a string is bowed or plucked, the weaker the vibrations, and the softer the sound that is produced.

and then they move again to the beat of the drum. Children are free to go in any direction they choose in the classroom rather than being required to go around in a circle. They spontaneously respond as they hear the beat of the drum. An individual response to sounds occurs when rice, rocks, bells, or other objects are placed into boxes of varied sizes. Children play a game of finding two boxes that have similar sounds, and they open the boxes to verify that the contents are the same.

Interactive Technology

Software programs for the computer, such as Kid Pix, can also be used to teach literacy through music. Teachers create a picture for each verse or phrase, record the children singing a song appropriate for that picture, and create a title page and an ending page. Put this information into the slide show format, and ta-da! Many favorite songs lend themselves well to pictures, singing, and dramatizations.

Music interactive tables called Noteput, developed in Germany by Jonas Friedmann Heur and Jurgen Grae, have made their debut with tangible notes that can be perceived by three senses: hearing, sight, and touch. Noteput is designed to make learning the classical notation of music easier and will be eventually available to children. Whole, half, and quarter notes differ in shape and in weight (long-note values are heavier than short ones). Children can play a note and hear various musical instruments using the same tone and hear various note values. Noteput and other new interactive music experiences can be found in *Touch of Code: Interactive Installations and Experiences* by Klanten, Ehmann, and Hanschke (2011) and are part of the way children can learn through interactive technology. Interacting with digital information via the physical environment of the senses will bring more of the senses to music.

Even though mathematical, scientific, and literary concepts can easily be integrated through music, teachers need to be cautious when they are using music *only* to teach other skills because children's musical experiences will become limited. Music is a subject that needs to be carefully planned, implemented, and assessed and should be recognized as having its own value for children.

SUMMARY

Music in early childhood is interwoven throughout the day and includes listening, singing, playing instruments, and moving to music. These musical activities help children develop spatial reasoning, a skill needed in math and science. Experiencing music is also helpful in math in learning number operations and patterns, and it has close connections with the physical science of sound. It promotes creativity and communication and collaboration with peers.

Mastery of the elements of music is not a goal in early childhood. Instead, we want young children to find pleasure in musical experiences such as listening, moving, singing, playing instruments, and creating music. These musical experiences should be play-based and include many kinds of musical interactions in one-on-one and in small and large groups. Regarding these experiences, teachers must be open and flexible in their implementation and base them on the developmental levels of the children. Providing a classroom climate where musical expression is nurtured and creativity flourishes means that music is present throughout the day, as was noted at the beginning of the chapter in the vignette about Ms. Waters. Musical experiences in early childhood can also be integrated within various content areas, including mathematics and science.

REVIEW AND REFLECT

1. Brainstorm what math concepts can be taught through music. Which of the Common Core Mathematics Standards would these concepts be related to?
2. Use the scientific method to experiment with some scientific concepts in physical science that are related to the study of sound. Which of the Next Generation Science Standards would these address? Tell what you did and what you learned about sound.
3. Look up the National Association for Music Education's (NAfME, 1991) position statement on music in early childhood. Use it as a way to promote an understanding of the importance of music education in early childhood. Using the position paper, develop a panel discussion of why music should be kept in the school. Include a panel member who can relate music to science and math.

COLLABORATION FOR CREATIVITY
A Plan of Action for Arts–STEM

It takes a village to raise a child.

—African Proverb

THINKING AND ACTING LIKE LEONARDO DA VINCI

The primary-age children described below were in an Arts–STEM after-school program in two low-performing schools in Denver, Colorado. They studied the work of Leonardo by reading *Who Was Leonardo da Vinci?*, a chapter book about Leonardo, his life, and his inventions by Roberta Edwards (2005).

The children learned that Leonardo had an insatiable curiosity toward life and an unrelenting quest for continuous learning. He tested knowledge through experience, persistence, and a willingness to learn from mistakes. He saw the connection between nature, art, math, and science. This interconnection was emphasized in the after-school program. Children carefully studied the dragonfly and saw how its wings were similar to both a helicopter and airplane, two inventions of da Vinci. They carefully studied the wingspan of birds and developed the vocabulary of *lift*, *gravity*, *thrust*, and *drag*. They related the study of flight to kites, balloons, helicopters, and airplanes, and they studied the special airfoil shapes of wings, which foils the pulling-down force of gravity by creating an upward force of flight—lift. They were shown some of the designs of helicopters, airplanes, and bridges that Leonardo drew. After designing and making paper airplanes, they tested them to see how far they would fly.

The children studied the physics of simple machines (wheels, gears, pulleys, inclined plane or ramp, lever, screw), examining them, and testing them for efficiency. Many concepts were learned from the study of simple machines. The children learned how a wheel helps things move and how a drive belt can help another wheel move. They saw the gears with cogs and compared them to their bicycles and saw that gears moved in opposite directions. The children examined pulleys and saw how they make lifting easier. They learned that a ramp makes it easier to push an object up or down, and a lever reduces the amount of effort to move something. They recorded how fast and how far a toy car traveled down ramps of varying heights. The scientific method was used to make predictions. They learned how a wedge, which is a double-sided ramp, drives things apart, and they examined the wedge of the nail and even the zipper. After examining a screw, which makes a longer but easier path to follow, they compared it to a water slide shaped liked a screw. Examination of everyday machines took place more often. The simple machines in the egg beater, ice cream scoop, pizza cutter, cork screw, can opener, nutcracker, scissors, and so forth were examined with a keen observation of the parts.

A professor from the Industrial Design Department of the local college visited the program and showed his inventions and the inventions of his students (see Figure 8.1).

A student of aeronautics came and pretended he was Leonardo and answered questions about Leonardo's life and aviation. The children were given the opportunity to be creative inventors. They were instructed to use at least one simple machine and show how it could help people. The children made such inventions as a pulley to help a mother feed her baby; a flying truck; video glasses; a pulley to help a grandmother in a wheelchair get up a ramp; a machine that cleans the floor; a robot that helps dust the furniture. They shared their inventions with their parents at a family night (see Figure 8.2).

Figure 8.1. Professor from Industrial Design Department with Inventions

Figure 8.2. A Girl Sharing Her Invention of a Machine for Picking Up Toys

All children have the right to express themselves creatively. A deeper, more authentic part of the human mind is expressed through creativity. Artists and scientists have always had a very strong need to express themselves. Therefore, educators must recognize the creative genius in children and actively advocate for their creative experiences in early childhood in the arts leading to the sciences. The purpose of this book is to demonstrate the essential relationship of the arts to science, technology, engineering, and math and show how to enable teachers to make that connection in their classrooms.

There is an immense body of literature indicating that what happens in childhood is related to subsequent creativity and innovation in adulthood. Many adults do not exhibit characteristics of creativity because they have not experienced, as children, the kinds of activities and playfulness that are needed in creative production (Dacey & Lennon, 1998). As pointed out in Chapter 1, the Partnership for 21st Century Skills (2008, 2009), which is composed of large corporations, national professional organizations, and state offices of education, is concerned because it foresees a need that goes beyond what is presently emphasized in our schools. Educational writers such as Robinson (2009, 2011) and Darling-Hammond (2010) emphasize the importance of creativity, critical thinking, problem solving, as well as communication and collaboration as skills needed for the 21st century. Current books on innovation and the future for the United States consistently emphasize the importance of both the arts and sciences for economic growth (Estrin, 2009; Friedman, 2007; Gardner, 2008; Issacson, 2011; Pink, 2006; Trilling & Fadel, 2009).

Currently much of the curriculum in U.S. early childhood classrooms focuses on helping children learn factual knowledge. The school systems judge individual talent mostly by standardized tests. However, the standardized tests rarely cover the nonacademic domains, such as creativity, communicating, and collaborative problem solving. There is little focus on the arts, which can help children with the understanding and pursuit of creativity. Teachers and families need to work with local organizations and agencies in order to become advocates for increasing expressive-arts opportunities for children both within the classroom and in the community. This chapter will look at effective advocacy methods for educators and conclude with specific recommendations for stakeholders in early childhood education who are committed to connecting the arts and STEM using 21st century skills.

EXPLORING METHODS FOR EDUCATORS TO PROMOTE THE ARTS–STEM CONNECTION

Advocate educators can be teachers, leaders, advisers, or researchers. Historically, early childhood teachers have maintained a low profile in being advocates for the arts and play. Today, the professional community of early childhood education needs to influence the professional growth of educators and the efforts of others who are committed to the needs of children in a changing society. In a day when legislatures are determining what is happening to young children, rather than qualified educators, teachers need extra training in desirable conditions, programs, and practices for children. The advocacy training should be centered on networking, communication, and political adeptness in order to promote alliances, legislation, and programs that are developmentally appropriate and in keeping with "best practices" for the whole child. Advocates need to be bold promoters of creative ideas that are constructive.

Advocacy work is mandated by Standard 6E of the NAEYC Standards for Initial and Advanced Early Childhood Professional Preparation Programs (NAEYC, 2010). This advocacy should continue for inservice teachers. This section will examine five major methods for building advocacy skills to promote the Arts–STEM connection: (1) making learning visible so that we can generate the interest of policymakers and community leaders in early care and education; (2) writing and utilizing position statements; (3) composing effective letters to the editor and opinion editorials; (4) structuring briefing papers; and (5) creating community awareness of the importance of the arts in the schools.

Making Learning Visible

One major issue in schools today is demonstrating accountability by specifying what children are learning. Posting test scores and grading schools is the way that politicians seek to make learning visible. One way that is deeper is to gather documentation of children's work so the public can see the abilities and thinking of children. Teachers need to show how literacy can be developed through art, music, movement, and play and integrated into STEM. Providing opportunities for teachers and community leaders to connect by studying the work of children is a step for generating the interest of policymakers in early care and education. This method of documentation has been used by Reggio Emilia preschools and can be used by U.S. schools to help parents and others see the growth in children's thought.

Developing Position Statements

Another opportunity for educators and community leaders to connect is by distributing and discussing position statements of nationally recognized organizations. A position statement is disseminated by an organization or organizations to promote a stand on an issue relevant to the organization's mission. These can be used to establish a viewpoint that promotes the development of children in the expressive arts. Members of these organizations can contribute to position statements. The National Association for the Education of Young Children (NAEYC) has a website (www.naeyc.org) that includes their position statements. NAEYC's statements are adopted by the Governing Board to state the association's position on issues related to early childhood education practice, policy, and/or professional development for which there are controversial or critical opinions. Current NAEYC position statements are grouped in two categories: "Where We Stand" summaries on selected issues and "Current Position Statements/Standards." Other professional early childhood organizations also have position statements such as the Association of Childhood Education International (ACEI), which has a position statement on the arts (Jalongo, 2003), and the National Association for Music Education, which has a position statement on music in early childhood education (NAfME, 1991).

Composing Letters to the Editor and Opinion Editorials

Educators and community leaders can also advocate for the education of young children by communicating with the news media through writing letters to the editor and op-eds. A letter to the editor of a newspaper is usually 250 words or less. It is a public expression of opinion on a given subject that helps build awareness for issues that are important on both personal and professional levels. These letters often respond to articles that have appeared in the newspaper. Following is an example of an appropriate letter to the editor:

Dear Editor,

I would like to address the issue of music and the arts being taken away from our schools' curriculum. The need for communication of ideas that both artists and scientists have is started early in life. If the arts are taken away from children, we will be taking away something so precious: expression. Participating in music and art is an important part of children's growth and development. More important, the arts can help children discover beauty, organization, and meaning in the world. I understand that STEM and literacy are also very important, but music and art can be incorporated into each of these content areas, and each of these areas can be incorporated into music and art as well. Throughout history, both artists and scientists have seen the connections between the arts and sciences.

Furthermore, music and art erase the borders of cultural, ethnic, and racial differences. Cultural education is just as important as content education. Music and art are universal learning tools for all children. If they are taken away, creativity is lost not only in the arts but in math and science. We should think about this long and hard before we take music and art away from a generation for whom the benefits could be greater than in any other era.

Sincerely,

John Doe, Early Childhood Teacher

Opinion editorials (op-eds) for newspapers should be about 400 words and support a position with pertinent facts. An op-ed is not a story that simply describes a situation, but rather it is your opinion about how to improve the situation. Remember, the majority of people reading the op-ed may not have an understanding of the issue, so give a brief background before venturing into your opinion. Readers want to know how the issue affects them and their community. Op-eds must be timely since newspaper editors are looking for columns that engage their readers about a current issue. Conclude with a call to action that is concrete and realistic.

Structuring Briefing Papers

A briefing paper supports a position, generally on a piece of legislation. An organization or group of interested people usually initiates it. Most briefing papers take the same format. First, an introduction identifies the topic and then previews what is to come. Next, the paper, using data, defines the problem and outlines steps on how to fix it. Write as though you are teaching readers about this issue. Keep it simple and easy to understand while still telling the whole story. Relevant research can be included to show how, for instance, the issue is handled in other U.S. localities and/or other countries to enhance the lives of children. Be sure to provide contact information such as email addresses for further inquiries about the issue.

Briefing papers can be sent by email to members of an organization, or sent to legislators in the form of individual letters. Some briefing papers are written by educators as a group to higher levels of management to define an issue such as the importance of qualified teachers for early childhood classrooms.

Creating Community Awareness of Arts–STEM in Your School

Conferences, festivals, open houses, tours of rooms, and shopping-mall activities are all ways to create an awareness of the arts and STEM. Special events at school could include speakers, researchers, or displays of children's Arts–STEM projects. Children from each room could be the guides, and artists, architects, inventors, and industrial designers could talk about their work and connections between the arts and STEM. In one Colorado school district, the superintendent, who is an advocate for the arts, has an ongoing display of children's work in the arts and sciences in the district administration building for the community to view throughout the year. This display has been successful in creating an awareness of the importance of the arts and sciences in the schools. Schools are starting to include invention fairs along with science fairs, which integrate Arts–STEM ideas.

RECOMMENDATIONS FOR PRESERVICE AND INSERVICE EDUCATION PROGRAMS TO ENHANCE CREATIVITY IN ARTS–STEM

The following recommendations regarding the Arts–STEM connection need to be emphasized at the college level in teacher education as well as in early childhood programs:

- The expressive arts (creative movement, drama, visual arts, and music) should be used in some form every day in every early childhood room, and every art form should be taught in early childhood teacher education. Courses on play need to be included in the early childhood programs, as well as current research on this important creative activity, so that teachers learn how to facilitate play for creative development and the promotion of Arts–STEM.
- Students of early childhood education should study creativity—the theories of creativity, research in creativity, characteristics of people with creativity, and how to promote creative behaviors in students. Courses on creativity should be part of licensure, and there should be professional development programs on creativity for in-service teachers.
- Teachers and teacher educators need to go out of their way to encourage learners to take risks both in the arts and the sciences, and this begins

with creative movement, the first of the arts studied in detail in this book. Play is the beginning of where the arts and sciences take place, and it is the child's first means of self-expression.

- Breadth and depth need to take place in our schools and in our teacher training institutions. Commonalities among the standards in the arts and STEM fields need to be studied. Along with meeting the standards, children should have the opportunity to pursue their interests in depth. The project approach (Helm & Katz, 2016; Katz & Chard, 2000) is one of the best ways to implement this breadth and depth in an interdisciplinary way.

- In both the arts and sciences the process skills of observation, comparison, classification, measuring, communication, inferring, and predicting should be used informally and formally. Although they are well defined in the sciences, they should be discussed in both the arts and sciences. The elements of design as well as form and function in the arts and sciences needs to be discussed.

- Beauty and organization in the world are discovered by understanding the arts, math, and sciences and their relationship to one another. In other words, science, math, and art are how the world is organized. Great scientists such as Leonardo da Vinci, Albert Einstein, and modern-day tech giant Steve Jobs connected these fields, although textbooks in the field tend to separate the arts and do not connect the STEM fields to the arts. The arts and STEM should not be separated because they work together to tackle the unsolved problems of the world. It is only through scientists and artists working together that iPads, iPhones, and many other inventions were made in the last 25 years. In early childhood classrooms children should be working together to promote designs that integrate art with scientific investigation.

- A shift must be taken from the importance of knowing the right answers to knowing how to behave when answers are not necessarily apparent. Artists and scientists do not always know the correct answer. They have to persevere to find the right answer.

- Creativity is not about a lack of constraints but working through the constraints to solve a problem or improve a situation. It is important to consider mistakes and take advantage of them. Mistakes are opportunities for tremendous growth.

- Children will need interactive experiences that merge hardware and software with architectural design to promote discovery, curiosity, and active participation. Schools will need to provide inspiration and thought for further ideas, innovations, and experiments in interactive technology.

- Children need to go outdoors and look at the natural world. They need to see the connection of nature, design, and math and science, as Froebel did in his minerals curriculum. Many creative thinkers, such as Leonardo da Vinci, Michelangelo, Francis Galton, and Charles Darwin, began in their childhood to record images of nature on paper and made use of those images later in their work. Observing nature exposes children to the beauty of flowers, trees, mountains, hills, meadows, lakes, and oceans. Inspiration for creativity can come from nature. Teachers should ask children questions about nature: Why do you think the trees lose their leaves? How do you think the mountains got there?

- Teachers should emphasize the diversity of music, math, and science. There are many different kinds of music from different cultures. Math and science inventions have come from many countries. The creativity in math and science from other countries needs to be acknowledged.
- To further enhance children's sensibilities toward arts and nature, class field trips should be part of early childhood programs. Children should visit, for example, art museums, children's museums, natural science museums, botanical gardens, butterfly pavilions, aquariums, and outdoor museums. Most museums have workshops for teachers as well as families and offer many activities parents can do at home with their children to enrich their aesthetic experiences.

RECOMMENDATIONS RELATED TO THE COMMUNITY AND PARENTS

The following are recommendations that would promote Arts–STEM and 21st century skills in museums, exhibits, schools, libraries, playgrounds, camps, as well as homes:

- Funding for programs in children's museums should be contingent on incorporation of Arts–STEM connections as well as 21st century skills. Children need exposure to interactive technological installations and experiences that promote linking of art, science, and design and address the curiosity of their audiences and take them to wonderful discoveries through sensual and interactive experiences.
- Professional development for staff in museums and community programs needs to focus on Arts–STEM connections and 21st century skills, with emphasis on understanding and developing creativity in children.
- Volunteers in museums should be trained in spatial development and in Arts–STEM connections so that every conversation and question and response with children enhances their curiosity. An emphasis on the NGSS standards (NGSS, 2013), the Common Core State Standards (NGA

& CCSSO, 2010), and the National Core Arts Standards (NCCAS, 2014) should be encouraged.

- Architecture exhibits need to emphasize how famous architects such as Frank Lloyd Wright or Buckminster Fuller, as children played with blocks in a systematic way using Froebelian blocks.
- Playrooms in museums and libraries should have booklets available for parents on art and science suggestions to use with children while playing in the room or at home.
- Parents, educators, and community leaders should advocate for collaboration among local, state, and national policies in promoting the Arts–STEM connection.
- Schools and parents should address obstacles to play and the arts, such as the large amount of TV and computer time, overscheduling of lives, and education that emphasizes only skills and not creativity.
- Mentoring and other support systems should be developed to promote and support play, creative arts, and STEM in schools, at home, after school, and in programs at camps, playgrounds, neighborhoods, and museums.

Only when experimentation in the arts and STEM takes place through play in early childhood will a creative ecosystem be developed that harnesses the imagination needed for the future. Cultivation of imaginative minds is a high priority for the communities of children. This generation is growing up in a rapidly changing world, and their experience with the arts can lead the way for innovations in STEM to promote positive change.

SUMMARY

This book has looked at the Arts–STEM connection with the arts leading the way. This conclusion provides specific ways that teachers can be advocates for integrating Arts–STEM throughout the curriculum and working with community members for the promotion of the expressive arts. By spearheading collaborative efforts, teachers can help parents and the general public have a greater awareness of the importance of the Arts–STEM connection. I hope that the skills you learn in this book will encourage you to further develop your leadership abilities in Arts–STEM in early childhood education, but most of all to be a creative teacher or parent who appreciates the creativity and beauty of each child's creation.

REVIEW AND REFLECT

1. Describe ways you can advocate for the arts.
2. Write a letter to an editor of a newspaper on why the Arts–STEM should be in the schools.
3. Describe a teacher exemplar of Arts–STEM for young children.
4. Take the following action to promote the importance of creativity in the early years in your community: Look online for local organizations that support the expressive arts, and expand your knowledge about the expressive arts through these organizations and determine how you could use these organizations to promote the Arts–STEM connection.
5. Determine how you could get local art museums, children's museums, and science and nature museums to collaborate and promote the Arts–STEM connection in your community.
6. To maximize your thinking on 21st century skills and innovation, read a book listed in the References by one of the following authors: Bellanca and Brandt (2010); Estrin (2009); Florida (2007, 2012); Gardner (2008); Pink (2006); Robinson (2011); and Zhao (2009). Propose how you would adapt 21st century skills for young children in one of the following: schools, museums, workspaces, towns. Share your ideas with the appropriate people online.
7. Some families may see the creative arts distracting from the academic curriculum, while others consider them important but want children to produce exact replicas of teacher-produced models. Using the information in this book, how might you address the concerns of parents but at the same time respect the creativity of the children?

REFERENCES

Aghababyan, A. R., Grigoryan, V. G., Stepanyan, A. Y., Arutyunyan, N. D., & Stepanyan, L. S. (2007). EEG reactions during creative activity. *Human Physiology, 33*(2), 252–253.

Althouse, R., Johnson, M., & Mitchell, S. T. (2003). *The colors of learning: Integrating the visual arts into the early childhood curriculum.* New York, NY: Teachers College Press.

Amabile, T. (1989). *Nurturing a lifetime of creativity.* Buffalo, NY: Creative Education Foundation Press.

America Competes Act. (2007). Govtrack.us/congress/bills/110/hr2272/summary

Ardley, N. (1991). *The science book of color.* San Diego, CA: Harcourt Brace Jovanovich.

Balfanz, R. (1999). Why do we teach young children so little mathematics? Some historical considerations. In J. V. Copley (Ed.), *Mathematics in the early years* (pp. 3–10). Reston, VA: NCTM; Washington, DC: NAEYC.

Bellanca, J., & Brandt, R. (2010). *21st century skills: Rethinking how students learn.* Bloomington, IN: Solution Tree.

Boyer, E. (1991). *Ready to learn: a mandate for the nation.* Special Report of the Carnegie Foundation for the Advancement of Teaching. Lawrenceville, NJ: Princeton University Press.

Bronowski, J. (1973). *The ascent of man.* Boston, MA: Little, Brown, & Company.

Brosterman, N. (2014). *Inventing kindergarten.* New York, NY: Kaleidograph Design.

Burrack, J. (2005). Uniting mind and music: Shaw's vision continues. *American Music Teacher, 55*(1), 84–89.

Cadwell, L. B. (1997). *Bringing Reggio Emilia home: An innovative approach to early childhood education.* New York, NY: Teachers College Press.

Cambourne, B. (1988). *The whole story: Natural learning and the acquisition of literacy.* Auckland, New Zealand: Ashton/Scholastic.

Chavez-Eakle, R. A. (2007). Creativity, DNA, and cerebral blood flow. In C. Martindale, P. Locker, & V. M. Petrov (Eds.), *Evolutionary and neurocognitive approaches to aesthetics, creativity, and the arts* (pp. 209–224). Amityville, NJ: Baywood.

Chua, A. (2007). Day of empire: How hyper powers rise to global dominance—and why they fall. New York, NY: Doubleday.

Clements, D. H., & McMillen, S. (1996). Rethinking concrete manipulatives. *Teaching Children Mathematics, 2*(5), 270–279.

Clements, D. H., & Sarama, J. (2003). Young children and technology: What does the research say? *Young Children, 58*(6), 34–40.

Clements, D. H. & Sarama, J. (2009). *Learning and teaching early math: The learning trajectories approach.* New York, NY: Routledge.

Copley, J. (2001). *The young child and mathematics.* Washington, DC: NAEYC.

Copple, C., & Bredekamp, S. (Eds.). (2009). *Developmentally appropriate practice in early childhood programs: Serving children from birth through age 8.* Washington, DC: NAEYC.

Corbin, C., & Lindsey, R. (1996). *Concepts of physical education with laboratories.* Madison, WI: W. C. Brown / Benchmark.

Corso, M. (1993). Is developmentally appropriate physical education the answer to children's school readiness? *Colorado Journal of Health, Physical Education and Dance, 19*(2), 6–7.

Counsell, S., Escalada, L., Geiken, R., Sander, M., Uhlenberg, J., Van Meeteran, B., . . . Zan, B. (2016). *STEM learning with young children.* New York, NY: Teachers College Press.

Csikszentmihalyi, M. (1990). *Flow: The psychology of optimal experience.* New York. NY: Harper.

Dacey, J. S., & Lennon, K. H. (1998). *Understanding creativity: The interplay of biological, psychological, and social factors.* San Francisco, CA: Jossey-Bass.

D'Agnese, J. (2010). *Blockhead: The life of Fibonacci.* New York, NY: Holt.

Danoff-Burg, J. A. (2003). Be a bee and other approaches to introducing young children to entomology. *Spotlight on Young Children and Science, 57*(5), 33–37.

Darling-Hammond, L. (2010). The flat world and education: How America's commitment to equity will determine our future. New York, NY: Teachers College Press.

Dewey, J. (1934). *Art as experience.* New York, NY: Minton, Balch.

Dewey, J. (1938). *Experience and education.* New York, NY: Macmillian.

Eckhoff, A. (2011). Creativity in the early childhood classroom: Perspectives of pre-service teachers. *Journal of Early Childhood Teacher Education, 32*(3), 240–255.

Eckhoff, A., & Urbach, J. (2008). Understanding imaginative thinking during early childhood: Sociocultural conceptions of imagination and creativity. *Childhood Education Journal, 36,* 179–185.

Edwards, C., Gandini, L., & Forman, G. (Eds.). (2012). *The hundred languages of children: The Reggio Emilia approach—Advanced reflections* (3rd ed.) Santa Barbara, CA: Praeger.

Edwards, R. (2005). *Who was Leonardo da Vinci?* New York, NY: Grosset & Dunlap.

Eger, J, M. (2011, May 31). National Science Foundation slowly turning STEM into STEAM. *Huffington Post.* Retrieved from huffingtonpost.com/john-m-eger/national-science-foundati_b_868449.html

Eisner, E. (2002). *The arts and the creation of mind.* New Haven, CT: Yale University Press

Ellis, A. K., & Fouts, J. T. (2001). Interdisciplinary curriculum: The research base. *Music Educators Journal, 87*(5), 22–26.

Erikson, E. (1950). *Childhood and society.* New York, NY: Norton Press.

Estrin, J. (2009). *Closing the innovation gap: Reigniting the spark of creativity in a global economy.* New York, NY: McGraw Hill.

Feuerstein, R., Feuerstein, R. S., Falik, L., & Rand, Y. (2006). *The Feuerstein instrumental enrichment program: Parts I and II.* Jerusalem, Israel: International Center for the Enhancement of Learning Potential.

Flaherty, G. (1992). The learning curve: Why textbook teaching doesn't work for kids. *Teaching Today, 67*(6), 32–33, 56.

Florida, R. (2007). *The flight of the creative class*. New York, NY: Basic Books.

Florida, R. (2012). *The rise of the creative class revisited*. New York, NY: Basic Books.

Friedman, T. (2007). *The world is flat*. New York, NY: Picador/Farrar, Straus and Giroux.

Fritz, J. (2001). *Leonardo's horse*. New York, NY: Putnam.

Froebel, F. (1895). *The songs and music of Friedrich Froebel's mother play* (mutter und kose lieder). New York, NY: D. Appleton and Company.

Froebel, F. (2001). *Education of man* (W. N. Hailmann, Ttrans.). New York, NY: D. Appleton. (Original work published 1887)

Frostig, M. (1970). *Movement education: Theory and practice*. Chicago: Follet.

Gandini, L. (2002). The story and foundations of the Reggio Emilia approach. In V. Fu, A. Stremmel, & L. Hill (Eds.), *Teaching and learning: Collaborative exploration of the Reggio Emilia approach*. Upper Saddle River, NJ: Merrill-Prentice.

Gandini, L. (2015). The amusement park for birds: Emergence and process of a project. In L. Gandini, L. Hill, L. Cadwell, & C. Schwall (Eds.), *In the spirit of the studio: Learning from the atelier of Reggio Emilia* (2nd ed., pp. 23–41). New York, NY: Teachers College Press.

Gandini, L., Hill, L., Cadwell, L., & Schwall, C. (Eds.). (2015). *In the spirit of the studio: Learning from the atelier of Reggio Emilia* (2nd ed.). New York, NY: Teachers College Press.

Garbarino, J. (1989). An ecological perspective on the role of play in child development. In M. Bloch & A. Pellegrini (Eds.), *The ecological context of children's play*. Norwood, NJ: Ablex.

Gardner, H. (1993). *Frames of mind: The theory of multiple intelligences* (10th ed.). New York, NY: Basic Books.

Gardner, H. (1999). *Intelligence reframed: Multiple intelligences for the 21st century*. New York, NY: Basic Books.

Gardner, H. (2006). *Multiple intelligences: New horizon in theory and practice*. New York, NY: Basic Books.

Gardner, H. (2008). *Five minds for the future*. Boston, MA: Harvard University Press.

Garreau, M., & Kennedy, C. (1991). Structure time and space to promote pursuit of learning in the primary grades. *Young Children, 46*(4), 46–51.

Geary, D. C. (1994). *Children's mathematical development: Research and practice*. Washington, DC: American Psychological Association.

Geist, K., Geist, E., & Kuznik, K. (2012). The patterns of music: Young children learning mathematics through beat, rhythm, and melody. *Young Children, 67*(1), 74–79.

Gelb, M.J. (1998). *How to think like Leonardo da Vinci*. New York, NY: Random House.

Gonzales, P., Williams, T., Jocelyn, L., Roey, S., Kastberg, D., & Brenwald, S. (2009). *Highlights from TIMSS 2007: Mathematics and science achievement of U.S. fourth- and eighth-grade students in an international context* (NCES 2009-001 Revised). Washington, DC: U.S. Department of Education, Institute of Education Sciences, National Center for Education Statistics.

Gowan, J. C., Khatena, J. , & Torrance, E. P. (1981). *Creativity: Its educational Implications*. Dubuque, IA: Kendall/Hunt.

Graham, G., Holt/Hale, S., & Parker, M. (2004). *Children moving: A reflective approach to teaching physical education* (6th ed.) Boston, MA: McGraw Hill.

Gruber, A., & Bodeker, K. (2005). *Creativity, psychology, and the history of science*. New York, NY: Springer.

Guilford, J. P. (1950). Creativity. *American Psychologist, 5,* 444–454.

Guilford, J. P. (1984). Varieties of divergent production. *Journal of Creative Behavior, 18,* 1–10.

Hannaford, C. (1995). *Smart moves: Why learning is not all in your head.* Arlington, VA: Great Oceans Publishing.

Harden, E. (1995). *Printmaking.* London, United Kingdom: Quarto Children's Books.

Haugland, S. W. (1999). What role should technology play in young children's learning? Part 1. *Young Children, 54*(6), 26–31.

Haugland, S. W. (2000). What role should technology play in young children's learning? Part 2. *Young Children, 55*(1), 12–18.

Helm, J. H. (2015). *Becoming young thinkers: Deep project work in the classroom.* New York, NY: Teachers College Press.

Helm, J. H., & Katz, L. G. (2016). *Young investigators: The project approach in the early years* (3rd ed.). New York, NY: Teachers College Press.

Honig, A. S. (2006). Supporting creativity in the classroom. *Scholastic Early Childhood Today, 20*(5), 13–15.

Hulme. J. N. (2005). *Wild Fibonacci: Nature's secret code revealed.* New York, NY: Tricycle Press.

Humphreys, L. G., Lubinski, D., & Yao, G. (1993). Utility of predicting group membership and the role of spatial visualization in becoming an engineer, physical scientist, or artist. *Journal of Applied Psychology, 78,* 250–261.

Isbell, R. E., & Raines, S. (2013). *Creativity and the arts with young children* (3rd ed.). Belmont, CA: Wadsworth Cengage Learning.

Isenberg, J., & Jalongo, M. (2014). *Creative thinking and arts-based learning* (6th ed.). Upper Saddle Back, NJ: Pearson.

Issacson, W. (2011). *Steve Jobs.* New York, NY: Simon & Schuster.

Jackson, P. W., & Messick, S. (1965). The person, the product, and the response: Conceptual problems in the assessment of creativity. *Journal of Personality, 33,* 309–329.

Jacques-Dalcroze, E. (2013). *Rhythm, music and education.* Worcestershire, England: Read Books. (Original work published 1921)

Jalongo, M. R. (2003). The child's right to creative thought and expression (International position paper of the Association for Childhood Education International). *Childhood Education, 79*(4), 218–228.

Jenkins, E. (1995). Music is culture. *Scholastic Early Childhood Today, 9,* 40–42.

Jensen E. (2001). *Arts with the brain in mind.* Alexandria, VA: Association for Supervision and Curriculum Development.

Johansson, F. (2004). *The Medici effect.* Boston, MA: Harvard Business School Press.

Johmann, C. A., & Rieth, E. (1999). *Bridges! Amazing structures to design, build, and test.* Nashville, TN: Williamson Books.

Johnson, H. (1966). *The art of block building.* New York, NY: Bank Street College of Education. (Original work published 1933)

Jones, E. (1999). The importance of play. In *The play experience: Constructing knowledge and a community of commitment.* Symposium conducted at the annual meeting of NAEYC, New Orleans, LA.

Katz, L. G. (2007). Viewpoint: Standards of experiences. *Young Children, 62*(3), 94–95.

Katz, L. G. (2010). STEM in the early years. In *Collected papers from the SEED (STEM in Early Education and Development) Conference. Early Childhood Research & Practice, 12*(2). Retrieved from ecrp.uiuc.edu/beyond/seed/katz.html

Katz, L. G., & Chard, S. (2000). *Engaging children's minds: The project approach* (2nd ed.). Stamford, CT: Ablex.

Katz, L. G., Chard, L., & Kogan, Y. (2014). *Engaging children's minds: The project approach* (3rd ed.). Santa Barbara, CA: Praeger.

Kemple, K., Batey, J., & Hartle, L. (2004). Music play: Creating centers for musical play and exploration. *Young Children, 59*(4), 30–37.

Kim, K. H. (2011). The creativity crisis: The decrease in creative thinking scores on the Torrance Tests of Creative Thinking. *Creativity Research Journal, 23*(4), 285–295.

Klanten, R., Ehmann, S., & Hanschke, V. (2011). *Touch of code: Interactive installations and experiences.* Berlin, Germany: Gestalten.

Kodaly, Z. (1974). *The selected writings of Zoltan Kodaly.* London, United Kingdom: Boosey Hawkes.

Krechevsky, M. (2001). Form, function, and understanding in learning groups. Propositions from the Reggio classrooms. In C. Giudici, C. Rinaldi, & M. Krechevsky (Eds.), *Making learning visible: Children as individual and group learners* (pp. 246–269). Cambridge, MA: Project Zero, Harvard Graduate School of Education; and Reggio Emilia, Italy: Reggio Children.

Laban, R. (1948). *Modern educational dance.* London, England: McDonald & Evans.

Lindqvist, G. (2003). Vygotsky's theory of creativity. *Creativity Research Journal, 15,* 245–251.

Lowenfeld, V., & Brittain, W. (1987). *Creative and mental growth.* New York, NY: Macmillan.

Lubart, T. I. (1990). Creativity and cross-cultural variation. *International Journal of Creativity, 25,* 39–59.

MacDonald, S. (2001). *Block play: The complete guide to learning and playing with blocks.* Beltsville, MD: Gryphon House.

Malaguzzi, L. (1993). For an education based on relationships. *Young Children, 49*(1), 9–12.

Meador, K. S. (1992). Emerging rainbows: A review of the literature on creativity. *Journal for the Education of the Gifted, 15*(2), 163–81.

Montessori, M. (1949). *The absorbent mind.* New York, NY: Henry Holt.

Montessori, M. (1965). *Dr. Montessori's own handbook.* New York, NY: Schoeken.

Moomaw, S. (2013). *Teaching STEM in the early years.* St. Paul, MN: Redleaf Press.

Moomaw, S., & Davis, J. A. (2010). STEM comes to preschool. *Young Children, 65*(5), 12–14, 16–18.

National Association for the Education of Young Children (NAEYC). (2010). *2010 NAEYC standards for initial and advanced early childhood professional preparation programs.* Washington, DC: NAEYC. Retrieved from www.naeyc.org/ncate/standards

National Association for the Education of Young Children (NAEYC) & National Council of Teachers of Mathematics (NCTM). (2010). Learning PATHS and teaching STRATEGIES in early mathematics [Position statement]. In *Early Childhood mathematics: Promoting good beginnings* (pp. 19–21). Washintgon, DC: NAEYC. Retrieved from www.naeyc.org/positionstatements/mathematics

National Association of Early Childhood Teacher Educators (NAECTE). (2008). *Position statement on early childhood certification for teachers of children 8 years old and younger in public school settings.* Retrieved from www.NAECTE.org/about/position-statements-by-laws-and-policies/

National Association for Music Education (NAfME). (1991). *Early childhood education* [Position statement]. Retrieved from www.nafme.org/about/position-statements/early-childhood-education-position-statement/

National Coalition for Core Arts Standards (NCCAS). (2014). *National Core Arts Standards.* Retrieved from www.nationalartsstandards.org

National Council of Teachers of Mathematics (NCTM). (2006). *Curriculum focal points: A quest for coherence.* Reston, VA: Author.

National Governors Association Center for Best Practices (NGA), & Council of Chief State School Officers (CCSSO). (2010). *Common Core State Standards.* Washington, DC: Authors. Available at the Common Core State Standards Initiative website at www.corestandards.org

National Mathematics Advisory Panel. (2008). *Foundations for success: The final report of the National Mathematics Advisory Panel.* Washington, DC: U.S. Department of Education.

National Research Council (NRC). (2006). *Learning to think spatially.* Washington, DC: National Academies Press.

National Research Council (NRC). (2007). *Taking science to school: Learning and teaching science in grades k–8.* Washington, DC: National Academies Press.

National Research Council (NRC). (2009). *Mathematics learning in early childhood: Paths toward excellence and equity.* Washington, DC: National Academies Press.

National Research Council (NRC). (2012). *A framework for K–12 science education.* Washington, DC: National Academies Press.

Nilsen, B. (2004). *Week by week: Documenting the development of young children* (3rd ed.). Clifton Park, NY: Thomson, Delmar

NGSS Lead States (NGSS). (2013). *Next generation science standards: For states, by states.* Washington, DC: National Academies Press.

Ohman-Rodrigu, J. (2004). Music from inside out: Promoting emergent composition with young children. *Young Children, 59*(4), 50–54.

O'Reilly, S. (1993). *Weaving.* New York, NY: Thomson Learning.

Osborne, M. P., & Boyce, N. P. (2009). *Leonardo da Vinci.* New York, NY: Scholastic.

Park, B., Chae, J.-L., Boyd, B. F. (2008). Young children's block play and mathematical learning. *Journal of Research in Childhood Education, 23*(2), 157–178.

Parnes, S. J. (1967). *Creative behavior guidebook.* New York, NY: Scribner.

Parsad, B., & Spiegelman, M. (2012). *Arts education in public elementary and secondary schools: 1999–2000 and 2009–10* (NCES 2012-014). Washington, DC: U.S. Department of Education, Institute of Education Sciences, National Center for Education Statistics.

Partnership for 21st Century Skills. (2008). *21st century skills, education & competiveness: A resource and policy guide.* Tucson, AZ: Author. Retrieved from www.p21.org/storage/documents/21st_century_skills_education_and_competitiveness_guide.pdf

Partnership for 21st Century Skills. (2009). *Framework for 21st century learning.* Tucson, AZ: Author. Retrieved from www.p21.org/storage/documents/P21_Framework.pdf

Phillips, J. (2008). *Leonardo da Vinci: The genius who defined the Renaissance.* Washington, DC: National Geographic Society.

Piaget, J. (1952). *The origins of intelligence in young children.* New York, NY: International Universities Press.

Piaget, J. (1959). *The psychology of intelligence.* London, United Kingdom: Routledge & Kegan Paul.

Piaget, J. (1974). *To understand is to invent: the future of education.* New York, NY: Viking.

Pica, R. (2012). *Experiences in movement and music: Birth to age eight* (6th ed.). Albany, NY: Delmar.

Pink, D. (2006). *A whole new mind: Why right-brainers will rule the future.* New York, NY: Riverhead.

Piro, J. (2010). Going from STEM to STEAM: The arts have a role in America's future too. *Education Week, 29*(24), 28–29. Retrieved from www.edweek.org/ew/articles /2010/03/10/24piro.h29.html

Pollman, M. (2010). *Blocks and beyond: Strengthening early math and science skills through spatial learning.* Baltimore, MD: Paul H. Brookes.

Rauscher, F. H., Shaw, G. L., Levine, L. J., Wright, E. L. , Dennis, W. R. & Newcombe, R. L. (1997). Music training causes long-term enhancement of preschool children's spatial–temporal reasoning. *Neurological Research, 19*(1), 2–8.

Rauscher., F. H., & Zupan, M. A. (2000). Classroom keyboard instruction improves kindergarten children's spatial–temporal performance: A field experiment. *Early Childhood Research Quarterly, 15*(2), 215–228.

Rinaldi, C.(2006). *In dialogue with Reggio Emilia: Listening, researching, and learning.* London, England: Routledge.

Robinson, K. (2009). *The element: How finding your passion changes everything.* New York, NY: Penguin.

Robinson, K. (2011). *Out of our minds: Learning to be creative.* West Sussex, England: Capstone.

Robinson, K., & Aronica, L. (2015). *Creative schools: The grassroots revolution that's transforming education.* New York, NY: Viking.

Rothenberg, D. (2011). *Survival of the beautiful.* New York, NY: Bloomsbury Press.

Rousseau, J. (1979). *Emile or On Education* (A. Bloom, Ed. & Trans.). New York, NY: Basic Books. (Original work published 1764)

Rozmajzl, M., & Boyer-White, R. (1990). *Music: Fundamentals, methods, and materials for the elementary classroom teacher.* White Plains, NY: Longman.

Sahlberg, P. (2011). *Finnish lessons: What can the world learn from educational change in Finland?* New York, NY: Teachers College Press.

Sarama, J., & Clements, D. (2009). *Early childhood education research.* New York, NY: Routledge.

Schirrmacher, R. (2002). *Art and creative development for young children.* Albany, NY: Delmar.

Seefeldt, C., Castle, S., & Falconer, R. C. (2010). *Social studies for the preschool/primary child* (8th ed.). Columbus, OH: Pearson Prentice Hall.

Seo, K. H., & Ginsburg, H. P. (2004). What is developmentally appropriate in early child-hood mathematics education? In D. H. Clements, J. Sarama, & A. M. DiBiase (Eds.), *Engaging children in mathematics: Standards for early childhood mathematics education* (pp. 91–104). Mahwah, NJ: Erlbaum.

Sharapan, H. (2012). From STEM to STEAM: How early childhood educators can apply Fred Rogers' approach. *Young Children, 67*(1), 36–40.

Sharp, C., & Le Métais, J. (2000). *The arts, creativity and cultural education: An international perspective* (International Review of Curriculum and Assessment Frameworks). London, England: Qualifications and Curriculum Authority (QCA). Retrieved from www.nfer.ac.uk/publications/CAA01

Shaw, G. L. (2004). *Keeping Mozart in mind* (2nd ed.). San Diego, CA: Elsevier Academic Press.

Shlain, L. (2014). *Leonardo's brain*. Guilford, CT: Lyons Press.

Silberg, J. (1998). *I can't sing book*. Beltsville, MD: Gryphon House.

Silberstein-Storfer, M., & Jones, M. (1997). *Doing art together*. New York, NY: Harry Abrams.

Slavin, R. (1994). *Educational psychology: Theory and practice* (5th ed.). Boston, MA: Allyn & Bacon.

Strom, L. L. (2008). *Leonardo da Vinci: Artist and scientist*. New York, NY:. Scholastic.

Sturloni, S., & Vecchi, V. (1999). *Everything has a shadow except ants*. Reggio Emilia, Italy: Reggio Children.

Suzuki, S. (1969). *Nurtured by love. A new approach to education* (W. Suzuki, Trans.). New York, NY: Exposition Press.

Tishman, S., MacGillivray, D., & Palmer, P. (2002). Investigating the educational impact and potential of the Museum of Modern Art's Visual Thinking Curriculum: Final report. In R. Deasy (Ed.), *Critical links: Learning in the arts and student academic and social development* (pp. 153–154). Washington, DC: Arts Education Partnership.

Tokuhama-Espinosa, T. (2011). *Mind, brain, and education science: A comprehensive guide to the new brain-based teaching*. New York, NY: Norton.

Torrance, E. P. (1995). *Why fly? A philosophy of creativity*. Norwood, NJ: Ablex.

Trilling, B., & Fadel, C. (2009). *21st century skills: Learning for life in our times*. San Francisco, CA: Jossey-Bass.

Van der Linde. C. H. (1999). The relationship between play and music in early childhood: Educational insights. *Genetic, Social, and General Psychology Monographs, 119,* 2–8.

Vecchi, V. (2010). Art and creativity in Reggio Emilia: Exploring the role and potential of ateliers in early childhood education. London, England: Routledge

Vygotsky, L. S.(1962). *Thought and language* (E. Hanfmann & G. Vakar, Eds. and Trans.). Cambridge, MA: MIT Press.

Vygotsky, L. S. (1978). *Mind in society*. Cambridge, MA: Harvard University Press.

Wagner, T. (2002). *Making the grade: Reinventing America's schools*. New York, NY: Routledge.

Wagner, T. (2010). *The global achievement gap: Why even our best schools don't teach the new survival skills our children need—and what we can do about it*. New York, NY: Basic Books.

Wallas, G. (1926). *The art of thought.* London, United Kingdom: C.A. Watts.

Walling, D. (2000). *Rethinking how art is taught.* Thousand Oaks, CA: Sage.

Weiner, E. (2016). *Geography of genius.* New York, NY: Simon & Schuster.

Weisman Topal, C., & Gandini, L. (1999). *Beautiful stuff: Learning with found materials.* New York, NY: Sterling.

White, M. (2000). *Leonardo: The first scientist.* New York, NY: St. Martin's Press.

Wolff, K. L. (1979). The effects of general music education on the academic achievement, perceptual-motor development, creative thinking, and school attendance of first-grade children (Doctoral dissertation) University of Michigan, Ann Arbor. (Diss. Abstr., 40:5359A)

Wolfgang, C. H., Stannard, L. L., & Jones, I. (2001). Block play performance among preschoolers as a predictor of later school achievement in mathematics. *Journal of Research in Childhood Education, 15*(2), 173–180.

Wright, S. (2003). *The arts: Young children, and learning.* Boston, MA: Allyn & Bacon.

Xie, Y., & Shauman, K. A. (2003). *Women in science.* Cambridge, MA: Harvard University Press.

Zhao, Y. (2009). *Catching up or leading the way.* Alexandria, VA: ASCD.

INDEX

An *f* or a *t* after a page number refers to a figure or table, respectively.

ABOUT THE AUTHOR

Mary Jo Pollman is professor emerita of early childhood at Metropolitan State University of Denver (MSUD). She received her PhD in early childhood education from Florida State University. A former lab school teacher at Florida State University as well as a kindergarten, 1st-, and 3rd-grade teacher, Dr. Pollman taught for 30 years in higher education and continued her study of early childhood education in Australia, Italy (Reggio Emilia), Japan, Germany, and Canada. She has spent the last 4 years developing Arts–STEM curriculum and teaching children in a primary afterschool program through a MSUD 21st Century College Readiness Center Program grant, a partnership between MSUD and the Denver Public School's Office of College and Career Readiness. Her curriculum titles include *Thinking and Inventing Like Leonardo da Vinci, Art + Math + Science = Creativity, I am a Scientist,* and *The Missing Fruits and Vegetables.*

At the national level, Dr. Pollman has been vice president in charge of membership of the National Association of Early Childhood Teacher Educators and a member of the professional development panel of the National Association for the Education of Young Children. Dr. Pollman is a past president of the Presidents' Council of the Association for Childhood Education International. She is a past president of the Alabama Association of Early Childhood Teacher Educators and the Colorado Association of Childhood Education International. She is currently a member of the National Association for the Education of Young Children, National Science Teachers of America, the National Council of Teachers of Mathematics, and their state affiliates. She has been an Arts–STEM presenter at NSTA, NAEYC, and ACEI conferences, as well as at the Cal Tech STEM Conference, Head Start Region 8 Conference, Froebel USA Conference, and the Rocky Mountain Early Childhood Conference. Additionally, she has been an Arts–STEM consultant and presenter in Chicago Public Schools preschools; Humboldt School District preschools in Prescott, Arizona; and four school districts in Colorado. Dr. Pollman has written articles in the STEM field and was a contributor to the 2016 SAGE Encyclopedia of Contemporary Early Childhood in the area of Spatial Development. She is the author of the book *Blocks and Beyond: Strengthening Early Math and Science through Spatial Development* (2010).